Galveston: Ellis Island of the West

SUNY Series in Modern Jewish History
Paula Hyman and Deborah Dash Moore, Editors

BERNARD MARINBACH

Galveston: Ellis Island of the West

State University of New York Press

ALBANY

Published by
State University of New York Press, Albany

© 1983 State University of New York

For information, address State University of New York
Press, State University Plaza, Albany, N.Y., 12246

Library of Congress Cataloging in Publication Data

Marinbach, Bernard, 1946–
  Galveston: Ellis Island of the West.

  (SUNY series on modern Jewish history)
  Bibliography: p.
  1. Jews—Texas—Galveston. 2. United States—Emigration and immigration. 3.
Galveston (Tex.)—Foreign Population. 4. Jews—Emigration and immigration. I.
Title. II. Series.
F395.J5M37 1983   304.8'73'0089924   82-10609
ISBN 0-87395-700-8
ISBN 0-87395-701-6 (pbk.)

10 9 8 7 6 5 4 3 2

Dedicated with everlasting love, esteem, and gratitude
to my parents,

GERSHON AND LEILA MARINBACH

Contents

List of Illustrations

Following Page 130

15. Jacob Billikopf, superintendent of the United Jewish Charities in Kansas City, Missouri.

16. Promotional literature prepared in 1907 by Jacob Billikopf of Kansas City.

17. "Announcement, to be posted in synagogues, study houses, and elsewhere" of groups leaving for Galveston.

18. ITO identification card carried by immigrants to Galveston.

19. Cover page of an 11-page pamphlet printed in Zhitomir in 1907 by the "ITO Central Emigration Bureau for all of Russia, in Kiev", entitled *Important Information about Emigration to Galveston (State of Texas)*.

20. Last page of a pamphlet printed in Zhitomir in 1907 by the "ITO Central Emigration Bureau for all of Russia in Kiev", entitled *Important Information about Emigration to Galveston (State of Texas)*.

21. Report sheet from Jacob Billikopf of Kansas City, Missouri, on progress of immigrants sent to him from Galveston.

22. A conference of the Jewish Territorial Organization, with Israel Zangwill standing in the center.

23. Israel Zangwill, founder and president of the Jewish Territorial Organization (ITO).

24. Galveston-bound emigrants in Bremen, with representatives of the Hilfsverein.

25. Boarding ship in Bremen for the voyage to Galveston.

26. Immigrants arriving at Galveston.

27. Ephraim Zalman (Charles) Hoffman, an immigrant who settled in Fort Worth after arriving at Galveston in 1913.

28. W. H. Novit, a Jewish immigrant from Russia, selling bananas in Gatesville, Texas (c. 1912).

29. Sarah Bernstein and Ephraim Zalman (Charles) Hoffman, two immigrants who arrived separately in Galveston in 1913, met in Fort Worth, and got married in 1915.

30. Ephraim Zalman (Charles) Hoffman (left), an immigrant who arrived at Galveston in 1913, as half-owner of a fruit, vegetable, and grocery store in Fort Worth (c. 1913–20).

Directory of Organizations

1. The *Jewish Territorial Organization*, with headquarters in London. (Its Yiddish acronym, ITO, was pronounced "EEtoe.") The department directly concerned with the Galveston Movement was the Emigration Regulation Department. Its Jewish Emigration Society, based in Kiev, managed the recruitment of emigrants from Russia.
2. *Hilfsverein der deutschen Juden*, based in Berlin, which operated an office in Bremen, the port of embarkation for Galveston. This office was operated with the cooperation of the ITO and was known as the ITO Emigrants' Dispatch Committee.
3. The *Jewish Immigrants' Information Bureau*, directed from New York but managed from Galveston. It is frequently referred to herein, as the JIIB. The JIIB's executive committee, which met in New York, was known as the Galveston Committee.
4. The *Industrial Removal Office*, which shared its offices with the JIIB in New York. Its manager, David M. Bressler, was also honorary secretary of the JIIB (though his activity was much more than honorary). The Industrial Removal Office encouraged Jewish immigrants to leave New York and other east-coast cities for points further west.
5. The *Jewish Colonization Association*, with headquarters in Paris. (Its Yiddish acronym, ICA, was pronounced "EEkah.") The ICA, which was involved in the organization of Jewish emigration from Russia, did not participate in the Galveston Movement. (It did, however, send funds to support the Industrial Removal Office.)

Preface

Most American Jews are descended from, or were themselves, immigrants who arrived at the Port of New York during the late nineteenth and early twentieth centuries. While Jews are now found in all areas of the country, many still retain family remembrances of life on the Lower East Side, or in other Jewish neighborhoods of New York. Those who arrived—or whose ancestors arrived— at the ports of Philadelphia, Baltimore, or Boston often recall similar stories about life in the "ghettos" of these or other north-eastern cities. These experiences have been incorporated into the success stories of many American Jews now living affluently in suburban areas throughout the United States. The arrival of the immigrant at the Ellis Island immigration station in New York, which was established in 1892, or at the immigrant stations of Philadelphia, Baltimore, or Boston, was the first of many steps leading toward his entrance into the mainstream of American life.

While this massive flow of Jewish immigrants to the northeastern port cities was taking place, a small trickle of Jewish immigrants found its way to the United States through the southwestern port of Galveston, Texas, situated on an island in the Gulf of Mexico. Between the years 1907 and 1914, about ten thousand Jews were admitted as immigrants at Galveston, settling in virtually every state of the West. The story of these people is one that has not yet been fully told. The descendants of these immigrants, now scattered throughout the United States, are mostly unaware of the unique story of their ancestors' arrival. Yet, this is a story which must be told, for it is the only substantial example of organized Jewish immigration to the United States. From their recruitment in Eastern Europe to their settlement in the American West, these immigrants were supervised and looked after by organized teams of agents. This project was known during its time as the "Galveston Movement."

The word "movement" here had a double meaning. In its plainest sense, it simply alluded to the fact that people were moving or being moved through Galveston. In a larger sense, however, the word "movement" implied something quite significant, for a movement can be defined as a heterogeneous group of organizations working toward a common goal. In this sense, the Galveston Movement represented a workable alternative to other concurrent attempts by Eastern European Jews to deal with the problems facing them, such as the Zionist Movement, the Bundist Movement, and the Yiddishist Movement. In retrospect, Zionism seems to dwarf the other Jewish Movements of its time, for it alone succeeded in achieving its major objectives. The chief advocates of the Galveston Movement, however, regarded their plan as being much more realistic and, hence, more likely to succeed. The competition between the Galveston Movement and the Zionist Movement was fierce, and ended only when the Galveston Movement ceased operations in 1914.

Some Jews from Eastern Europe attacked the Galveston Movement, for they considered it to be an artificial solution to their problems, imposed upon them by the American-Jewish Establishment—affluent Jews of German extraction who, they felt, often failed to understand the true needs and aspirations of the new immigrants. However, Jacob H. Schiff, who founded and funded the project, and others who were active in its implementation, were convinced that spreading Jewish immigrants throughout the West was crucial for the future well-being of American Jewry. More immediately, they felt that it would serve to minimize the agitation for legislation to restrict further immigration to the United States.

Unlike other Jewish movements, the Galveston Movement did not have to face serious financial problems, for Schiff generously supported the project from his own personal fortune. The mere availability of funds, however, was not enough to insure its success, for money alone could not buy the hearts and minds of the Jewish people. The project, furthermore, ran into a series of obstacles that could not have been foreseen. Soon after the inception of the Galveston Movement the American economy suffered a depression, making it difficult to secure jobs for the immigrants. Subsequently, the Russian government took action against the organization which recruited the immigrants for Galveston. During the administration of President Taft, the U.S. Department of Commerce and Labor instituted deportation proceedings against Jewish immigrants arriving at Galveston, and threatened to declare the entire project illegal. Later, during the Wilson Administration, the issue was raised once again. These and other problems, along with the attempts to overcome them, serve as themes of the chapters which make up this book. The chapters are arranged in chronological order.

In our examination of the Galveston Movement, we meet a number of great personalities in various parts of the world. Israel Zangwill, well known for his successful literary efforts, added a new dimension to his complex personality, as president of the London-based Jewish Territorial Organization (ITO). Dr. David S. Jochelmann, the energetic and heroic secretary of the ITO's Jewish Emigration Society of Kiev, practically worked himself to death on behalf of the refugees. David M. Bressler, honorary secretary of the Jewish Immigrants' Information Bureau (JIIB) in New York, was the organizational genius who created and supervised a network of local committees throughout the West, to receive the arriving immigrants. A succession of able managers, including the widely esteemed Morris D. Waldman and the controversial Henry Berman, greeted the immigrants on behalf of the JIIB and sent them off to their final destinations. Dr. Henry Cohen, the charismatic rabbi of the Galveston Jewish community, lent the managers his invaluable support. The prestigious members of the JIIB's executive committee, known as the "Galveston Committee," met in New York to plan their strategy for combating the hostility of the Administration in Washington. Presiding over them, as well as over the entire Galveston Movement, was the stately Jacob H. Schiff, whose beneficence made his name a household word in thousands of Jewish homes throughout America.

While these men were running the project, the immigrants were arriving and being settled. Like other immigrants, they faced the tasks of adapting themselves to new surroundings, finding homes, and obtaining suitable jobs. The Galveston Movement tried to help them resolve these problems but, inevitably, some of the immigrants never quite managed to do so. While describing the various events and circumstances surrounding the project, we have tried, at the same time, to emphasize the problems and the experiences of the immigrants themselves. The arrival of the immigrant and his attempt to adjust to an alien environment is a theme which pervades this study.

My search for sources of material relating to the Galveston Movement took me, both literally and figuratively, to various unlikely locations throughout the world. (The qualification "figuratively" is needed here, because in some cases the documents were photocopied or microfilmed and mailed to me, without necessitating a trip on my part.)

Most of the paper work for the Galveston-based Jewish Immigrants' Information Bureau (JIIB) was handled in New York, where the meetings of the Galveston Committee were held. With the advice and consent of Jacob H. Schiff, chairman of the Galveston Committee, most policy decisions for the JIIB were made by its honorary secretary, David M. Bressler, who was also general manager of the Industrial Removal Office. Besides setting policy, Bressler tightly supervised all aspects of the JIIB from his office in New York. The office files of the JIIB were included with those of the Industrial Removal Office, and together they eventually found their way to the archives of the American Jewish Historical Society. These archives were located in New York City until 1968, when they were moved to the campus of Brandeis University in Waltham, Massachusetts. I looked through the files of the Industrial Removal Office when they were still in their original boxing crates, and I sorted out the JIIB files, photocopied most of them, and ultimately used them in preparing this work. Since then, the files of the JIIB have been indexed and catalogued under the heading of "Galveston Immigration Plan," by the American Jewish Historical Society. These papers are extremely revealing about all aspects of the Galveston Movement, especially about the arrival and distribution of the immigrants in the United States.

In Europe, the project was run by the Jewish Territorial Organization (ITO), an offshoot of the Zionist Movement that became one of Zionism's most bitter competitors. In one of the ironies to which historical researchers are accustomed, the ITO papers are now found in the Central Zionist Archives, in Jerusalem, Israel. These papers, which are filed under Section A36 of the Archives, include the correspondence of the Kiev-based Jewish Emigration Society as well as that of the Emigration Regulation Department, which operated out of ITO headquarters in London. After I perused them in Jerusalem, the documents which I selected were microfilmed and sent to me in New York, where I then lived. They reveal much about the way the immigrants were recruited in Europe and sent to America. The JIIB papers and the ITO papers are my two most important documentary sources, and I have cited them frequently throughout this study.

I have also relied heavily on the papers of Jacob H. Schiff, which contain important correspondence between Schiff and many other prominent personalities, among them several key leaders of the Galveston Movement. These papers were originally held in the library of the Jewish Theological Seminary of America but were consumed by fire in 1967, along with many other priceless manuscript collections. Luckily, six years before the disastrous fire, the Schiff Papers had been microfilmed by the American Jewish Archives, which is located on the campus of the Hebrew Union College-Jewish Institute of Religion in Cincinnati, Ohio. With the kind permission of Dr. Jacob R. Marcus, director of the archives, the two relevant microfilm rolls, numbers 4 and 18, were sent to me in New York where I had copies made.

The Schiff papers are frequently complemented by documents which we have from other sources. For example, they include many letters written to Schiff by Israel Zangwill, but the corresponding letters from Schiff to Zangwill are often missing. Frequently, the opposite may be the case, for the Schiff papers do include copies of many of Schiff's letters to Zangwill, but the corresponding letters from Zangwill to Schiff are often not to be found. More often than not, the missing half of the correspondence appears among the ITO papers at the Central Zionist Archives in Jerusalem. To complete the picture, we often find relevant correspondence exchanged by Schiff and Bressler, or by Zangwill and Bressler, among the JIIB papers, which are filed under "Galveston Immigration Plan" at the American Jewish Historical Society in Waltham, Massachusetts. When the JIIB papers, the ITO papers, and the Schiff papers are all put together, they give us a nearly complete picture of the inner workings of the Galveston Movement.

In contrast with the archival material mentioned above, there is an additional, large collection of documents representing a source which was mostly antagonistic toward the Galveston Movement. These are the records of the Bureau of Immigration and Naturalization of the United States Department of Commerce and Labor, which can be found at the Civil Archives Division of the Legislative, Judicial, and Fiscal Branch of the National Archives and Records Service, in Washington, D.C. The immigration files are located in Record Group No. 85. The documents I have used are from Immigration Files Nos. 52,779/29 and 52,961/11, which contain the internal correspondence of immigration officials who dealt with the legality of the Galveston Movement in 1910. Upon visiting the National Archives and Records Service in Washington, I located these documents and had them photocopied. Without them, chapters four and five of this work, dealing with the deportation crisis and its aftermath, could scarcely have been written.

Throughout the study, I rely heavily on the immigrant arrival records which are kept by the Immigration and Naturalization Service, now under the administration of the United States Department of Justice. The San Francisco office possesses, on microfilm, the arrival records of all immigrants who entered the United States through the Western ports, including Galveston. There are sixteen rolls of microfilm containing records of all immigrants who arrived in Galveston between the years 1907 and 1914. At my written request, these microfilm rolls were duplicated and mailed to me. Generally, they furnish the following information, appearing on the manifest of every arriving ship: the name of each immigrant, his date of arrival, age, marital status, place of birth, last permanent residence, destination in the United States, name of the person to whom destined, biographic and physical description, accompanying passengers, amount of money in possession, nationality, and, most important for our purposes, race. Under the last category, all Jews were listed as members of the "Hebrew race." Thus, we have detailed lists of all Jewish immigrants arriving in Galveston during the period of the Galveston Movement. It is not always easily recognizable how many of these Jewish immigrants were participating in the organized project and how many were arriving entirely on their own. Nevertheless, these records have proven to be extremely valuable by providing detailed information concerning arriving groups of Jewish immigrants about which we often have little other information.

The archival sources listed above are, by far, the most important of those which I have examined. Together, they provide the basis upon which this book was written. There are other sources, however, which also proved quite useful, especially the Henry Cohen Collection at the American Jewish Archives. Box no. 2538 of this collection contains Rabbi Cohen's correspondence with Jacob H. Schiff, Israel Zangwill, David M. Bressler, and others, concerning the Galveston Movement. The American Jewish Archives also houses the Felix M. Warburg Papers, of which Box No. 165 contains several relevant items.

The bulk of Rabbi Henry Cohen's correspondence can be found at the Barker Texas History Center, which is located in the General Libraries of the University of Texas at Austin. Those of the Henry Cohen Papers which relate to the Galveston Movement are located in Box Number 3M226-234, and 3M323. I wish to thank Mrs. Ruth Horowitz for locating these letters, having them photocopied, and bringing them to me for my study.

At the American Jewish Historical Society, the Baron de Hirsch Fund Archives include a file on "Immigration Statistics," which contains statistics concerning Jewish immigrants to all ports of the United States. The society also houses papers of Max J. Kohler, including some which are relevant to the Galveston Movement. In New York, the archives of the American Jewish Committee yielded some interesting material from among its minutes and correspondence. Finally, the Central Archives of the History of the Jewish People, situated on the campus of the Hebrew University in Jerusalem, yielded only one relevant document, which was a duplication of a document available at the Central Zionist Archives.

I was led to many of the above sources by the late Zosa Szajkowski, whose fields of erudition included a wide range of topics in modern Jewish history. Mr. Szajkowski was a veritable mine of information about Jewish archival sources throughout the world. It was he who first made me aware of these sources, and for this I remain grateful.

I wish to thank Mr. Reuven Koffler of the Central Zionist Archives in Jerusalem and Mrs. Nachama Shalom of the Weizmann Archives in Rehovot, Israel, for helping to locate certain photographs and documents. I am also grateful to Mr. Aryeh Sadan for his help in the reproduction of photographs, to Mrs. Regina Langenauer for her help in researching Yiddish newspaper articles, and to Mr. Dan Haruv for his help with Russian material.

I would like to express my appreciation to Mrs. Fanny Cockerell of London and Mrs. Sonia Benari of Ramat Gan, Israel, for providing me with information about their father, Dr. David S. Jochelmann. Mrs. Benari's husband, Dr. Yehuda Benari, formerly president of the Jabotinsky Institute in Tel Aviv, was kind enough to escort me to the Institute archives, where we located file number PA 105, containing letters and papers of Dr. Jochelmann which Dr. Benari had brought from London. These letters and papers are from the period after the Galveston Movement had ceased operations and thus do not bear upon the subject of this book. At the same time, however, Dr. Benari's personal reminiscences of

Dr. Jochelmann were fascinating by themselves, making the trip more than worthwhile.

Professor Ismar Schorsch originally suggested this topic to me as one which was important but had been little investigated. At first, I pieced together the basic story of the Galveston Movement almost exclusively from magazine articles and other secondary sources. My interest in the topic deepened as I sensed the drama of the story and as I began to realize that a wealth of primary source material had barely been touched—indeed, much of it had yet to be located. I, therefore, chose *The Galveston Movement* as the topic of my doctoral dissertation, which was awarded the Louis Finkelstein Prize of 1976 by the Jewish Theological Seminary of America. The present book is an outgrowth of that manuscript. I am indebted to Professor Schorsch, who kindly agreed to serve as my mentor, for his constant encouragement and for his wise suggestions.

I was privileged and fortunate to have Professor Henry L. Feingold as my second mentor. His expertise in American Jewish history, especially in matters dealing with immigrants and refugees, was immensely valuable in providing me with a sense of perspective. I am very grateful to Professor Feingold for his continual help.

I also wish to gratefully acknowledge Professor Lloyd Gartner for reading the manuscript and for offering excellent advice and constructive criticism. I take sole responsibility, however, for any and all mistakes which may be found herein.

My mother, Mrs. Leila Marinbach, typed a good portion of the manuscript, for which I owe her much thanks. Any success I may achieve, whether from this book or from any other endeavor, I owe to her and to my father, Professor Gershon Marinbach. Besides inspiring me intellectually and spriritually, my father and mother have sustained me throughout my life with their love, their devotion and their faith in me. I shall never be able to repay them, but I dedicate this book to them as a small token of my everlasting gratitude.

Jerusalem, August, 1983

CHAPTER 1

Origins

The first large-scale pogroms broke out ostensibly as a reaction to the assassination of Czar Alexander II on March 13, 1881. They began at Easter and continued into the summer. In a hundred localities throughout the southern provinces of Russia, the scene was always the same. At first, rumors and threats were circulated. Then the Jewish quarter was invaded by laborers supported by peasants. Houses were destroyed, sacked, and burned. The Jews were savagely beaten, many being wounded or killed. The police and the troops, who were called out too late, were passive when they arrived on the scene. The Russian government did nothing to assure the Jews that more devastating pogroms would not follow. On the contrary, it encouraged any development that would cause its Jews to emigrate. "A veritable panic seized the Jews of southern Russia."[1] By the end of the summer of 1881, thousands of Jews were fleeing westward across the Russian border. The May Laws of 1882, which prevented the Jews, with minor exceptions, from living on the land, further accelerated the pace of emigration.

During the preceding decade, Jews had been emigrating from Russia at a slow but steady rate. A small number had settled in Germany, but the majority, about four thousand annually, had chosen the United States as their final destination. That was the beginning of the third wave of Jewish immigration to America, following the early Spanish-Portuguese and the more recent German immigration.[2]

The vast majority of the Russian-Jewish immigrants settled in the northeastern port cities of Philadelphia, Baltimore, Boston, and

New York, notably the latter. In these cities, especially in New York, the Jewish immigrants crowded into slums, which were soon labeled ghettos. The German Jews, many of whom were by this time well established and "Americanized," were dismayed and not a little embarrassed by the spectacle of their Russian coreligionists living in squalor. By the end of 1881, a Hebrew Emigrant Aid Society (not to be confused with the later Hebrew Immigrant Aid Society) was organized, seeing as its chief task the dispersion or "removal" of Jewish immigrants from the northeastern slums to the rural areas of the country. Its endeavors in this direction were taken over at the end of the following year by the United Hebrew Charities, which succeeded in dispersing 3,440 immigrants by 1889. This organization, which had been founded in 1874 as a union of five New York City charitable associations, had no intention, however, of letting its resources become overtaxed by a multitude of unemployed persons. Between 1882 and 1889, the United Hebrew Charities returned 7,534 unemployed immigrants to Europe.[3] In fact, from 1870 to 1891, when America as a whole was pro-immigrant, organized American Jewry was restrictionist in its approach.[4] There was still hope that the Russian government could be moved to alter its anti-Jewish policy and that large-scale emigration could be avoided.

In 1891, a new wave of pogroms, combined with the expulsion of thousands of Jews from Moscow, Kiev, and other cities of the Russian interior, convinced world Jewry that the only solution to Russian Jewry lay in emigration. In that year, the Jewish Colonization Association (ICA) was founded in London. Capitalized at $10 million, all of which was contributed by Baron Maurice de Hirsch (1831–1896), a German Jew, the ICA remained for a long time the world's greatest Jewish philanthropic organization. Meeting annually in Paris, its governing board assisted and promoted Jewish migration from countries where they were being oppressed to territories promising opportunity, notably Argentina. At the same time, recognizing that the main stream of Jewish migration was to North America, Baron de Hirsch contributed two and a half million dollars to set up a special fund in New York, known as the Baron de Hirsch Fund, to aid in the settling of Jewish immigrants throughout the United States. Its trustees were chosen from among the lay leaders of American Jewry, including such personalities as Oscar S. Straus, Myer S. Isaacs, Mayer Sulzberger and, most important, Jacob H. Schiff, the leading American Jewish philanthropist of the time (perhaps, of all times).

2

If the Baron de Hirsch institutions throughout the world could be said to share a specific ideology, that ideology would be the dispersion of the Jews and the encouragement to settle on the land. Accordingly, the Jewish Colonization Association and the Baron de Hirsch Fund joined together in 1900 to establish a credit institution for the establishment and maintenance of agricultural and industrial homesteads, known as the Jewish Agricultural and Industrial Aid Society.[5]

Apart from the creation of rural settlements, the Jewish Agricultural and Industrial Aid Society, with the help of the ICA, created a separate organization whose job it was to remove Jewish immigrants on an individual basis to small urban centers throughout the United States. The new organization, founded in 1901, was called the Industrial Removal Office. Based in New York, with numerous committees extending throughout the South and West—usually organized by local B'nai B'rith Lodges—the Industrial Removal Office acted as a sort of nonprofit employment agency. The local committees usually committed themselves to accept a certain number of immigrants per month and would constantly keep the main branch informed as to what jobs were available in their cities and towns. The New York office placed advertisements in the Yiddish newspapers encouraging men with the called-for skills to apply at the office for placement.

The Industrial Removal Office operated until 1922 and distributed 79,000 immigrants. (This figure includes 5,000 removed by the Philadelphia and Boston branches.)

> On the basis of an immigration of one and one-half million Jews in the United States between 1901 and 1913, and a distribution—direct and indirect—of 100,000, it appears that the Industrial Removal Office removed between six percent and seven percent of the total number of arrivals. The hope of the Industrial Removal Office that every family removed would attract others appears to have been substantially realized.[6]

A major reason for its success lay in the ability and devotion of David M. Bressler, a young lawyer, who became its general manager in 1903 and remained in that position until his resignation in 1916, when the war had greatly reduced the flow of immigrants. As we shall see, Bressler was equally active in the workings of the Galveston Movement. In fact, the *modus operandi* of the Galveston Movement was patterned after that of the Industrial Removal Office, and its succcess was dependent, to a large extent, upon the cooperation of that organization.

The official United States government attitude was highly favorable to the removal idea. Commissioner-General of Immigration Franklin Pierce Sargent, in his annual report of 1903, declared that removal was much more important than anything concerning immigration actually provided by law, since it prevented the creation of "immigrant colonies." Furthermore, two government bodies similar in function to the Industrial Removal Office were formed. These were the National Labor Bureau of New York and the Division of Information of the Department of Commerce and Labor. It soon became clear, however, that the vast majority of Jews who came to New York City would never leave. Indeed, the Ellis Island Experiment, a project undertaken by the Industrial Removal Office to convince immigrants while still at the immigration station not to settle in New York, lasted only from 1902 to 1904 and was a self-acknowledged failure.

In 1903 and 1904 new pogroms broke out in Russia, even more vicious than those which had taken place before. It appeared imperative to American Jewish leaders that something be done to distribute the Russian-Jewish refugees throughout the United States. With each passing year, Congress came closer and closer to passing a bill restricting immigration. The arguments used by the restrictionists included charges that the northeastern ghettos were hotbeds of disease, sedition, and moral depravity. A book issued in 1907 by the National Liberal Immigration League, which opposed the restrictionists, pointed out that "artificial distribution is of itself one of the strongest advocates of unrestricted immigration and will continue to be so as long as it is effective."[7] It was feared, however, that artificial distribution, or "removal," as it was known, was not effective enough to forestall the restrictionists, for the vast majority of Jewish immigrants remained in the ghettos of New York in spite of the efforts aimed at their "removal." There seemed only one way to change this: to prevent the immigrants from reaching Ellis Island by rerouting them to immigration stations in other areas of the country. The first suggestion that this be done came from Jacob H. Schiff, the universally acknowledged philanthropic leader of American Jewry.

The problem of spreading the immigrants throughout America had concerned Mr. Schiff for quite some time. As early as 1891, Schiff, in reply to a request from Baron de Hirsch to investigate conditions in Mexico, said that while he would be happy to do so, "in the last analysis the United States remains the best field for colonization . . . especially in the states west of the Rocky Mountains. What we are now doing is [trying] to induce those who are already here to relieve the tremendous congestion in the seaboard cities."[8] Schiff was a founder of the Industrial Removal Office in 1901 and remained one of its staunchest supporters. By the end of 1904, however, he had reached the conclusion that only by rerouting immigration could immigrants be induced to settle in cities other than New York.

On December 28, 1904, Jacob H. Schiff wrote a letter to Dr. Paul Nathan, secretary of the *Hilfsverein der deutschen Juden*. In this letter, Schiff wrote:

> I suggest to you the following suitable ports, to which part of the emigration could be advantageously directed: Philadelphia, Baltimore, Boston, New Orleans, Charleston, Savannah, and Galveston; also Montreal.[9]

His reason for addressing the letter to the *Hilfsverein* was that most Russian Jews who emigrated did so through the German ports of Hamburg and Bremen. (Schiff's attempt of July 1904, to relieve congestion there by helping to establish a direct shipping line to New York from the Latvian port of Lebau had failed.) Thus, the cooperation of the *Hilfsverein*, which was the all-encompassing German-Jewish relief organization, was essential to the success of any venture to channel Jewish immigration.

The German Jews, for their part, were all too anxious to facilitate emigration of the destitute Russian refugees who were flocking to their ports. In July 1905, the Hamburg branch of the *Hilfsverein* came up with a plan, which it presented to the Industrial Removal Office. It proposed that the Industrial Removal Office cooperate by giving the *Hilfsverein* regular and reliable information as to the industrial situation all over the United States in order that those whose transportation expenses they assisted might be forwarded to the interior rather than to New York. The Industrial Removal Office rejected this proposal as being likely to create the impression among United States immigration authorities that these immigrants were "assisted" and, therefore, illegal.[10] No action was taken during 1905 concerning any plan to divert immigration from New York. At this time, however, unrelated events in Switzerland were working to create an organization which would eventually deal with this problem.

The Seventh Zionist Congress meeting in Basle from July 27 to August 2, 1905, was the first which took place without the presence of its great leader, Dr. Theodor Herzl, who had died during the previous year. The 1905 Congress marked the climax of a stormy debate on the issue of whether to accept the British offer of a territory in East Africa, commonly referred to, somewhat inaccurately, as the Uganda scheme. At the congress, the "Zion Zionists," mostly Russian Jews who refused to consider any substitute for Palestine, gained the upper hand and voted to reject the British offer. Most members of the opposition accepted the decision of the majority, but a small group of diehard "Uganda" advocates, led by Israel Zangwill, Dr. Max E. Mandelstamm and Dr. David S. Jochelmann, withdrew from the congress and, meeting separately in Basle, formed the Jewish Territorial Organization (ITO), with Zangwill as president.

Israel Zangwill, the celebrated English writer, was best known for his sympathetic sketches of Jewish immigrant types, such as those portrayed in his novel *Children of the Ghetto*, which was based on his own experiences. Himself the child of a poor Russian family that had emigrated to London, Zangwill demonstrated in his writings a binding emotional attachment to the values of the Jewish past contrasted with an irresistible impulse to break away from the physical and spiritual restrictions of the ghetto. The dilemma of choosing between the ghetto and the surrounding world, never fully resolved in a satisfactory manner, was a theme which ran through Zangwill's life and work, emphasizing the paradoxical nature of modern Jewish existence in the Diaspora. Zangwill was one of Herzl's earliest supporters. Besides being the most popular contemporary Jewish writer in the English language, he was an extremely witty and even brilliant orator. Zangwill's election as president of the Jewish Territorial Organization greatly enhanced its prestige, and he continued to hold this office throughout the entire twenty-year period of the ITO's existence. At the same time, the contradictions inherent in Zangwill's approach to the Jewish experience prevented the ITO from ever establishing a clearly defined policy.

Dr. Max Emmanuel Mandelstamm, a renowned ophthalmologist, had been one of Herzl's most influential supporters among the Jews in Russia. Mandelstamm's enthusiastic advocacy of Jewish nationalism was in marked contrast to his ideological upbringing. Two of his uncles had been leading advocates of Russian-Jewish assimilation, and from childhood on he had been given a thorough secular education. After the pogroms of 1881, however, Mandelstamm was convinced that emigration was the only solution for Russian Jewry, and he became an avid supporter of the budding Zionist Movement. In his visionary novel, *Altneuland*, Herzl used him as a model for the president of his imaginary Jewish state ("an ophthalmologist from Russia, Dr. Eichenstamm"). After Herzl's death, Mandelstamm joined Zangwill in founding the Jewish Territorial Organization and became the head of operations in Russia, with his home in Kiev serving as headquarters. His overriding concern was to find a haven for the masses of Jewish emigrants from Russia. Despite many attempts by leading Zionists to tear him away from Territorialism, Mandelstamm, a beloved figure, remained the ITO's leading advocate among Russian Jews, until his widely mourned death in 1912.[11]

Dr. David S. Jochelmann,* born near Vilna, had spent his youth studying in a yeshiva, preparing to become a rabbi. At age eighteen, financial circumstances forced him to cut short his studies, and he went to work in a Jewish agricultural colony, where he became an avid advocate of farming among Jews. His enthusiasm for Jewish agricultural work led him into the Zionist Movement. Along with many other young Russian Jews, Jochelmann obtained his higher education in Switzerland, beginning his studies at the University of Berne in 1900 and earning his doctorate in philosophy several years later. During this time, Jochelmann became chairman of Berne's Zionist Academic Society and a leader in the Democratic Faction. The latter was a group initiated by young East European Jews studying in Switzerland and Germany who opposed Herzl's characteristic preoccupation with the attainment of international recognition and called, instead, for social and cultural action among the Jewish people as the main activity of the Zionist Movement. The Democratic Faction, which was Herzl's main opposition within the Zionist Movement from 1901 to 1903, was led, among others, by Chaim Weizmann, then a student at the University of Geneva, who was a friend of Jochelmann's. When Herzl first presented the British East Africa proposal in 1903, the Democratic Faction joined other "Zion Zionists" in fierce opposition. At that time, Jochelmann, a "Uganda" advocate, broke from the Democratic Faction, combining his political defection with personal estrangement. Weizmann regretted the loss of Jochelmann as a friend, commenting, "It is strange how Uganda divides and unites people." Two years later,

* Years later, during the First World War, when Jochelmann was living in England, he changed the spelling of his name to "Jochelman." (See the end of chapter 9.)

when the proposal was finally defeated, it was Jochelmann who organized the walkout from the Seventh Zionist Congress, persuading Zangwill to accept the leadership of the Territorialists.[12]

Far from considering themselves renegades, most of the Territorialists viewed themselves as the representatives of true political Zionism, referring to themselves at first as "Herzlian Zionists." They recalled that Herzl, along with some other early Zionist leaders and theorists, had seen the overwhelming necessity of a legally recognized, autonomous Jewish territory and would have initially considered any land that was suitable for such a purpose. It was only when he sensed the romantic appeal of the Land of Israel that Herzl had turned his attention toward that land. By 1903, when he had realized that he was unable to attain legal recognition for an autonomous Jewish settlement in Palestine, Herzl had been willing to sacrifice the dream of Palestine for the reality of East Africa or of any other territory that would offer such legal autonomy.

Herzl's death in 1904 was followed by the defeat of the British East Africa proposal at the Seventh Zionist Congress in 1905. Zangwill and his associates saw this as a rejection of political Zionism, which aimed for the establishment of an autonomous Jewish state, in favor of practical Zionism, whose chief advocates seemed to be engaging in haphazard pioneering work in Palestine, while giving no thought to achieving autonomy there. Although Zangwill admired them for their pioneering efforts, he considered the practical Zionists to be, basically, irresponsible adventurers who were sowing the seeds of yet another expulsion of the Jews.[13]

The Territorialists viewed themselves, then, as the true standardbearers of orthodox Herzlian Zionism. In characteristically dramatic fashion, Zangwill expressed this position as follows:

> Alas! The Palestine Charter is at present out of the question. Some suggest that we should go back to the methods of the Chovevei Zion [members of early Zionist groups founded in the 1880s] and merely establish agricultural colonies in Palestine. But Palestine without a Charter offers no security of land tenure, no open method of holding property. Zion without Zionism is a hollow mockery. . . . No, better Zionism without Zion than Zion without Zionism.[14]

As soon as it became organized, the Jewish Territorial Organization (ITO) informed the British government that it was ready to accept its offer of a territory in East Africa. The government, however, hastily withdrew the offer following its rejection by the

Seventh Zionist Congress, and it considered the matter closed. (The plan had aroused considerable opposition among British settlers in East Africa, and the government was somewhat relieved at its rejection by the Zionists.)

Having eliminated Palestine as being both unattainable and impracticable, the ITO established a geographical commission composed of some internationally known Jews whose object was to locate a territory suitable for Jewish colonization on an autonomous basis. Such a territory became known, in Territorialist parlance, as "ITOland." The search for such a territory took the geographical commission to such unlikely locations throughout the world as Cyrenaica, Angola, and Mesopotamia. Other territories which were briefly considered at various times were the Guianas, Mozambique, Cyprus, Northern Australia, and Mexico. Years later, Zangwill admitted "there was not a land on earth that we did not think about."[15]

Curiously, the Territorialists never doubted their ability to direct the masses of Russian Jewish emigrants to ITOland, once such a land would be found. Their abilities, however, were never called to the test, for none of their plans was actualized. Ultimately, the search for ITOland was an abject failure. In retrospect, it would seem that, while the practical Zionists were building up the Land of Israel, the Territorialists were searching for a land that did not exist. After its first year of existence, the ITO remained an organization in search of a project, and its members were demoralized by frustration.

At this low point in its activity, the Jewish Territorial Organization was given a tempting offer to enter into a grand project which, however, completely belied its ideology and everything for which it stood. This project was first proposed to Zangwill by Jacob H. Schiff.

In the beginning of 1906, according to Schiff's own recollection, he had been approached by United States Commissioner-General of Immigration Franklin Pierce Sargent, who knew of Schiff's ardent wish to relieve immigrant congestion in eastern port cities. Sargent suggested that the most effective way to accomplish this would be to divert immigration to the U.S. ports on the Gulf of Mexico. This suggestion from a high public official inspired Schiff to formulate a plan of action, which he outlined in his letter to Zangwill, dated August 24, 1906.[16]

Schiff was unalterably opposed to Territorialism. In addition to regarding its goal as being unattainable, he felt that attempts to establish Jewish autonomy in one territory would arouse doubts about the patriotism of Jewish citizens in other countries throughout the world. Schiff was convinced, furthermore, that America offered the best hope for the masses of Jewish refugees from Eastern Europe. His efforts, therefore, were directed at facilitating Jewish immigration to the United States, and he was now convinced that this immigration had to be diverted from the congested cities of the Northeast.

Schiff was so convinced of the necessity to reroute American Jewish immigration that he decided to enlist the aid of the Territorialists in this plan, despite his complete opposition to their ideology. In fact, Schiff later confided that he had purposely invited the participation of the Territorialists in a conscious effort to divert their attention from what he considered to be their dangerous ideology.[17] For their part, the Territorialists, too, realized that by accepting Schiff's plan they would be compromising their principles, but at least it offered a constructive outlet for their energies, a chance to get their feet wet in channeling the stream of Jewish migration. After all, they would be gaining valuable experience in the business of sending Jewish refugees to a safe haven. While agreeing to work on Schiff's project, however, they never abandoned their search for an autonomous Jewish territory.

The Jewish Territorial Organization's task in this project, as outlined in Schiff's letter to Zangwill, would be "to make propaganda to Russia itself for a change of this flow of emigration to the United States, from the Atlantic ports to New Orleans and other Gulf ports, to arrange with steamship lines to furnish the necessary facilities and to do all the manifold work which is necessary to promote a large immigration into the indicated channels." As an indication of the seriousness of his commitment, Schiff offered to personally contribute $500,000 to the American end of the project, with the assumption that the European end would be sponsored in Europe.[18]

Three days after Schiff wrote his letter to Zangwill, he sent a copy of it to Dr. Nathan, expressing the hope that Nathan would help convince Zangwill to undertake the project. [19] A personal feud, however, broke out between Nathan and Zangwill. The latter demanded total control of the project, including the American end. This Schiff refused, since he feared that Zangwill would attempt to establish an autonomous territory in the West. Arguments between Zangwill and Nathan delayed the inauguration of the project through the first part of 1907, but they were eventually resolved in the following manner: While remaining secretary of the *Hilfs-verein der deutschen Juden*, Nathan agreed to become an active member of the Jewish Territorial Organization's newly formed Emigration Regulation Department, which took charge of the European end of the project. Thus, while Nathan exerted a strong influence on the operation through the *Hilfsverein*, he was also accountable to Zangwill through the ITO.

Schiff attempted to secure the participation of the Jewish Colonization Association as well, but it proved impossible to get the Jewish Colonization Association and the Jewish Territorial Organization to cooperate in the same venture. Only July 15, 1907, Schiff wrote to Cyrus L. Sulzberger:

> It is a pity that it is so difficult for Zangwill to get along with people, or it should have been possible for him to assure the cooperation of the ICA which, I am convinced, at heart, these gentlemen are desirous to give, if it were not for Zangwill's brusque manner, in which he endeavours to claim everything for the ITO, and his unwillingness to give others their due.[20]

Another, underlying cause for the ICA's refusal to cooperate—it too, like the ITO, demanded exclusive control—may have been political rivalry between the Paris-based ICA and the Berlin-based *Hilfsverein*, which Schiff, of German family connections, might be expected to favor.

Schiff resigned himself to doing without the ICA's cooperation, satisfying himself with the participation of the Jewish Territorial Organization and the *Hilfsverein*. But while Schiff now had a European organization he still lacked an American one. For this purpose, he enlisted the cooperation of the Industrial Removal Office, managed by David M. Bressler in New York.[21] The Industrial Removal Office agreed to take the first steps toward the establishment of a new organization, which would be in charge of the project. Bressler's assistant, Morris D. Waldman, was assigned the task of locating a new port suitable for receiving mass Jewish immigration.

Zangwill wrote Schiff that it might be a good idea to bring Jewish immigrants to the South, since he had heard that more whites were needed, to diminish the influence of blacks. Schiff vetoed this idea for precisely that reason; he did not want the Jews to be used as pawns in the poisoned racial politics of the South.[22] Nevertheless, in November 1906, he sent Morris D. Waldman to Charleston,

11

South Carolina, to see if that might be an appropriate port of entry for his project.

Waldman reported that Charleston was inhospitable to Jewish immigrants; they encouraged only "Saxon and Anglo-Saxon immigrants." He recommended that New Orleans and Galveston be favored for Jewish immigration. They were, after all, closer to the West, which offered much better economic opportunities than the South, and were far from the northeastern ghettos, whose congestion the Industrial Removal Office wanted to relieve. Between New Orleans and Galveston, Waldman recommended the latter,[23] and his recommendation was accepted for several reasons. First, Europeans feared New Orleans as a center of yellow fever epidemics. Second, Galveston was closer to the West and, in fact, served as a large terminus for railroad lines from every portion of that region. At the same time, Galveston had the advantage of not being a big city. Schiff, after all, did not want the immigrants to congregate in the port of arrival, but to spread throughout the country. New Orleans, with its many economic opportunities, might have tempted the immigrants to stay.

The most important reason that Schiff chose Galveston over New Orleans was that in Galveston a direct passenger line, run by the Bremen-based Nord Deutscher-Lloyd, or North German-Lloyd Shipping Company, was already in existence and, in fact, European immigrants had been arriving there for some time. New Orleans did not have a direct passenger shipping line from Germany. Schiff's efforts to persuade the Hamburg-American Line to run a passenger steamer to New Orleans failed.[24] Thus, Galveston became the port of entry for Schiff's project.

Galveston proved to be a fortunate choice from still another standpoint, for it was the home of a dynamic spiritual and communal leader, Rabbi Henry Cohen. Cohen, a circuit-riding rabbi to many Jews in southeastern Texas, was a colorful figure. He was very active in civic and state affairs, and his influence ranged far beyond the members of his local reform congregation. Interestingly enough, Cohen had been born and raised in London, was a contemporary of Zangwill's and knew him well from the days when both studied at the Jews' Free School in London's East End.

On January 3, 1907, Schiff received word from Europe that Zangwill and Nathan had finally resolved their differences. (Actually, this information later proved to be a bit premature, but their differences were eventually resolved.) Without further delay, Morris Waldman was instructed to proceed to Galveston to organize the project.[25] Waldman, who had been a practicing rabbi before going into social work, formed a fast friendship with Rabbi Cohen. As soon as he was approached, Cohen began devoting himself wholeheartedly to the new enterprise.

On January 28, 1907, after some discussion regarding its name, the Jewish Immigrants' Information Bureau (JIIB) was established in Galveston, with Waldman as general agent. With the help of Rabbi Cohen and other local Jews, Waldman began to lay the groundwork in Galveston for welcoming the first party of immigrants, which was expected soon after Passover.[26] David M. Bressler, general manager of the Industrial Removal Office in New York, agreed to serve as the JIIB's "honorary secretary." This title was a misnomer, for Bressler's role in the Jewish Immigrants' Information Bureau was much more than honorary. In effect, Bressler ran both the Industrial Removal Office and the JIIB from the same New York office.

Bressler and Waldman were of similar background. Coincidentally, they shared a common date of birth, having both been born in Europe on May 1, 1879, and each had been brought to America when he was four or five years old. [27] More importantly, the two men were personal friends, sharing a youthful enthusiasm for the newly inaugurated project, and they worked on it very well together—Bressler from New York and Waldman from Galveston.

At about this time, a bill was proposed in Congress calling for the establishment of an immigration station in Galveston. Schiff used his influence in lobbying successfully for passage of the bill. He was helped in this endeavor by his friend Oscar S. Straus, secretary of Commerce and Labor, under whose jurisdiction immigration lay.[28]

To carry out the active recruitment of Russian-Jewish emigrants for Galveston, ITO's Emigration Regulation Department formed the Jewish Emigration Society, with Dr. Max E. Mandelstamm as president, Dr. David S. Jochelmann as secretary, or manager, and Joseph Michaelowitz as assistant manager. The Jewish Emigration Society was based in Kiev and operated many committees throughout Russia for the purpose of recruiting emigrants for Galveston. Dr. Jochelmann was authorized to organize the first expedition to Galveston, and he immediately instructed his agents to begin recruiting the emigrants.

The Jewish Immigrants' Information Bureau sent the Jewish Territorial Organization a set of guidelines to be used by Jochelmann's agents in their recruitment of emigrants for Galveston.

These guidelines indicated the types of immigrants that could be most easily absorbed. According to this list, strong laborers below the age of forty were needed. Men of the following trades were also encouraged to come: ironworkers, carpenters, cabinetmakers, butchers, tinsmiths, painters, paper-hangers, shoemakers, tailors, masons, plumbers and machinists.[29]

Among the guidelines laid down by the Jewish Immigrants' Information Bureau was one which became a considerable point of controversy: "Nor should *Schochtim* (ritual slaughterers), *melamdim* (Hebrew teachers) and others who do not work on the Sabbath be sent." Zangwill, who was not at all religiously observant—he was married to a Christian woman and refused to have his first son circumcised[30]—professed himself to be scandalized by this rule. Ironically, Schiff, who was quite well known for his refusal to conduct business matters on Saturday, [31] saw nothing wrong with this stipulation. He defended it as being entirely consistent with the labor conditions of the West. He accused Zangwill of using this issue as a pretext to promote his ideology that large autonomous settlements offered the only solution to the Jewish problem.[32] In the end Zangwill backed down, but he brought up the issue again several times in later years. For its part, the Jewish Immigrants' Information Bureau agreed to slightly modify its wording, which now read as follows: "It is but proper that intending immigrants should understand that economic conditions everywhere in the United States are such that strict Sabbath observance is exceedingly difficult and in some cases almost impossible."[33] Even with this modified wording, it was obvious that the JIIB was giving notice that it had little patience for the religious sensitivities of its future protégés.

In anticipation of the arrival of the first group, Waldman visited various cities throughout the West. Before his first visit to Galveston, Waldman had stopped off in Chicago, where he obtained the support of Adolph Kraus, president of the Independent Order B'nai Brith. This endorsement proved to be very valuable in convincing locally prominent Jews to participate actively in the reception of Jewish immigrants from Galveston. In each community, Waldman established a committee which accepted responsibility for finding jobs for a certain number of immigrants.

Waldman jokingly referred to himself as a travelling salesman who was in the business of "selling Jews." Here and there, however, he encountered a bit of "sales resistance." For example, the owner of a large shoe establishment in a small Kansas town recalled that he had once provided work for a poor immigrant shoemaker who had been sent to him from New York by the Industrial Removal Office. Within two years, he complained, this destitute refugee had become his biggest competitor. The gentleman finally agreed to cooperate with Waldman provided that no shoemaker would be sent to this town. Generally, however, the Jewish communities were very receptive. Waldman attributed this to the profound sense of shock they had experienced as a result of the Russian pogroms of 1905.[34]

In Galveston, the Jewish Immigrants' Information Bureau rented an empty warehouse, which it remodeled as a shelter for the immigrants for the few days during which they were to be selected and routed. It installed washrooms, showers, baths, and various items of furniture designed to make the immigrants' stay a pleasant one. The chairman of the local committee, a prominent citizen, was the leading insurance agent of Galveston. Naturally, Waldman asked him to provide coverage for the new fixtures. The contract job was finished on a Saturday evening, and the insurance was to be placed on Monday morning. At midnight, before the insurance went into effect, a fire broke out which destroyed the whole building. At the time Waldman happened to be in New York, where he had returned for a conference, and he had to answer directly to Schiff on the matter. Upon his return to Galveston, Waldman found another building, but Schiff had to pay for the new installations. Years later, Waldman wrote of this incident, "It was my first lesson in the direction of business hazards and the importance of taking business precautions."[35] In any event, the Jewish Immigrants' Information Bureau was now ready to receive immigrants.

The first immigrants who were recruited by Jochelmann's agents in Russia began arriving in Bremen during May 1907. The North German-Lloyd Shipping Company had arranged for kosher hotel accommodations for these emigrants. However, this kosher hotel-restaurant, which was called the *Stadt Warschau*, was closed at the time, for disinfection. The local innkeepers seized the opportunity to take advantage of the emigrants by charging them exorbitant rates. Fortunately, the Jewish Territorial Organization's Emigration Regulation Department was able to undo the damage by forcing the return of the overcharged expenses to the emigrants. One of the innkeepers was actually summoned before a court of law. In addition, the director of the Lloyd Company reprimanded the exorbitant businessmen, warning them not to repeat their repugnant behavior.[36]

The Russian-Jewish emigrants found the Germans to be obnoxious toward emigrants in general and toward them in particular. Dr. Jochelmann, who came to Bremen to see them off, advised the emigrants to choose from among themselves someone who would act as their spokesman. The captain agreed to meet daily with this representative. The S.S. *Cassel*, bound for Baltimore and Galveston, left Bremen on June 6 with approximately 1,500 passengers on board. Of these, eighty-seven were Jews bound for Galveston—sixty-six men, six women and fifteen children. Of the eighty-seven, fifty-six had been recruited in Russia by the Jewish Territorial Organization. Jochelmann accompanied the group to sea for about an hour, returning on a cutter, together with the American Consul. The Galveston Movement was on its way.[37]

After stopping in Baltimore, where it discharged half its passengers, the S.S. *Cassel* continued on its way to Galveston at a deliberately slow speed in order to conserve fuel. The ship entered the Galveston harbor early in the morning of July 1, 1907, which was the first day in which a new U.S. immigration law went into effect. Among other provisions, this law made the steamship companies subject to a $100 fine for transporting physically or mentally defective immigrants, or those afflicted with loathesome or contagious diseases. More important, it replaced the $2 head tax per immigrant with one for $4, thus doubling the expense to the steamship companies. Thus, while saving between $100 and $200 worth of coal, the captain had cost his company over $1600 in taxes![38]

The S.S. *Cassel* arrived at her pier at 7:30 A.M., and by 8:00 passengers were coming down the gangway. By prior arrangement, the eighty-seven Jewish passengers were allowed to disembark first, followed afterward by the cabin and general steerage passengers. After they had passed inspection by the Port Marine Surgeon, interrogation by the immigration inspectors and examination of baggage by the customs officers, the Jewish immigrants were loaded with their belongings onto large wagons. They were then taken about half a mile to the headquarters of the JIIB, which impressed many of them with its roominess, good lighting, and ventilation. There, they were given the opportunity of taking baths, after which they were treated to a fine kosher dinner. The immigrants were very appreciative of the kind hospitality shown them by their American coreligionists, especially after the poor treatment they had suffered in Germany.[39]

The immigrants were met in Galveston by Rabbi Cohen, Morris Waldman, and his assistant, Mr. J. Lippman. Also on hand was Jacob Billikopf, newly appointed superintendent of the Federation of Jewish Charities in Kansas City, Missouri, who came especially to assist in welcoming the new arrivals. Formerly superintendent of Charities in Milwaukee, Billikopf had cooperated closely with the Industrial Removal Office in that city. Together with Bressler and Waldman, Billikopf was one of the leading figures in the field of Jewish social work. He proved to be instrumental in making Kansas City a showplace for the Jewish Immigrants' Information Bureau.

The JIIB had received from the ITO a list containing the occupation of every immigrant in the group. The immigrants were called up individually to tables, where this information was verified. Working mainly on the basis of the immigrants' occupations, the JIIB officials assigned them to various locations throughout the West—nineteen cities in all.

During the afternoon, the mayor of Galveston, Mr. Landes, visited the headquarters of the Jewish Immigrants' Information Bureau. Rabbi Cohen called the immigrants together and, speaking in Yiddish, told them in glowing terms of the democratic country to which they had come. Then he introduced Mayor Landes, whose words he translated into Yiddish. "You have come to a great country," the mayor said. "With industry and economy all of you will meet with success. Obey the laws and try to make good citizens." He then shook hands with each member of the party. One of the immigrants, formerly a school teacher in sourthern Russia, responded in halting English to the mayor's words of greeting, with the assistance of Rabbi Cohen:

> We are overwhelmed that the ruler of the city should greet us. We have never been spoken to by the officials of our country except in terms of harshness, and although we have heard of the great land of freedom, it is very hard to realize that we are permitted to grasp the hand of the great man. We will do all we can to make good citizens.[40]

Most of the immigrants were sent off that very day. The rest of them spent the night there and were dispatched during the following day. Billikopf took nine men back with him to Kansas City. Three immigrants, who had arrived in Galveston ahead of the first group,[41] were already in Kansas City, making it the leading host city for immigrants sent by the JIIB, a distinction which it continually retained throughout the existence of the Galveston Movement.[42] Seven men were sent to Saint Joseph and two to Saint Louis, making Missouri the largest receiving state of Jewish immigrants from Galveston. Minnesota came in second, with nine immigrants being sent to Minneapolis, three to Saint Paul, and one to Duluth. Iowa was represented by five cities, more than any other state: Cedar Rapids received three immigrants, Des Moines and Dubuque two apiece, and Davenport and Sioux City one each. The rest of the immigrants were distributed among the following cities: Denver and Pueblo, Colorado; Lincoln and Grand Island, Nebraska; Quincy, Illinois; Milwaukee, Wisconsin; Oklahoma City, Oklahoma. The State of Texas was represented by Fort Worth, which took in four immigrants. None of the new arrivals remained in Galveston. In keeping with its policy, the Galveston Movement discouraged its immigrants from staying in that city longer than necessary.[43]

On July 14, 1907, the second party, consisting of twenty-six Jewish immigrants, arrived in Galveston. These immigrants complained of the poor treatment they had suffered on board the ship, the S.S. *Frankfurt*. The Jewish Immigrants' Information Bureau relayed this complaint to the *Hilfsverein*, which took the matter up with the North German-Lloyd Co. in Bremen. Some of the passengers on board the *Frankfurt* had originally been booked for the *Cassel*, which carried the first group, but, for various reasons, they actually sailed with the second group.[44] Among these was a woman with six children, whose husband had gone ahead with the first group and had been sent to Pueblo, Colorado. Naturally, his wife and children were sent there to join him. The rest of the immigrants were distributed among the following cities: Des Moines, Sioux City, and Burlington, Iowa; Duluth and Saint Paul, Minnesota; Topeka and Leavenworth, Kansas; Joplin, Missouri. One man, a baker, was sent as far north as Fargo, North Dakota.[45]

Having disposed of the second group, Waldman decided to visit some of the cities where the first immigrants had been sent, beginning with the twin cities of Minneapolis and Saint Paul, Minnesota. In Saint Paul, Waldman was glad to note that the three immigrants who had arrived with the first group were quite pleased with their situation. One, a shoemaker, worked at his trade for $7.50 a week, with a promise for an eventual salary of twice as much. The second man, who claimed to have been a watchmaker in Russia, had really been an unskilled hand in a watch factory. The local committee decided to send him to school to learn how to become a barber. The third immigrant, formerly a noodle and macaroni maker, was given a job washing cars. A fourth immigrant, a member of the second group, was also living in Saint Paul. He had been a grain dealer in Russia, but he arrived in America too weak to work. The committee decided to buy him a horse, a wagon and some stock and send him on the beaten path to fortune. The immigrants were generally pleased with their reception in Saint Paul.

The immigrants in Minneapolis were much less satisfied, being bitterly disappointed with the salaries they were receiving. They did not find fault with the local committee but, rather, they blamed the Russian agents of the ITO for exaggerating the opportunities in America. Three of the immigrants stated that Dr. Jochelmann and his representatives had explicitly promised them salaries of between $12 and $18 per week. In reaction to Waldman's report, the JIIB wrote Jochelmann asking him to discontinue these empty promises.[46]

Waldman next visited Cedar Rapids, Iowa, where he had sent three immigrants from the first party. One immigrant, who said he had been a farmer, was given a job at the Quaker Cereal Factory. The other two men claimed to be carpenters, so they were put to work at that trade. Neither of them qualified, however, and they were soon dismissed. One of them, who was quite mediocre, was placed in another carpentry position with a starting salary of $12 a week. The other "carpenter," however, was discovered to be a fraud, as he could not even tell the difference between a saw and a plane. In addition, he was not used to hard labor. The local committee finally found him an easy job in a packing house at $1.25 per day. This incident illustrates a problem which was to plague the JIIB in its placement of immigrants: Frequently, immigrants claimed to be members of certain professions in the hope of being able to learn on the job. The failure of these men, once placed in positions, to demonstrate even the minimum necessary skills, reflected badly upon the credibility of the Jewish Immigrants' Information Bureau.[47]

Before returning to Galveston, Waldman visited Kansas City, Missouri, where he had sent twelve immigrants including three who had preceded the first group. He discovered that they were doing fine and generally earning comparatively good wages for immigrants. Two carpenters were earning salaries of $12 per week. A tailor was receiving $8 weekly plus room and board. Another tailor was earning enough to support himself and his wife, who was not working. A laundry presser was making $8 with the promise that he would eventually make $15 per week. An unskilled laborer was earning $9 a week in a junk yard. A factory hand was working at a packing house for $1.75 per day, steady work, and had already sent 20 rubles to his family. Another man who was working at the packing house was actually a mason, but could not do teamwork because of his ignorance of English. After going through four jobs as a bricklayer, he was given a job at the packing house for $10.50 per week. As in Cedar Rapids, the lowest-paying jobs were reserved for those who could not demonstrate the skills they claimed to have. One man, who declared himself to be a tailor, had to satisfy himself with a job as a pants presser for $6 a week. Another immigrant did not tell the truth when he claimed to be a bookbinder. He was put to work in a factory at a weekly salary of $5.[48]

The men who were sent by the Jewish Immigrants' Information Bureau to Kansas City were doing better than most immigrants who had arrived there on their own. Unfortunately, many of them had been led to believe, by Dr. Jochelmann and his agents in Russia, that they would be earning even more money. Their complaints, however, were not as vociferous as those of the immigrants in Minneapolis. Waldman attributed this to the fact that Billikopf met with them twice a week, taught them English and otherwise encouraged them in their endeavors. By taking a personal interest in their progress, Billikopf had a profoundly uplifting effect on the morale of the immigrants in Kansas City. It soon became clear that, as a general rule, the personal attitudes of the local representatives of the Jewish Immigrants' Information Bureau often contributed to the degree of adjustment shown by the immigrants in the various cities.

Largely satisfied with the results of his trip, Waldman returned to Galveston to prepare for the reception of the third immigrant party.

CHAPTER 2

1907: Activity and Controversy

The groups of Jewish immigrants arriving in Galveston during the summer of 1907 established a certain routine which, allowing for modification to meet changing conditions, remained throughout the history of the Galveston Movement. At its peak, the ITO's Jewish Emigration Society, based in Kiev, operated a network of eighty-two committees throughout the Russian Pale of Jewish settlement. These committees distributed literature in Yiddish describing the opportunities waiting for immigrants in the American West. Jews applying for emigration at these local offices paid a price which included transportation to Bremen and lodging there, plus a ticket for the next available steamship bound for Galveston. They also received letters of introduction which they were to present to the *Hilfsverein der deutschen Juden* in Bremen and to the Jewish Immigrants' Information Bureau in Galveston.

The *Hilfsverein* saw to it that the immigrants were not taken advantage of while in Bremen. It also obtained assurances from the North German-Lloyd Shipping Company that the Jewish immigrants would be treated fairly aboard ship, but these assurances were often violated. As each ship left Bremen, the *Hilfsverein* cabled Bressler at the Jewish Immigrants' Information Bureau in New York. Every cablegram contained the name of the ship and the number of ITO immigrants on board. As soon as Bressler received such a cablegram, he sent a copy of it to the JIIB manager at Galveston. (Waldman remained manager only during the first year of operations.)

Bressler also usually received two separately prepared lists, one from the Jewish Emigration Society and one from the *Hilfsverein*, each containing the names, ages, cities of origin, and occupations of the immigrants. When the lists conflicted with each other, which was often, the *Hilfsverein* list usually proved more accurate, since some immigrants sent from Russia did not reach Bremen in time for the ship which they had intended to take. Sometimes, though, the *Hilfsverein* lists were incorrect due to last-minute arrivals or changes of heart on the part of some prospective immigrants. Inaccurate as they were, the lists served as some indication to the manager in Galveston as to approximately how many immigrants he would have to distribute, and what their occupations were. As much as possible, he planned to send them to cities in which their professed skills would prove useful.

The manager usually had a choice of about twenty to thirty towns and cities among which to distribute the immigrants. Here, the help of the Industrial Removal Office and the B'nai B'rith was crucial. The local branches of these organizations organized special committees to look after the immigrants for a short time until they could be provided with work. The willingness of these committees to accept this responsibility fluctuated with local economic conditions and other factors. At one time or another, over two hundred Jewish communities cooperated in this manner. To each, the Jewish Immigrants' Information Bureau gave an allowance of ten dollars per immigrant or twenty-five dollars per family, whichever was less.

Many of the local committees, usually consisting of businessmen who were also active in other affairs, found little time for the immigrants after they had provided them with jobs. If the jobs proved to be unsatisfactory, the committees, especially if they existed in small towns, would often send the immigrants to the nearest large city, thus eliminating the problem from their midst. This caused the JIIB to establish paid employment agents in several large cities, with salaries of about sixty dollars per month, in addition to the allowance per immigrant or per family. If a small boatload of immigrants (that is, under twenty-five) arrived at Galveston, they were distributed among the small towns. If, however, a larger shipment arrived, many were sent to the bigger cities, such as Kansas City and Minneapolis, whose agents had fixed salaries.

The Galveston Jewish community agreed to host the JIIB on the presumption that Galveston would not serve as a center for immigrant settlement but, rather, as a temporary depot from which the immigrants would move out to other cities throughout the

West. To insure that this be the case, it was considered essential that the immigrants be sent on to their ultimate destinations as quickly as possible after they had been processed by the United States immigration authorities. If possible, they were sent out that very day. If not, they were provided with food and shelter at the headquarters of the Jewish Immigrants' Information Bureau, for a few days at the most. After that, they were given free transportation to their ultimate points of destination (for which the JIIB paid the railroad companies specially reduced charity rates, amounting to one-half the normal first-class rate). Each immigrant received a letter of introduction which he was to present to the agent or committee chairman to whom he was sent. Thus, out of the ten thousand immigrants handled during the course of the Galveston Movement, less than three hundred remained in Galveston, while the remainder were settled throughout the West.[1]

After sending off a group of immigrants, the manager sent to Bressler in New York a full report, which included the final destination of each immigrant. Bressler passed on this information to the *Hilfsverein* and to the London headquarters of the Jewish Territorial Organization. The ITO, in turn, informed the Jewish Emigration Society in Kiev as to the whereabouts of each immigrant. If the family of any immigrant wished to contact him, they could obtain his address through the Jewish Emigration Society.

The third party, consisting of seventy immigrants, arrived in Galveston on August 6, 1907. They were distributed among twenty-one cities in the states of Missouri, Iowa, Minnesota, Wisconsin, Ohio, Nebraska, Colorado, and Texas.[2]

At first, Bressler was wary of concentrating Jews in Texas and asked the ITO, in its recruitment campaign, "not to emphasize Texas and especially Galveston, in fact to say that Galveston offers no opportunity for the immigrant."[3] Soon, however, Bressler realized that this was unnecessary. He informed the ITO that the JIIB had "added several cities in the State of Texas, because while we wish special stress laid on the fact that Galveston itself offers no opportunity for the immigrant, the State of Texas is otherwise not barren of opportunities for the newcomer."[4]

Of the third party, four immigrants were sent to Fort Worth, five to Dallas, and five to Houston. The Houston group consisted of a shoemaker, a baker, a blacksmith, a bookbinder, and a common laborer. The first three were all given work at their respective trades. Only the bookbinder had difficulty finding a job. As for the laborer, he was sent to work in the countryside near Houston.[5]

Kansas City took in nine immigrants from the third party, more than any other city. One man had actually intended to go to Boston, where three of his brothers lived, but had somehow found himself on the ship to Galveston. After spending two weeks in Kansas City, he left for Boston. The others did quite well in Kansas City, including a shoemaker who opened up his own shop.

The men of the third party made an average of about $9.50 per week in Kansas City. Women typically were given lower salaries than men. For instance, two immigrants of opposite sex were provided with work in a packing house, with the man earning $8 and the woman only $6 per week. As things turned out, this couple decided to get married, so they eventually pooled their resources to support the expenses of a common household.[6]

Not all the members of the third group found their places in America. One immigrant, a shoemaker, was sent to Fort Worth, where he secured immediate employment and, in fact, was able to save over $50 in about two-and-a-half months. He was homesick, however. Returning to Galveston, he purchased a steamship ticket to Bremen and returned to his family in Europe.[7]

The fourth group, which arrived in Galveston on August 24, consisted of eighty-nine Jewish immigrants, more than any previous group. They were distributed in twenty-six cities throughout the states of Wisconsin, Minnesota, North Dakota, Illinois, Iowa, Missouri, Kansas, Nebraska, Oklahoma, Texas, and Colorado. One immigrant was sent as far west as Los Angeles, California.[8]

It was inevitable that some immigrants would become disillusioned and wish that they had gone to New York, like most of their contemporaries. One immigrant who arrived with the fourth party and was sent to Sioux City, Iowa, sent a letter to his wife in Europe imploring her to sell everything in order to send him the fare from there to New York.[9] There were, of course, many others like him who, nevertheless, eventually adjusted to living in what they at first considered alien surroundings.

Despite the dissatisfaction of some immigrants with their reception in the United States, most of their complaints centered about the poor treatment which they received in Germany. In response to these complaints, Clement I. Salaman, honorary secretary of the Jewish Territorial Organization, made a special trip from London to Bremen to investigate conditions there, timing his trip to coincide with the sending of the fifth party to Galveston. To his dismay, Salaman discovered that many of these complaints were well founded. The office where the emigrants were received in Bremen was very small, overcrowded, poorly ventilated, dirty, and of foul odor. It was a haven for all beggars and homeless Jews who happened to find themselves in Bremen. Instead of being granted private interviews, different people with varying problems were dealt with collectively. The resulting confusion can be left to the imagination. There was neither order nor system in dealing with the emigrants.[10]

The manager of the *Hilfsverein* immigration office in Bremen at this time was Dr. Jacob Klatzkin, himself a Jew from Russia. In 1909, Klatzkin was to offer his talents to the World Zionist Organization, for which he energetically worked thereafter on the intellectual as well as organization level. Klatzkin established for himself a brilliant career as a Hebrew and German essayist and philosopher, arguing for a strictly territorial definition of Zionism, without any traditionalist sentiment. It is interesting to recall that until he became active in promoting the Zionist cause Klatzkin was, in Salaman's words, the special representative of the Jewish Territorial Organization in Bremen. Klatzkin tried his best to help the ITO emigrants, as well as many other Jewish emigrants in the teeming port of Bremen, but he had almost no staff to support him.[11]

The paid secretary of the *Hilfsverein* in Bremen, a Mr. Goldsmidt, was also a teacher and *shochet* (ritual slaughterer). Thus, he had little time for his *Hilfsverein* duties. The secretary usually spent about two hours a day at the office, but on the day before the departure of the fifth group he did not put in an appearance at all. Rabbi Dr. Leopold Rosenak, president of the Hilfsverein's Bremen branch, dropped in at the office every once in a while to assist in the work. He was very energetic and sincerely dedicated, but his many communal and pastoral duties absorbed most of his time and energy. Rosenak also aided thousands of other Jewish refugees, bound for other destinations.[12]

After visiting the *Hilfsverein* office, Salaman went on to inspect the lodging houses, where the emigrants were kept during their stay in Bremen. He reported as follows:

> The [house] most frequented by Jewish emigrants was *Stadt Warshau*. I might add at this point that emigrants have no choice as to the house in which they shall lodge, but are allotted by the police authorities to the various lodging house keepers. *Stadt Warshau* is the joint property of the *Nord Deutscher Lloyd* and its largest and richest agent. It is a large rambling building and is not constructed on the best principle. The Jewish kitchen and dining hall are on the ground floor, the windows open into a narrow yard, and immediately opposite are the latrines. The dining room and kitchen were infested with flies,

parts of the wall were simply black with them, but no means were taken to abate the nuisance. The dormitories in this building are exceedingly unsatisfactory. They are large but ill-ventilated, and contain from twenty to forty or more beds in a room. These beds are not separated but are in long rows without any division between them. As the windows in most cases are immediately at the back of the rows of beds, and can only be opened wholly or not at all, it is obvious that those sleeping under the window would prefer the stuffy air to the draughts which would come from the open windows immediately behind them. There are no means by which the emigrants may retain the same bed on consecutive nights. The close proximity of the sleepers and the danger of occupying a bed which has been previously used by a person suffering from a contagious disease must be great. . . .

The bulk of our emigrants were allotted to a temporary building situated in the gas works which is under the direct management of the Nord Deutscher Lloyd. At present owing to the cholera scare and the quarantine regulations, all Russian emigrants are now relegated to this building. I paid two visits to an establishment, and I am afraid I can give no adequate idea of the horrible conditions which prevailed. The building is a large L-shaped barn and is licensed to hold 400 emigrants. The approach is through a kitchen. The heat and smell of the large temporary field stoves, added to the appalling smell of humanity, baffle description. The beds are ranged in two tiers, one above the other, around the walls and in the center. Every bed appeared occupied, men, women and children sleeping together. I know that one family consisting of husband, wife and three children had two beds between them. The disorder and dirt can hardly be imagined. . . . Dancing and fighting, I am told, continued through the whole night. Needless to say the complaints of our emigrants, some of whom were most respectable men, were great.[13]

Salaman reported that conditions for emigrants in Hamburg were much better than those in Bremen. Unfortunately, though, the Hamburg-America Line did not send ships to Galveston. Even the conditions in Hamburg, however, were inferior to those in the ports of emigration in England. In addition, the prices charged by the German lodging houses were exorbitant compared to those charged in England.

On Thursday, August 22, Salaman went down to the port to see off the fifth ITO group, which consisted of some seventy-three Jewish emigrants. The S.S. *Frankfurt* was licensed to carry 1,600 passengers, but it carried only 1,400. Yet, even with this reduced number, it appeared to Salaman that the emigrants were packed much too tightly for comfort. At about the time of his visit, an American commission was also investigating emigration conditions in Europe. Upon its return to the United States, the commission recommended a small increase in the amount of air space allowed to each emigrant, a minor improvement which was not to be enacted until 1909.

The arduous and lengthy voyage added to the already bedraggled appearance of the emigrants. Many of them had arrived in Bremen with barely more than a change of clothing, crudely wrapped together in a knapsack. The *Hilfsverein* tried to help them by providing cast-off clothing, but this often added to the incongruity of their appearance. As Salaman pointed out, "a young man calling himself a laborer will hardly give an impression of efficiency when clothed in a shabby genteel frock coat originally made for a portly gentleman, and a pair of trousers to match, nor is his appearance improved by a frayed and dirty linen shirt."[14]

Far more important than poor appearance, some immigrants had symptoms of trachoma, an infectious eye disease which led to automatic exclusion by the U.S. inspectors at Galveston. The S.S. *Frankfurt*, which arrived with the fifth group on September 14, returned to Bremen with four Jewish passengers who had arrived as members of previous groups and had shown signs of trachoma. These were the first deportees among the immigrants of the Galveston Movement.[15]

In order to minimize the number of deportations and to facilitate the smooth running of the Galveston Movement, the ITO issued a Yiddish pamphlet, which it prepared in consultation with the JIIB. This pamphlet advised emigrants how to dress, pack and otherwise prepare for the voyage to Galveston. It also contained useful instructions on behavior aboard ship. For example, "the emigrants are cautioned against the practice of bathing their eyes with salt water, which might lead to their rejection."[16]

Although the pamphlet alluded to some difficulties which the emigrant might encounter, it tended to minimize them, for its aim was not to discourage emigration to Galveston, but to facilitate it. For example, the following statement was included in the preface, which was written by Zangwill:

> The passage to Galveston has indeed the drawback of being longer than the passage to New York, but the real troubles of a sea-passage are those which occur in the first few days; the latter part of a voyage, after the passenger has found his sea-legs, is generally agreeable, and as long sea-voyages are invariably recommended by the doctors to worn-out patients, the emigrant is likely to arrive in the New World with new strength for his new struggle.[17]

Despite Zangwill's description, it is doubtful whether many physicians would have advised their "worn-out patients" to embark on lengthy voyages in the steerage compartments of overcrowded ships.

While the fifth group was in mid-voyage, the next ITO emigrants were making their way from Russia to Bremen, where the sixth group was scheduled to depart on September 12. Several of them, however, were arrested on the frontier and never made it to Bremen. One of these would-be emigrants, Jacob Gorodetsky, returned to his home near Kiev, where he raised a considerable fuss, demanding the return of his luggage.[18] Eventually, Gorodetsky's case was resolved and he found his way to Galveston among the members of the eighth group.[19]

In the meantime, the sixth group sailed according to schedule, arriving at Galveston on October 5. The Jewish Immigrants' Information Bureau had been notified by the ITO to expect sixty-five immigrants, but the group actually consisted of eighty. Nevertheless, the JIIB encountered no unusual difficulties in assigning these people to various localities throughout the West. Unfortunately, though, five of the immigrants were detained—two for trachoma and three for tuberculosis.[20]

During this time, Salaman's report, which exposed the terrible conditions in Bremen and on the steamships, was brought to the attention of the ITO Emigration Regulation Department in London. As a means of bringing pressure to bear on the North German-Lloyd Shipping Company, the ITO decided to virtually suspend the Galveston Movement for one shipment. Consequently, the seventh group, which left Bremen October 3 and reached Galveston October 26, consisted of only nine immigrants.[21] In order not to discourage potential applicants, the officials announced that the "suspension" was taking place due to the advent of the Jewish holidays.[22]

During the last week of September 1907, Zangwill and Salaman visited Bremen. There, in consultation with the local *Hilfsverein* and ITO committees, they drew up a list of demands, which they presented to the general director of the North German-Lloyd, Dr. Weigand. Dr. Weigand received the delegation in a friendly manner and even accompanied it on a tour of the *Stadt Warshau* lodging house. He agreed to institute major hygienic and social improvements there and on his ships to Galveston, taking Jewish sensitivities into special consideration. For example, he announced the establishment on each ship of a kosher kitchen, to be supervised by a representative of Rabbi Rosenak. (Until then, the only kosher meat available came packaged in tin cans.) Dr. Weigand also promised to eventually institute a direct and speedy passenger service to Galveston. For its part, the *Hilfsverein* undertook to establish, with the cooperation of the ITO, an efficient Bremen office, which became known as the ITO Emigrants' Dispatch Committee. The promises were written down in the form of a contract, which was signed by representatives of both the *Hilfsverein* and the North German-Lloyd Shipping Company.[23]

While the agreement looked quite impressive on paper, many of its provisions were carried out only grudgingly, if at all. At the very least, by providing for periodic inspection by the *Hilfsverein*, it helped to keep the most serious abuses to a minimum. Some of its provisions, however, were simply never implemented. For example, ships to Galveston continued to make at least one stop, either at Baltimore or at Philadelphia, and they remained as slow as ever, averaging about twenty-four days for the journey.

The virtual suspension of the seventh group caused the next group to be very large. The eighth group, which left Bremen October 24, consisted of one hundred eighty-nine Jewish emigrants, or more than twice that of any previous group. The *Hilfsverein*-run ITO Emigrants' Dispatch Committee sent along one of its active members, Dr. Oscar Nacht, as an official observer and intermediary. This was one of the few times that the North German-Lloyd Shipping Company allowed an official representative of the ITO or *Hilfsverein* to accompany a group to Galveston, and to intercede for them. Dr. Nacht kept careful notes and submitted a full report upon his return to Bremen. This is the only detailed report we have on the sea voyage of a group of Jewish immigrants to Galveston. In his report, Dr. Nacht vividly described overcrowded steerage conditions, lack of adequate food distribution, improper medical care, and abuse of the passengers by the anti-Semitic crew. He included in his report many recommendations for the future, but it is doubtful whether many of them were carried out. The experiences recorded by Dr. Nacht, then, were typical of those undergone by immigrants in later years, as well.[24]

As described by Dr. Nacht, the first sight of the cramped steerage quarters was enough to depress anyone who saw it. Although each immigrant had been designated a specific sleeping space, the first two days were spent in a desperate attempt to obtain more favorable accommodations, every man for himself. Eventually, the immigrants realized that their efforts were in vain, and that "some 180 persons . . . [would] have to lie close to and over one another in a single cubicle for three weeks." Naturally, this in itself created a mood of dissatisfaction, which persisted for the remainder of the journey.

There was not much that Dr. Nacht could do to improve conditions for members of the eighth group of ITO immigrants, but sometimes his intercessions proved effective. For example, when he visited a Jewish steerage section on the first morning of the voyage, he saw that the passengers had problems conducting a proper prayer service in those crowded conditions. At their request, Nacht obtained permission for the Jewish passengers to conduct a daily service in the adjacent dining hall, each morning before breakfast.

The newly inaugurated kosher kitchen was a great boon to the Jewish immigrants, but it was, unfortunately, too small and did not contain enough proper utensils. The cook, who also served as superintendent, was overwhelmed with work. Moreover, the dining hall did not have enough room to seat all the passengers at once. Dr. Nacht described the eating arrangements as follows:

> The people have to come up four times a day, one after another, pushing on for an hour before their bit of food is thrown into their vessel, while neither their fellow-passengers, nor those who distribute it, are very considerate in the process. . . . Many passengers have the feeling of being fed almost like cattle. . . . The present arrangements and the steerage as a whole are unworthy of human beings.[25]

Except for beer, no refreshments were sold in the steerage compartment, ostensibly to prevent members of the crew from embezzling food products and selling them to the passengers. Thus, the steerage passengers were totally dependent on the meals which they received in the dining hall.

During the second week of the voyage, the Jewish passengers began to discover that their meat was no longer fresh, so they went without it until they arrived at the port of Baltimore, after two weeks at sea. At Baltimore, kosher meat and sausages were provided for the remainder of the journey. In accordance with Jewish practice, food for the Sabbath was prepared on Friday, but especially warm weather made its taste objectionable to some of the passengers.

Although most other food supplies were satisfactory, the bread rations were quite meager, leading to grumbling among the Jewish passengers. During the last ten days of the voyage, from Baltimore to Galveston, Nacht managed to secure them a double allowance of bread. Other instances of stinginess, while of lesser importance, were no less aggravating. When, for example, a half-emptied tea-kettle was filled up, the corresponding amount of sugar was added only after Nacht's repeated requests. After the ship's stopover in Baltimore, where it discharged many of its passengers and loaded up with fresh supplies, the shortage of meat, bread, and sugar was alleviated.

Whenever possible, Dr. Nacht tried to remedy unnecessary hardships. Although he officially represented the Jewish immigrants, he often interceded for the benefit of all the passengers, as in the following incident, which he recorded:

> It was raining for several days, while owing to the heavy rolling of the vessel, the people could not remain in their compartments, and ran upon the deck. Nevertheless, it was only after I got to know that there existed some means of protection in such cases and spoke to the captain about it, that the tarpaulins were put up. It is thus often possible to save the steerage much hardship by a trifling act which, however, remains undone.[26]

Other unnecessary inconveniences were due less to the callous attitude of crew members than to the habitual enforcement of thoughtless measures, as in the followig example:

> The straw bags that serve as mattresses are put in white cases at the beginning of the journey, but are removed a few days before reaching Baltimore, so that the passengers to Galveston have to sleep during ten or twelve days on uncovered straw bags. In consequence, I would hear the people complain: "We are treated like cattle!" After their having been used to cover bedding, the removal of the cases makes a still worse impression. The alleged reason for such a measure is the apprehension that many passengers would carry the cases away with them on their landing at Baltimore. But if this measure be really necessary, we ought to demand that after Baltimore, the bedding be covered anew for those who go further.[27]

Every morning, all of the passengers had to report to the ship's physician, after which their cards were to be punched as a sign that they had passed inspection. The "inspections" soon became the object of bitter sarcasm, as Nacht observed, for "the doctor only paid attention to the cards that have to be punched without bestowing a glance on the immigrants themselves." Dr. Nacht reported additional examples of poor medical treatment:

> A passenger, who had been lying ill for eight days in his nook, was at last discovered by his fellow-passengers, and then taken to the

doctor. Though the patient, whose stomach had not exercised its functions during eight days, was in a most pitiable condition, shivering in his whole body, awfully emaciated, and in the greatest anxiety, the doctor merely dispensed purgatives which the patient vomited immediately. To my question whether nothing else should be done for the patient, the doctor replied that so far there was no occasion for it. Half an hour later I found the man on the deck, lying on the ground and writhing with pain. I fetched the doctor, who only now saw fit to order the man to be taken to the hospital. But even there the nursing left much to be desired. It was proved to me that in spite of his terribly reduced state, the patient never received special refreshments, being kept on ordinary steerage food, so that the patient at last ran away from the hospital, where hardly anyone took notice of him.

Another patient, who was visibly very hot and feverish, applied to me for advice, and I sent him to the doctor. But on knocking at the door, it was signified to him very roughly (according to the man's own story, he received a knock in the chest), that he could only be admitted during the reception hour. A little later I found the man on the deck, naturally imagining his condition more dangerous than it really was, while his companions were shaking their heads at the inconsiderateness of the doctor, who could not even know whether it was not a very serious case.[28]

In general, Nacht commended the captain, the officers, and other superior officials for their sympathetic attitude towards the passengers. Immigrants traveling in steerage, however, had little contact with those officials and were treated roughly by the guards and the sailors. A contempuous attitude toward steerage passengers by members of the crew was typical of German ships, as Dr. Nacht pointed out:

I have found out that the treatment on the English vessels differs very favorably from that on German ships. The vessels plying between Great Britain and America are also fitted out with much more accommodation for emigrants, though the cabins on German vessels are preferred to all others, even by Englishmen. I noticed, indeed, that while the steerage passengers are not supposed to have any wishes or to deserve scarcely any consideration beyond the requirements of animal life, all the wishes of the cabin passengers are carefully anticipated, and nothing is too difficult that may increase their comfort. Whereas the stewards almost renounce their own human dignity towards the cabin passengers, they behave in the opposite manner towards the steerage passengers, expecting a similar renunciation from the latter.[29]

Just as the immigrants complained about the members of the crew, the latter had their own complaints about the immigrants of whom, they said, the Jews and Germans were the "worst." The German immigrants, it seems, felt that they were entitled to a privileged position on board a German ship, and they objected to being treated like the others. As for the Jews, they were sensitive, sometimes overly so, to the least injustice, and protested the loudest when their rights were violated. The Bulgarians and the Poles were rated the "best" immigrants, for they never complained about anything. Clashes occurred most frequently between Jewish immigrants and German crew members, since many of the latter were anti-Semitic to begin with. Nacht was convinced, as he put it, "that no great improvements will ever be attained in this respect on German vessels, as it is not in the nature of a German to be considerate towards strangers of the steerage passengers' class, especially to the Jews among them."[30]

Since Nacht did not expect his report to result in any great improvements, he asked the Jewish representatives in Bremen to warn the immigrants of the hardships they would have to face and to advise them to submit to the irksome regulations without complaint. In addition, he recommended that the immigrants should be asked to be more considerate of each other. He had noticed that the crowded steerage conditions had led, unfortunately, to clashes among the Jewish immigrants themselves.

On November 18, the S.S. *Frankfurt* finally arrived at its destination, where the warm welcome given to the newcomers was all the more appreciated after the hard voyage. The eyes of the immigrants "sparkled with gratitude" as Nacht put it, "when after a long interval they found themselves once more treated like human beings and brothers." Dr. Nacht had never seen "more active and kindly workers than Rabbi Cohen and Mr. Waldman."[31] The immigrants were quickly distributed throughout as many as sixty-six cities in eighteen states.[32]

Despite the original reluctance of the JIIB to accept *shochtim* and *melamdim*,[33] a ritual slaughterer and a Hebrew teacher were, indeed, among the arriving immigrants. They were sent, along with nine other new arrivals, to Kansas City. There, the *shochet* was put to work at his trade with the local butchers, but the *melamed* was simply given a menial job at one of the many liquor companies in that city. Perhaps he also gave Hebrew lessons on the side.

At another Kansas City liquor company, a twenty-five-year-old man and a twenty-eight-year-old woman, both from Warsaw, were provided with work. The woman earned $6 per week while the man was given a job as a salesman for $8.50. These were typical—

and typically unequal—starting salaries in Kansas City for female and male immigrants. After a month or two of experience, salaries were generally increased a dollar or two. At about this time, the average salary for a JIIB immigrant now working in Kansas City was $10.25 per week.[34] This enabled many of them to save enough money to send for their families. By this time, in fact, many of the previous immigrants had already sent their loved ones over a hundred dollars. As for the newly arrived couple from Warsaw, they got married in Kansas City. For them, at least, the voyage of the eighth group ended on a romantic note.[35]

As for some other members of the group, their experiences were anything but romantic. New Orleans took in twelve immigrants, which was more than any other city. Apparently, however, the local committee had difficulty providing work for these men. Barely a week passed before a letter signed by four of the immigrants appeared in the *Yiddishes Taggeblatt*, a New York Yiddish daily which catered to an Orthodox readership. The letter read as follows:

> We, the undersigned four immigrants, find ourselves in New Orleans in great distress. We are among those who, in Russia, let ourselves be persuaded, by those who promised us all fortune, that we should travel with the ITO to America through Galveston. We have all our friends in New York and Philadelphia who would help us find work. We are carpenters who are well skilled in our trade and would have no difficulty finding work. We were told, though, that the representatives of the ITO provide the immigrants with work. We came, therefore, with a party of immigrants to Galveston. From there they sent us to New Orleans, where there are few Jews, and those that are here do not interest themselves in us and do not want to help us. And among Christians we cannot find work, because we don't understand the language. We are, therefore, in great distress.
>
> We hope, dear editor, that by your printing this letter perhaps our friends will learn of us and come to our aid. And secondly, you will prevent other Jews from letting themselves be talked into going through Galveston.
>
> Sincerely yours,
>
> Noah Izvolensky [Oswolinsky],
> Berl Izvolensky [Oswolinsky],
> Jacob Porefsky [Porisky], and
> Moses Lytinsky [Yshintzky],

all from Hozerkov, Kiev province.[36]

To supporters of the Galveston Movement, it seemed that the New York Yiddish newspapers were altogether too anxious to print sensational negative criticism of its work. Schiff accused the New York Yiddish press of malicious intent to subvert the movement, because if Jewish immigrants would be diverted from New York, it would lose potential readers.[37] This accusation, however, had little justification. By their general endorsement of the Industrial Removal Office and of other Baron de Hirsch projects, the Yiddish papers disproved Schiff's charge that they were against spreading the immigrants throughout the country. In fact, two days after it printed the letter from New Orleans, the *Yiddishes Taggeblatt* ran an editorial which was designed to minimize the effects of this letter. The editorial read, in part, as follows:

> We believe . . . that one must be careful in judging the work of the ITO on the basis of this letter. We know that in the best thing there are "kickers" who find fault, and especially in a matter concerning immigration. Surely, those who came through Galveston must suffer a little in the beginning. Anybody who comes to another country has to suffer in the beginning, and those who wrote this letter do not know that if they would have been in New York or in Philadelphia they would have had it any better, and especially they do not know if, in the near future, New Orleans will not be better than the biggest cities in the East.
>
> The information which we heard from other sources, that the representatives of the ITO care for the newcomers, and that they adjust themselves in the new places, puts us even more in doubt about the tragic letter that we printed.
>
> Our readers know that we were never very enthusiastic about the Galveston Plan and about the whole immigration to the South. We said, though, that this is a useful work, and we also say now that one should not get impressed about the "Galveston *glikn*" [fortunes], and it is only an experiment and we will wait to see what will be later.[38]

While the conservative *Taggeblatt* was willing to give the Galveston Movement the benefit of the doubt, the socialist *Jewish Daily Forward* showed no such consideration. In August 1907, the prestigious London monthly *Nineteenth Century* had featured a shocking study of the convict lease system and the chain gangs of the American South in an article by Mary Church Terrel entitled "Peonage in the United States."[39] The next month, the *Forward*, in an editorial, summarized the above article and used it to attack the Galveston Movement as follows:

> The Territorialists are the most practical of the Zionists. They finally see the truth, that in Palestine there is no hope. But they do not realize that there is no hope anywhere to settle Jews in another country.

They still do not realize that the only hope for Jews is when there will be equal rights for all men in the countries where they live . . . The Territorialists have not yet woken up from their sweet dream. They still hope to settle Jews "someplace else." Meanwhile, they started to make a little experiment in the Southern states of America. Since these states are working very hard to attract immigrants, the Territorialists have begun to send Jews there.

Let us see what is going on there . . .

. . . Since the convict lease system is such a good business, they fabricate convicts. They simply catch poor people that have no work and they lock them up as tramps. They are already prisoners and they can sell them as slaves!

But this is not yet the worst. According to the laws of those states if a worker breaks the contract with his employer, he may be punished with imprisonment. A contract, though, is made with almost every immigrant. He is given work and made to sign a paper. He thanks God that he gets work, but what does he know what he is signing for? However, this is a contract. And when he finds out that he has been harnessed to slave labor and he escapes, he is, according to law, just like a slave was when slavery was lawful. They look for him with police, and when they catch him he gets put in jail for breaking the contract. And then, he is already a convict, and the law allows him to be "hired out" as a "slave."[40]

The above editorial aroused little attention in America, but it was reprinted in two Yiddish newspapers in Russia. Realizing the importance of public relations in recruiting immigrants for Galveston, Cyrus L. Sulzberger wrote a letter to the *Forward*. After giving a short description of the Galveston Movement, Sulzberger went on to refute the implications contained in the *Forward* editorial:

The Jewish immigrants who came already were provided with jobs in which they make a nice living in those states from Texas northward up to the Canadian border. Not many remained in Texas, not because there is a danger of slavery but because there were better conditions for them elsewhere.

There are absolutely no grounds to fear that any of the Jewish immigrants, now or in the future, are in the least danger of becoming enslaved. Of this, I give my word of honor. Our only concern is for the welfare of our brethren.[41]

The *Forward* answered Sulzberger's letter with another editorial. After praising Sulzberger's sincerity and integrity most highly, the editorial went on to state:

But naturally he has his opinion of what is meant by being "enslaved" and we have our opinion.

We never gave anybody reason to believe that those who send the Jewish immigrants to the South mean to make them, God forbid, into slaves. We also do not have anything against the movement to spread Jewish immigrants throughout the country.

However, the movement of the ITO to send Jews to the South is understood by the masses of Jews as a "redemption"—as if the South could become a new Palestine. About this we remarked—and we stick to it—this, a region where sold slavery still rules, can not offer for Jewish masses a better outlook than a region where we have a workers' movement, and where the newcomers, in time, work themselves up to a higher standard of living and are taken up with the thought of freedom from slavery, by which we mean capitalistic wage-slavery.[42]

As long as the *Forward* editorialized, using its familiar socialist terminology, it was easy for the leaders of the Galveston Movement to dismiss its attitude as being motivated by ideology. In December, however, the newspaper printed a sensational letter written by one Moishe Opotowski, an immigrant who had arrived in Galveston as a member of the fourth group. The *Forward* featured Opotowski's letter on the front page under a headline that screamed, "Russian Jews Tricked into Slavery in America." Alongside the letter there was a photograph of Opotowski and an illustration depicting a Jew being beaten. The letter read as follows:

As the Territorial Organization Information Bureau in Warsaw, 10 Marianka Street, writes in the newspapers that those wanting to go to America should go to their colonies in the state of Texas, as they promise to provide the immigrants with everything that is necessary, like a brother, and promise that one can earn between eighteen and twenty dollars a week and provide them with a good ship, and that one would travel only ten days, with good food and good service so I, Moishe Opotowski, want to inform you that all this is not true. I and another seventy-five people started out from the office in Warsaw October 1st, traveled twenty-five days, were given food not fit for pigs, besides which we were beaten murderously.

We complained to the officers on the ship, but it didn't help. When we came to Galveston we were led into a big horse stable where they, without paying attention to our protests and screams, cut off our beards.

Then they put me and three of my friends on a train that went to Pueblo, Colorado, where we were met by a man by the name of Onina. We slept the night at his house, and the next morning we had to go nine miles on foot to a wood warehouse where they assigned us to cut wood. Our hands, naturally, were not used to such work, so the Negroes, our foremen, hurried us with cat-o'-nine-tails and with whips. About food, there is nothing to talk about. They teased us that we are Jews and, to spite us, they gave us pork. But a fortunate opportunity presented itself, and we ran away, leaving our baggage and prayer-shawls with our tormentors. The Negroes ran after us, but fortunately we came to Lincoln, Nebraska, from where a Jewish society sent us to Omaha. From there we came to Chicago, and from there they sent us to New York. I write this to you, that you may warn the Russian immigrants about these murderers.[43]

Sulzberger answered Opotowski's letter with another letter, which the *Forward* buried on its last page. In the name of the Jewish Immigrants' Information Bureau, Sulzberger rebutted Opotowski's charges, beginning with the claim that his beard had been forcibly cut off:

As soon as [Opotowski] came, he and the others were told that their chances of securing employment in a region where there are few Jews will be much better if they do not have such long beards. He and a few others with him allowed their beards to be trimmed. Those, however, who preferred to keep their long beards as before were allowed to keep them. Nobody had his beard shaved off.

Opotowski was sent to Pueblo, where he arrived on August 28th. On October 24th the president of the Pueblo Jewish Congregation, who is also chairman of the local committee, reported to the Jewish Immigrants' Information Bureau that Opotowski is a restless person, that he had already had a few jobs and lost them all due only to his own fault, and that he had left for Semper[?], Colorado. There he went on his own free will, without informing the local committee. Naturally, the Pueblo bureau and committee did not know what happened to him after he left. Anyway, the statement that there exists a form of slavery in the state of Colorado is one that, until now, was not made by anyone else in the history of this country.

At first he declared that he was only in Pueblo for five days. Next, he changed it to fourteen days. But when he was shown proof, it was demonstrated that he was there over two months.

He declared that in his wanderings throughout the United States he could not find employment, ignoring the fact that from August 28th to November 1st this land was in the midst of blooming prosperity, and there was a great demand for workers in all parts of the country. He was asked yesterday if he wants to have a job in New York, and he answered no.

The character of this man shows itself through a letter which was just received from Warsaw dated November 14th asking if we know where the man is, because his wife has not heard one word from him since he left Russia. In this whole story this man shows himself to be a swindler and a cheat. It would not have hurt if the press would have first tried to investigate the story before printing it.[44]

The *Forward* did not let Sulzberger have the last word. It was convinced—and it was right—that forms of peonage did exist in certain parts of the country. In the same issue in which Sulzberger's letter appeared, the *Forward* carried a front-page item about Hungarian immigrants being held in bondage in Louisiana, a scandal which had caused the Austro-Hungarian government to issue an official protest to the United States.[45] The next day, in an editorial, the *Forward* used this story to bolster its view that no Jewish immigrants should be sent to the South. After discussing this report, the *Forward* addressed itself to Sulzberger's letter:

> We have the highest respect for Mr. Sulzberger. This conservative, far from socialist Jewish citizen, is one of the most sincere and warm-hearted philanthropists we have. Surely he means the best for his poor brethren.
>
> Mr. Sulzberger wrote us that the immigrants are not sent to Galveston to remain there but, rather, in order to spread them throughout the whole Mississippi territory. The troubles also appear, though, in other regions. In the state of Mississippi itself, many contractors were sued for tricking immigrants who cannot read English into signing contracts that bound them to slave labor. The suits, however, did not help. The government of that state works hand-in-glove with these slave-contracts, and the United States government declared that it does not have the right to interfere in the internal affairs of the states.
> . . .
> The bottom line is that the help for the poor Jewish masses, as for the poor masses of Hungarians, Austrians, Germans, Italians, and so on, does not lie in which part of the sky they find themselves under, but it depends upon *how strong the workers' movement is* in the struggle against exploitation in the place where they settle down.
>
> We do not mean this to influence against the plan to spread the Jewish immigrants over the whole country. The plan is useful.
>
> We do not even expect great things of it. We know that if the Jewish trades in the great Eastern states will become busy again, the far-flung Jews will pack up again. With tricks one can never go against the stream that pulls people to a different place where they can expect to live a life that they think will be better. Since so many tens of thousands of Jews find a way to New York—when it is busy here—those from American cities will surely find their way to New York. When they will again be able to make a better living in the towns, they themselves will be drawn away from the various big cities of the East.
>
> Then it can be useful for the gentlemen of Sulzberger's office to help our immigrants who come anyway with the intention of spreading out over the land.[46]

Since the JIIB settled most of its immigrants in the West, rather than in the South, the *Forward's* criticism was a bit misdirected. Furthermore, those immigrants who were sent to the South were usually provided with work in the cities to which they were sent.

It cannot be denied, however, that, as it became harder to find work in the cities, some local agents did assign some immigrants to labor in the surrounding countryside, where they were open to various abuses.

In Russia, the recruitment machinery of the ITO's Jewish Emigration Society was now entering high gear. The record-breaking eighth group was followed by another large group of 164 Jewish emigrants, which left Bremen on November 14. In Galveston, however, the Jewish Immigrants' Information Bureau was not looking forward to the coming of the ninth group and, in fact, had tried to stop it by sending a cable to the ITO in London three days before embarkation. In subsequent communications, the JIIB explained why it considered it necessary to suspend the Galveston Movement.[47]

In October 1907, a panic had taken place on Wall Street. During the following month, large industrial establishments, banks and financial houses in New York began to fail, and practically all business activity slowed down. Businesses throughout the United States were forced to cut expenses, and there was widespread unemployment. Consequently, the local committees of the Jewish Immigrants' Information Bureau found it extremely difficult to find work for the immigrants, who were placed at a special disadvantage by their ignorance of the English language. On November 18, the JIIB cabled the ITO to restrict further shipments to fifty emigrants. As the year ended, business practically came to a standstill and the United States entered into a period of acute depression.[48] On November 28, the JIIB asked the ITO to halt all shipments until further notice.[49]

At this time, however, the Jewish Territorial Organization, which was just beginning to see successful results in its recruitment campaign, was reluctant to suspend its operations. Zangwill warned:

> It is very dreadful to contemplate the misery that will be caused by refusing to forward those who have acted on our advice and invitation by selling their homes . . . The whole movement is in peril . . . It was not an easy matter to gain the confidence of the people, and if we lose it, it will be almost impossible to regain it.[50]

Waldman had a hard time distributing the 164 Jewish immigrants of the ninth group, who arrived in Galveston on December 7. He managed to distribute 130 of them right away, but the rest had to wait in Galveston about as long as a week before places could be found for them.[51] Although most of the immigrants were settled in the West, a significant number were sent to the South, including twelve to Memphis, Tennessee. One of these, a 20-year-old laborer named Okon, later sent a letter home to his parents in Russia. Luckily for the public image of the Galveston Movement, the letter did not find its way into the hands of the press. Instead, Okon's parents turned it over to the ITO, who forwarded it to Bressler's office in New York. The letter read as follows:

> Last Thursday I was sent away from Memphis to a country place, Wedley [?], and from there to a village, where we were told that we should have to dig earth and raise a terrace for a railway. There we saw three of our people working very hard, knee-deep in water, and we heard from them that they were earning nothing but their food. To our observation that this was hardly worthwhile, they replied:
>
> "We are sold into slavery. We have signed a contract presented to us, and we must not run away after such an agreement."
>
> To our question, how they could be such fools, they replied:
>
> "We have signed it under threats of being shot down."
>
> . . . On hearing this, I and my two companions, who come from Warsaw, wanted to leave immediately, but we were threatened with being shot down, to which we intimated by mute signs: "Fire away then!"
>
> As soon as the boss went to the townlet for purchases, we got up and ran away. I thanked God for not being burdened with any parcel while my two companions had to carry parcels . . . But we managed to escape in spite of their heavy parcels. After having wandered about for seven hours, we discovered a house at a distance. We went up to it and found there a couple of Blacks, husband and wife. We asked them whether there was something to eat, and he said there was shipbread. So he gave us bread which we ate with onions. Then he put his horse to his cart and took us to the town of Wenley [?], where we found a Jew, who gave us a dollar and a half each and sent us off to Memphis. Now we are thanking and praising our dear God for having saved us from evil hands.[52]

After the receipt of this letter, the leaders of the Jewish Immigrants' Information Bureau realized that there might be some validity, after all, to the charges of the *Forward*. The Bureau, thereupon, instructed its agents to strictly refrain from sending its immigrants to work in gang labor.[53]

The tenth group, which left Bremen on December 5, consisted of 102 emigrants. These people had already left Russia before they could be informed that the Galveston Movement was suspending operations. They arrived in Galveston on December 30. Like the group which had preceded them, many immigrants were kept in Galveston for as long as a week until places could be found for them in various communities. Although he was reluctant to do so, Waldman was forced to assign seven immigrants to live in Galveston itself.[54] (Since the beginning of the Movement, Waldman had allowed only three immigrants to remain in Galveston.)

The Jewish Territorial Organization reluctantly limited the eleventh group to only twenty emigrants, who sailed from Bremen on December 27.[55] The Jewish Immigrants' Information Bureau agreed to accept this number as the maximum per shipment, provided that the twenty emigrants would be carefully selected.[56]

From June 1907 until the end of the year, some nine hundred Jewish emigrants had participated in the Galveston Movement. Of this total, 833 (672 men, eighty-two women and seventy-nine children) were recruited in Europe by the responsible organizations. Of these, 688 were recruited in Russia and thirty-seven in Rumania, by the agents of the Jewish Territorial Organization. The *Hilfsverein* recruited ninety-six in Germany, and an additional seven emigrants for New York had their tickets changed in Bremen and joined the ITO groups in Galveston. Five emigrants from London joined by contacting the ITO headquarters in that city and traveling from there to Bremen. The remaining "unrecruited" immigrants sailed from Bremen on their own responsibility but, upon arriving in Galveston, applied for and were granted assistance by the Jewish Immigrants' Information Bureau. To be sure, some Jewish immigrants to Galveston neither applied for nor received any assistance at all, but the number of such cases was small.[57] During this period, twelve Jewish immigrants were deported from Galveston—five for trachoma, three for tuberculosis, and four for "poor physique."[58]

Of the 672 "recruited" male emigrants, seventy-six were listed by the ITO as unskilled laborers and an equal number as salesmen, clerks, or bookkeepers. Seventy-five were listed as being involved in the tailoring trade and fifty-seven in woodwork (including carpenters, joiners, cabinet-makers and wood-turners). There were fifty-four bootmakers listed, thirty-nine locksmiths, twenty-six metalworkers, twenty-four blacksmiths, twenty bakers, nineteen painters and paperhangers, eighteen "agriculturalists," seventeen butchers, and others skilled in various assorted trades. Among the eighty-two "recruited" female emigrants, twenty-two were listed as belonging to the tailoring trade.[59] It should be remembered, of course, that many of these self-professed tradesmen possessed few or, in some cases, none of the required skills. Thus, the number of unskilled laborers was actually much higher than that which appeared in the official lists of the Jewish Territorial Organization and the Jewish Immigrants' Information Bureau.

Be that as it may, the ITO, the JIIB, and the *Hilfsverein* had a right to be proud of the work they had accomplished during 1907. In little more than half a year they had successfully demonstrated a new, organized approach to the hitherto anarchical emigration of East European Jewry. They had taken up the cause of defenseless emigrants against a powerful shipping company and ruthless innkeepers. They had opened up a new avenue of migration to an area of great opportunities.

That most of the immigrants had adjusted well to their new lives is demonstrated by a letter written by Jacob Billikopf of Kansas City in late October 1907, just before the beginning of the depression:

> Of the fifty-five or more immigrants we received thus far every one with the possible exception of one or two is employed. The skilled men are working at their trades; the unskilled ones at what I consider "light work". Most of them, particularly those who do not work overtime, attend our night school and are picking up the language with remarkable rapidity. They are mighty good at formation of sentences. Now and then they make mistakes. For instance, one immigrant has *flesh for dinner* and the other one has *meat on his body*. But they are making progress alright.[60]

The leaders of the Jewish Immigrants' Information Bureau looked ahead anxiously to the year 1908, hoping that economic conditions would quickly improve so as to permit an early resumption of the Galveston Movement.

CHAPTER 3

1908–1909: The Economic Depression

In January 1908, Waldman sent his assistant, Henry P. Goldstein, on a tour of the West, in which he visited the Jewish communities of thirty-two cities. Fourteen of these communities had not previously been connected with the Galveston Movement, and the other eighteen communities, while having been so connected, had recently discontinued cooperation due to the depressed state of industry throughout the country. Goldstein's mission was to persuade these communities to agree to accept limited numbers of Jewish immigrants from Galveston, in spite of the hard economic times. In many cases, he succeeded.[1]

During the months of February and March, however, industrial conditions worsened, and many of these communities were forced to renege on their pledges. The following letter from Topeka, Kansas, was typical:

> We regret to inform you that some time ago we agreed with your representative to continue to assist you in taking care of the immigrants, but at the present time we are compelled to cancel the order. Our only source of employment is the Santa Fe Railway shops, and they are daily letting out employees. Just today they dropped two hundred employees out of one department. Therefore, do not send us any more until later, when we will write you again.[2]

In February, Waldman embarked upon a tour of his own, to see for himself how bad conditions were throughout the West. Writing to Bressler from Saint Louis, Waldman commented, "What I have seen thus far is enough to make one blue—men out of work everywhere, starvation staring them in the face. The charities here are crowded with applicants and some of them Galveston men."[3] He concluded that it was useless at this time to persuade well-meaning communities to accept immigrants if these communities were actually unable to provide work. Upon receiving this grim assessment, Bressler instructed Waldman to reduce his staff in Galveston and to continue to operate on a minimal basis only.[4] On March 3, Bresler's office sent Zangwill a cable instructing him to send no more immigrants until further notice.[5] Thus, the Galveston Movement ground to a halt.

Morris D. Waldman's experience as chief organizer and manager of the Jewish Immigrants' Information Bureau had strengthened his reputation as one of the leading Jewish social workers of his day. At this time, Waldman welcomed the opportunity to return to New York as manager of that city's United Hebrew Charities, the largest agency of its kind in the world.[6] Louis Greenberg, a member of the JIIB's office staff in Galveston, was named acting manager of the JIIB, and Henry P. Goldstein continued to serve as a sort of traveling agent.[7]

In early April, Schiff stopped off in London on his way back to America after a tour of Europe and Palestine. Zangwill had arranged a committee meeting of the ITO's Emigration Regulation Department to coincide with this visit, which he deemed of sufficient importance to require the summoning of Jochelmann from Kiev. At the meeting, it was agreed that the ITO would cautiously resume operations by periodically sending a few hand-picked emigrants to Galveston—just enough "so that the Galveston machinery might be kept going."[8]

On his last day in London, Schiff found another opportunity to confer with Jochelmann, who was still in town. Jochelmann revealed to Schiff a piece of upsetting news: the Czarist government had revoked its legal recognition of the ITO's Jewish Emigration Society, thus forcing it to close its branches throughout Russia. Fortunately, a few of these centers were still allowed to remain open. Jochelmann assured Schiff that these few centers were able to supply more than enough immigrants for the presently reduced needs of the American labor market. Upon his return to Russia, Jochelmann hoped to regain full legal status by engaging in intense lobbying.[9]

In Saint Petersburg, Jochelmann met with some high level politicians, who promised to use their influence on behalf of the ITO. He was also offered support by the editor of *Novoe Vremya*, a notoriously anti-Semitic Russian newspaper. Although Jochelmann was tempted to accept the editorial support of this paper, his advisers counseled against it, for they feared that such support would be misunderstood by the masses of Russian Jews. Jochelmann continued his lobbying efforts through the rest of the year.[10]

In all of 1908, the ITO and the *Hilfsverein* sent only 126 Jewish immigrants to Galveston in ten separate shipments. They were largely distributed in the main territory used by the Jewish Immigrants' Information Bureau, that is, between the Mississippi River and the Rocky Mountains. Over three-fifths of them were settled in the states of Texas, Missouri, and Iowa.[11] Arbitrary quotas imposed by the JIIB, however, could not prevent Jews from traveling to Galveston outside the organizational framework of the Galveston Movement. During that same year, at least as many Jewish immigrants came to Galveston entirely on their own and did not bother applying for assistance by the JIIB.[12]

General immigration to Galveston and to the United States as a whole was quite low in 1908, due to the unfavorable American economic conditions. In fact, more aliens left the United States than entered it during this time.[13] Compared to other immigrant groups, the Jews had a very small percentage of persons returning to their countries of origin.[14]

In September 1908, Henry P. Goldstein went on another tour of the West, visiting sixteen cities in the states of Iowa, Nebraska, and Missouri. Goldstein's object was to ascertain whether the economic situation there warranted an early resumption of the Galveston Movement. He reported as follows:

> I found conditions . . . a great deal improved over what they were several months ago, inasmuch as the factories have resumed work in some cities to the full extent and in others to a lesser degree. The consensus of opinion of the men that I have interviewed both on the committee[s] and others was that the present business volume and activity had increased already to about 80% of its former size and that it was with them no longer so much a question of industrial depression due to internal causes but rather the usual condition occasioned by the uncertainty incidental to a change in office at a presidential election.[15]

(This was a reference to the upcoming contest in November between William Howard Taft and his Democratic opponent, William Jennings Bryan. Most businessmen—including Schiff—favored Taft, the Republican candidate, as being more likely to end the depression.)

In spite of the improved economic prospects, Goldstein encountered a general reluctance on the part of the local committees toward resuming cooperation with the Jewish Immigrants' Information Bureau. One of the main reasons given was that the committees were not satisfied with the types of immigrants they had been getting. Goldstein wrote:

The feeling was that those coming were not such as really merited the good services rendered in their behalf, and also that in a large number of cases such men were selected as could only with difficulty be assimilated in the mass of American workmen . . . In many instances, the committees complained that extravagant promises are alleged to have been made to the immigrants at home . . . as to the kind of employment and wages he was to receive, with the result that the immigrant expressed either a feigned or real disappointment at the conditions he met, making him dissatisfied and imposing a more difficult task upon our correspondents in finding employment.[16]

Complaints by the local committees about the immigrants were not new. Besides complaining about their lack of skills and unsuitability for hard labor, some committees had long complained about the political leanings of many of the immigrants. For instance, the chairman of the committee in Des Moines, Iowa, had written as follows:

The majority of the [immigrants] we receive are more or less permeated with Socialism and Nihilism which, applied to this country, means anarchy. The first thing we had to do . . . was to break up a band which they organized here, and in getting out among other Jews we find they quit their jobs . . . You ought to be very careful as to who[m] you allow to land here and inform your European countries no anarchists need to come as you will see that they are deported. . . . You can find out from the immigrants themselves, after a few minutes' talk with them, as to who is who, etc.[17]

Goldstein promised the local committees that he would relay their complaints to the Jewish Immigrants' Information Bureau. He managed to persuade eleven committees to agree to the absorption, between them, of thirty-one immigrants per month. These were communities which had suspended all cooperation during the industrial depression. The prospects for 1909, then, were not altogether discouraging.

In October 1908, a delegation of Russian ITOists, headed by Jochelmann, arrived in New York to discuss the possibility of actively resuming the Galveston Movement. Zangwill, who was in New York at the time, joined them in a meeting with Bressler, Sulzberger, and Schiff at the latter's Fifth Avenue mansion. At the meeting, Sulzberger submitted that in the event of a resumption, the ITO would have to screen out all immigrants who were not physically or vocationally desirable. In the future, he said, the JIIB would not aid any immigrants who arrived at Galveston without ITO certificates in their possession, except for immigrants who were joining their heads of family. The ITO delegation agreed to be careful in its future selection of immigrants.[18]

Dr. Jochelmann then gave a detailed report of his activities in Russia. He had made little progress in his attempt to restore the former legal status of the ITO's Jewish Emigration Society. Of its original fourteen branches, only three were allowed to remain open. These three branches, however, were able to send an adequate number of emigrants to Galveston during the depression of 1908. Jochelmann was confident that the Czarist government could soon be induced to allow the Jewish Emigration Society to reopen all of its centers. (He did not specify in what form these "inducements" would take place.[19])

On December 8, Dr. Jochelmann left New York, bound for Russia.[20] On the way, he received some very disturbing news: his house had been raided by the police and all his correspondence confiscated, including documents incriminating him of engaging in emigration work. Despite a good chance of being arrested, Jochelmann nevertheless returned to Russia.[21]

In Saint Petersburg he entered into negotiations with some of the highest officials of state, who regarded him with great respect. Paradoxically, while these negotiations were going on, in February 1909, Jochelmann was living the life of a fugitive, for he could not remain openly in the capital. By day he slept secretly at a friend's house, and by night he strolled through the streets of Saint Petersburg, in order to avoid a surprise visit by the police.[22]

In March 1909, Jochelmann's efforts began to bear fruit. The governor of Kiev ordered the police to return the confiscated documents to Dr. Mandelstamm, president of the Russian branch of the ITO's Emigration Regulation Department, which was officially responsible for the Jewish Emigration Society.[23] By April, though the Russian bureaucracy slowed things down considerably, legalization was on its way. While awaiting formal legalization, the governor of Kiev permitted the Jewish Emigration Society to go on with its emigration work.[24] It was not until June that full governmental sanction was granted.[25]

Although Dr. Jochelmann was no doubt elated over the outcome of his struggle, his strenuous efforts left him physically and emotionally drained. Moreover, Jochelmann had a history of heart trouble. At a conference of the Jewish Territorial Organization held in early July, he almost fainted. Zangwill insisted that he retire to the seashore for a vacation.[26] After resting for two weeks, Jochelmann returned to his duties, but he never fully recovered. Jochelmann was plagued by health problems for the rest of his life.

The American depression of 1908 continued through the first half of the following year. Happily for the JIIB, no Jewish immigrants came to Galveston in January 1909.[27] In February, forty-eight arrived,[28] but the JIIB was only responsible for twenty-seven of them,[29] who had been sent by the ITO and the *Hilfsverein*. The rest had arrived independently. During 1909, as in the previous year, only slightly more than half of all Jewish immigrants to Galveston were sent by the ITO and the *Hilfsverein*, and thus were entitled to placement by the Jewish Immigrants' Information Bureau.

The Jewish immigrants who came to Galveston in March 1909 were especially poor. Some arrived almost barefooted and were not even wearing shirts. After consulting with Rabbi Cohen, Greenberg bought some shoes and shirts for the most unfortunate cases.[30] Bressler approved the emergency measure, but he wrote to his European colleagues reminding them of their responsibility to see that the emigrants were sent off properly clothed.[31]

Cohen and Greenberg looked after more than merely the material needs of the immigrants. A man and woman who arrived with the April group were each listed as single in the list prepared by the *Hilfsverein*, but they claimed to be married, and they proved it by producing a *ketubah* (Jewish marriage contract). Although it was almost certainly unnecessary, Greenberg asked Rabbi Cohen to reaffirm the status of the couple by marrying them once again.[32] The incident was repeated in May with another couple who arrived under similar circumstances.[33]

By June 1909, Western industries were beginning to emerge from the depression. Since many communities had cancelled their affiliation with the Jewish Immigrants' Information Bureau, it became necessary for the organization to reestablish a network of cooperating communities, to which new immigrants could be sent. The Industrial Removal Office was also engaged in such an effort, for during the depression it had been forced to reduce its activities by one-third.[34] In his dual capacity as general manager of the Industrial Removal Office and as honorary secretary of the JIIB, David M. Bressler set out on a tour of the Midwest. He discovered that, while Jewish communities were perfectly willing to accept removals from New York, they were reluctant to accept new immigrants from Galveston. The latter, besides being ignorant in English, had exaggerated ideas of the salaries they could command in the American labor market, and they were therefore more prone to discontentment. In contrast, those who were sent by the Industrial Removal Office had generally experienced unemployment in New York and were happy to find any sort of work.[35]

Bressler managed to convince several communities to accept immigrants from Galveston, but sometimes only after using the utmost powers of persuasion. Even when he succeeded in convincing a particular committee to accept an allotment of immigrants, the committee was likely to be concerned that its local Jewish constituency would not support such a decision. In Saint Paul, Minnesota, Bressler elicited an authorization for one family per month by promising that he would return for the Jewish holidays in October and speak from the synagogue pulpit, in order to arouse renewed enthusiasm among the members of the community.[36]

Louis Greenberg set out on a mission of his own to regain the support of the Jewish communities of Texarkana, Marshall, Tyler, and Palestine, all in northeastern Texas. The cooperation of these communities was particularly valuable, because the railroad transportation from Galveston, at the half-priced charity rate, was only four or five dollars. It became clear to Greenberg that Henry P. Goldstein, in his earlier visits to these towns, had failed to garner true community support for the project, and had merely consulted with one or two men in each locale, to the resentment of the rest of the community.[37] This made it necessary for Greenberg to establish real community backing for the first time. After several acrimonious meetings, Greenberg was able to report to Bressler as follows:

Texarkana will receive two men monthly, and a family every three months. They must be men with trades. Marshall has agreed to receive one man per month. Restricted to carpenters, tailors, blacksmiths, or wagonmakers. Tyler will take a man per month. Must be a shoemaker or carpenter. They will also take care of a family, the head of which must be a tailor. Allowances for all above-mentioned cities is $10 per individual and $25 per family.[38]

Bressler wrote to Jochelmann that he should send as many tradesmen as possible.[39]

By July 1909, Schiff, Sulzberger, and Bressler felt that the Jewish Immigrants' Information Bureau was ready to accept larger groups of immigrants. In order to coordinate matters of policy in an organized fashion, and to share some of the responsibility with others, they established a JIIB executive committee, known as the "Galveston Committee," with Schiff as chairman, Sulzberger as vice-chairman and treasurer, and Bressler as secretary. (Actually, his title remained "honorary secretary.") The other members of the Galveston Committee were Morris D. Waldman, Rabbi Henry Cohen, Reuben Arkush, president of the Industrial Removal Office, and Dr. Morris Loeb, Schiff's brother-in-law.[40] Dr. Loeb, a well-known professor of chemistry, was also active in the Industrial Removal Office and in other Jewish immigrant organizations. Nathan Bijur, a juridical expert on immigration who became a Justice of the New York State Supreme Court, was added to the committee in November. Rabbi Cohen was the only member of the Galveston Committee who actually lived in Galveston; the others lived in New York. Meetings were held about once every month or every two months at the office or residence of Jacob H. Schiff. At these meetings, Schiff often called upon the members for advice or organized subcommittees to prepare reports, which were then discussed by the rest of the committee. On important policy matters, however, especially those involving the expenditure of funds, the committee members invariably deferred to Schiff's wishes. After all, the Jewish Immigrants' Information Bureau continued to be completely financed out of Schiff's personal fortune.

Although no real complaints were voiced about Louis Greenberg's work as acting manager of the JIIB, he was apparently never considered seriously as a permanent replacement to Waldman. Since the beginning of 1909, Bressler had been seeking candidates with recognized stature in the field of social work. Among the distinguished men who were offered the position was Dr. Sidney E. Goldstein, associate rabbi and director of the Social Service Department of the Free Synagogue in New York. Rabbi Goldstein decided, however, that "it would be unwise for me to surrender a permanent position with promise in New York and go to the uncertainty in Galveston."[41] Finally, in August, Henry Berman, an experienced social worker from Philadelphia, was appointed manager, with Greenberg remaining as assistant manager.[42]

Until July 1909, the JIIB had asked the ITO to send no more than thirty immigrants per shipment. This was a convenient arrangement for the ITO, as well, because until then that organization had been preoccupied in its battle with the Russian government. By now, this problem had been successfully resolved, and the JIIB felt justified in increasing the quota to fifty immigrants per shipment.[43] Responding to Schiff's appeal for more immigrants, Zangwill came up with a typically ambitious scheme:

> I shall . . . propose to the [ITO] London Committee to establish a Branch to tap the Galician emigration which is almost as great as the Russian, and it is even possible that something may be done in Paris, too, which gets congested with refugees, many of whom get foisted off on New York.[44]

Taken aback by the boldness of Zangwill's plans, Schiff attempted to temper his enthusiasm by advising that "until the new management, which we have instituted at Galveston, has had time to thoroughly get into the saddle, we had better go somewhat slowly."[45]

Schiff, however, had no reason to fear that Zangwill's organization would send more immigrants than the Jewish Immigrants' Information Bureau could handle. During the second half of 1909, the American economy gradually recovered from the depression. More Jewish communities throughout the West agreed to absorb immigrants from Galveston. Henry Berman, buoyed by a spirit of enthusiasm which was understandable for a new manager, continuously organized new towns, calling, at the same time, for increases in the sizes of shipments from Bremen. At first, he was satisfied with groups of up to seventy-five. Then, in October, he asked for an increase to 100. The following month he announced his ability to place 125 immigrants per shipment.[46] Schiff encouraged Berman in his zeal, stating

> that unless we could before long reach a point where we could properly distribute and place at least an average of two hundred a month or twenty-five hundred a year, so that within a decade we shall have, through the placement of twenty-five thousand, laid the seed for the natural inflow of a much larger Russian Jewish population west of the Mississippi, I should not consider the movement a success.[47]

Whenever Berman wrote to Bressler that he wished to receive larger groups, Bressler relayed this request to Jochelmann via cable. This was often followed by a letter from Schiff to Zangwill, urging immediate compliance with Berman's request.

The Jewish Territorial Organization, however, had difficulty keeping up with the demands of the Jewish Immigrants' Information Bureau. Apparently, the stream of immigrants could not be turned on and off as if with a water faucet. Zangwill reminded Schiff that before the depression the ITO had mustered almost two hundred emigrants per group. After such a long lapse in activities, Jochelmann and his agents would have to begin reacquainting prospective Jewish immigrants with the advantages of going to Galveston. It would take time to reestablish a climate of opinion favorable to mass recruitment. The Czarist government still intermittently caused legal problems for the ITO's Jewish Emigration Society, based in Kiev. Besides, Zangwill pointed out, many would-be recruits were being swayed from the Galveston route by attacks in the German and Yiddish press or by the sheer length of the voyage.[48]

Schiff showed little patience for Zangwill's excuses. He wanted to begin sending immigrants to New Mexico, Arizona, California, and the Northwest. Bressler reminded Schiff, though, that the JIIB presently had more than ample territory east of the Rocky Mountains without opening up new areas of settlement.[49] In fact, the Jewish Immigrants' Information Bureau often found itself in an embarrassing position. After finally persuading a community to accept a requisition of immigrants, the bureau would later realize that it did not have any to send. This left its future credibility open to serious question. Sulzberger suggested that the Industrial Removal Office make up the deficiency by sending some of its applicants to these communities. Schiff did not wish to mix up the work of the two organizations, but he agreed to telegraph Berman for his opinion on this idea. Berman replied with the following telegram:

> Would not advise using Bureau requisitions for Removal Office. It is intention of Bureau to have agencies make up in future for present small consignments and agencies have been so notified. I doubt whether communities would regard interchange of institutional activity favorably. The impression might also be harmful so soon after renewed cooperation.[50]

Schiff felt strongly, as he wrote to Zangwill, "that unless we can, during the next two years, make an unquestioned success of the

Galveston Movement, that this scheme will collapse, after the expenditure of much energy and very considerable resources."[51] He therefore proposed to Zangwill that the Jewish Colonization Association (ICA) be invited to send immigrants to Galveston. Anticipating Zangwill's negative reaction, Schiff communicated this proposal in the form of a telegram, in order to stress its urgent nature.[52] At about the same time, Bressler wrote a letter to Zangwill, criticizing the quantity and quality of the last few shipments of immigrants.[53] Zangwill forwarded Bressler's letter to Jochelmann, who was offended by its tone. As Schiff explained to Bressler, "In Russia they are, no doubt, used to another manner of correspondence than we, who write our letters in the shortest possible sentences."[54]

It may not have been Bressler's sentence structure, however, which angered Jochelmann; it may have been his arithmetic. According to Bressler's reckoning, the ITO had fallen hopelessly behind in its ability to fill the quotas provided by the JIIB. This analysis, however, was not necessarily supported by the statistics. In December, for example, Bressler wrote the following:

> The total number of persons in the last four consignments . . . fell far short of the agreed number. They (the ITO) had the right to send 75 per month up to Oct. 29th. On that day, we cabled them to increase the number to 100 . . . Had they lived up to the agreement with us, they should have sent in the last four consignments 325 persons (excluding women and children), yet they sent altogether 200 persons, including women and children.[55]

Actually, it is not known to what extent the JIIB had made it clear that it had only been counting adult males in the quotas which it had set our for the ITO. In the correspondence which we have from Bressler to Jochelmann and from Schiff to Zangwill, this distinction had never come up. Let us now take a careful look at the facts. The first of the four consignments alluded to by Bressler left Bremen on July 22, 1909, with thirty-nine ITO immigrants. This was at a time when the JIIB quota was still set at fifty, not at seventy-five, as stated by Bressler. The following group, which left Bremen on August 26, contained seventy-six ITO immigrants, which should have been exactly enough to satisfy Bressler. The next group left Bremen on September 23 and contained only fifteen ITO immigrants, presumably due to the Jewish holidays. The last of the four groups left Bremen on October 30, or one day after the JIIB sent a cablegram increasing the quota to 100.

This group contained eighty-six ITO immigrants, which should have been more than enough to satisfy Bressler, since it actually left under the old quota of seventy-five. In summary, during a period when the JIIB had requested a maximum of 275 immigrants (without clearly specifying adult males), the ITO had sent 216 (including women and children).[56] This does not seem like such a low figure, especially in view of the fact that 132 additional Jewish immigrants arrived independently, on the same four ships to Galveston.[57]

Schiff and Bressler must have realized that the Jewish Territorial Organization was doing its best to keep up with their consignments. They agreed to indefinitely postpone their proposal to call upon the help of the Jewish Colonization Association. As Schiff wrote to Bressler,

> We all appear to agree that we should give the ITO further time to show what they can henceforth do through their organization, but I think it would be unwise to name any definite period were it six months or a year, during which they shall have the combined opportunity to cooperate with us. In the first place, they might consider the setting of a time limit as offensive, and secondly it would be unwise if we tied our own hands.[58]

During the year 1909, 733 Jewish immigrants had arrived in Galveston.[59] Of this number, 426 had been sent by the Jewish Territorial Organization, with the help of the *Hilfsverein der deutschen Juden*, and were distributed by the Jewish Immigrants' Information Bureau.[60] About three-quarters of the immigrants arrived during the latter half of the year, when the U.S. economic depression and the issue of the legality of the ITO in Russia no longer presented themselves as significant problems. The outlook for 1910, then, seemed to call for an attitude of guarded optimism.

CHAPTER 4

1910: Deportations!

The seemingly endless stream of immigration which was coming in from Southern and Eastern Europe triggered a growing nativist sentiment among many Americans whose ancestors had come from Britain and Western Europe. These "old stock" Americans bitterly complained that the new immigrants were changing the "racial" complex of America.[1] In addition, the organized labor movement, many of whose members, ironically, were themselves of "new stock," was complaining that immigrants were undercutting American workers by accepting low wages. These groups lobbied in Washington for revision of the existing statutes with a view toward restricting further immigration.[2] Their activity came to a head in 1910, when the United States Immigration Commission, which had been created in 1907 and consisted of three senators, three congressmen, and three presidential appointees, invited statements and recommendations from all major societies and organizations interested in the subject of immigration. At this time, many restrictionists came forward to recommend the introduction of drastic limitations on immigration.[3] Senator William P. Dillingham, chairman of the Immigration Commission, then introduced a bill which contained a provision for a literacy test and other restrictionist measures.[4]

In opposition to these groups were those who favored retaining the current liberal immigration laws, with little or no revision. The industrialists, many of whom depended on inexpensive immigrant labor, exerted political pressure against any new legislation to restrict immigration.[5] Various immigrant groups also expressed their opposition to this legislation. Most active, by far, in the fight against the restrictionists, were the leaders of American Jewry. Of all the immigrant groups, only the Jews organized an effective lobbying campaign. This was because the Americanized Jews of German extraction, who had arrived a generation or two earlier, were willing and able to take up the cause of their Eastern European brethren.[6]

Several of the leading American Jews of German origin who fought against the restrictionists were concurrently active in the Galveston Movement. For example, Cyrus L. Sulzberger, among others, represented the American Jewish Committee, in March 1910, at a hearing of the Committee on Immigration and Naturalization of the House of Representatives. Sulzberger, it will be remembered, was vice-chairman of the Jewish Immigrants' Information Bureau Executive Committee, propularly known as the "Galveston Committee." Appearing together with Sulzberger at the hearing were Max J. Kohler and Abram I. Elkus, both of whom represented the Independent Order of B'nai B'rith.[7] These two prominent lawyers lent their legal talents to the cause of liberal immigration. Their abilities were soon recognized, and they were invited several months later to become members of the Galveston Committee.

Simon Wolf, a well-known Washington lawyer, also represented the B'nai B'rith at the House Committee hearing. While not a member of the Galveston Committee, Wolf, nevertheless, often used his influence in Washington on behalf of Jewish immigrants facing deportation from Galveston, as well as from other ports. As chairman of the Board of Delegates on Civil Rights of the Union of American Hebrew Congregations, Wolf often came into contact with the highest government officials, including presidents of the United States. In fact, he was considered a personal friend of President William Howard Taft.[8] The members of the Galveston Committee, however, were usually reluctant to include Wolf in their lobbying efforts, because of his tendency to compromise and to appease the government. Wolf's offer to become a member of the Galveston Committee was politely declined, but his close government connections were utilized by the Galveston Committee on various occasions.[9]

The governmental department which was responsible for matters pertaining to immigration was the United States Department of Commerce and Labor, which maintained a Bureau of Immigration and Naturalization. The head of this Bureau was the Commissioner General of Immigration, Daniel J. Keefe. Keefe came to his post after having spent most of his life as a labor leader, including five years as a vice-president of the American Federation of Labor. During his tenure as Commissioner General of Immigration (December 1908-May1913) he felt frustrated by the immigration statutes, which he regarded as inadequate. Keefe's annual recommendations to apply further restrictions on immigration did not result in the passage of any significant legislation.[10] However, he consistently applied the existing laws in a restrictionist fashion wherever possible.

The Bureau of Immigration and Naturalization maintained a number of administrative districts throughout the United States. The most important of these districts, by far, was the one whose headquarters were at Ellis Island, the immigration station at the Port of New York. The Commissioner of Immigration in that district was William Williams who, like Commissioner-General Keefe, was a restrictionist. In 1910, Williams, with Keefe's backing, embarked upon a campaign to restrict immigration through a series of administrative measures which were applied at the Port of New York. One of these consisted of a rule that an immigrant who did not possess twenty-five dollars would be excluded on the grounds that he was likely to become a public charge. All offers of aid, except from those legally obligated to support the immigrants, were to be discounted; only a husband supporting his wife and children was allowed to offer aid. Even bonds against the immigrants' becoming public charges were disallowed. Subordinates who failed to carry out these policies were judged incompetent, then demoted or removed.[11]

The attitude of the Inspector in Charge of the Immigration Service at Galveston, Texas, stood in marked contrast to the policies of Keefe and Williams. Inspector in Charge E.B. Holman publicly advocated the establishment of a new immigration station at Galveston with the intention of attracting more immigrants to that port. His efforts were supported by many citizens of Galveston, who were aware of the financial benefits which could accrue to their city as a result of an increase in port activity through the attraction of new shipping lines.[12] In keeping with his policy of encouraging immigration to Galveston, Holman did not normally order immigrants to be deported, except in extreme cases.

Inspector in Charge Holman maintained a special understanding with Rabbi Cohen in which all immigrants sent to Galveston by the Jewish Territorial Organization were discharged directly to the Jewish Immigrants' Information Bureau, which agreed to look after them. By this process, Holman was able to bypass the three-member Board of Special Inquiry, which had the authority to order the deportation of immigrants. Holman knew that his friendly attitude toward the JIIB and toward immigration in general was not shared by his superiors in Washington. He confided to Louis Greenberg, who was then acting manager of the JIIB, that Commissioner-General Keefe was "not very much in favor of increased immigration, Jewish particularly."[13]

While Keefe may not have been aware of Holman's verbal agreement with Cohen, he was undoubtedly displeased with Holman's liberal attitude toward immigration in general. In November 1909, Holman was suspended from his duties as Inspector in Charge of the Immigration Service at the Port of Galveston, pending the investigation of charges not made public.[14] A few months later, he was replaced by a man named Alfred Hampton. In addition, the old immigrant inspectors were replaced by a new team.

Until 1910, immigration officials refrained from deporting immigrants handled by the Jewish Immigrants' Information Bureau, even in cases where a strict interpretation of the law might have permitted them to do so. Only rarely did they order a deportation and, if so, never in more than one case per month.[15] Suddenly, without warning, the deportation figures soared. The S.S. *Frankfurt* arrived on February 7, 1910, with seventy-one Jewish immigrants. Of these, seven, or about 10 percent, were deported. The following month, another nine Jewish immigrants were deported from Galveston.[16]

Soon, a disturbing pattern emerged. Many Jewish immigrants were being labeled as having "poor physiques" and as being "likely to become public charges," which were sufficient grounds for exclusion. These classifications were broad enough to include anyone whose appearance did not meet the fancy of the medical examiner at the Port of Galveston. The medical examiner by himself could not exclude immigrants, but his reports usually carried considerable weight. Max J. Kohler, the Galveston Committee's expert on immigration law, explained the matter as follows:

> The situation in Galveston is not materially different than at other Ports. The Physicians make their medical examination without regard to the evidence in the case of showing the occupation of the Immigrant, and his condition as to breadwinning, or even, in the case of women and children, whether they are accompanying their husbands or fathers who may be well able to support them. In theory of law, the Board of Special Inquiry should apply the medical report to all the facts in

the case. In fact, however, in view of the present chaotic administration of our Immigration laws, and the desire to curry favor by making a record for exclusion, Immigration Officials are commonly adopting the medical report, no matter how little significance it has. In addition, the medical officers have been instructed from Washington to make their examinations more rigid.[17]

It developed that the Galveston medical examiner, Dr. Corput, may have had another motive for making his examinations more rigid. Henry Berman, manager of the Jewish Immigrants' Information Bureau, reported that he had heard on good authority that Dr. Corput had been making anti-Semitic remarks, saying that he would do everything in his power to make it as difficult as possible for Jewish immigrants to enter. When Jacob H. Schiff was informed of the matter, he called a special meeting of the Galveston Committee.[18] Kohler suggested that Dr. Corput's attitude be brought to the attention of his superiors.[19] Apparently, the protest had a temporary effect, for in early April, although about 150 Jewish immigrants arrived, all were admitted without incident. Berman reported that "a better spirit appear[ed] to prevail, because of the tendency of the new inspectors to override the opinions of the marine surgeons."[20]

Berman's mention of "new inspectors" was a reference to the new team of immigrant inspectors headed by Alfred Hampton, who, at this time, officially assumed the position of Inspector in Charge of the Immigration Service at Galveston. Berman's optimism, however, was short-lived. In his new position, Hampton was out to make a name for himself as a vigorous enforcer of the immigration statutes.

In late April, about another 150 Jewish immigrants arrived in Galveston. One of the immigrants, Tewja Breidberg, twenty years old, arrived with his eight-year-old sister, Schifra, whom he tried to pass off as the child of another family. When Hampton's inspectors discovered the deception, they forced Breidberg to accompany his sister on the next ship back to Bremen, since they felt that he would not be able to care for her adequately in the United States. In late July, having accompanied his sister back to Russia, Breidberg returned to Gaveston and, after being subjected to a thorough scrutiny, was finally admitted.[21]

Had Holman still been Inspector in Charge of the Immigration Service at Galveston, Breidberg and his sister would probably have been admitted immediately, since they would have been discharged directly to the care of the Jewish Immigrants' Information Bureau.

Hampton, however, was against this procedure. He noted that in the latest group most of the immigrants had very little money, and that many of them had neither relatives nor friends in the United States who could support them while they looked for work. In early May, Hampton wrote a letter to Commissioner-General Daniel J. Keefe, in which he exposed the special understanding that had existed between Holman and the JIIB. He requested a ruling as to whether the JIIB was actually entitled to accept responsibility for these immigrants or whether the immigrants really ought to be deported on the grounds that they were likely to become public charges.[22]

Hampton waited over a month for an answer from Commissioner-General Keefe. When he had still not received a reply by the second week in June, Hampton traveled to Washington, where he brought the matter to Keefe's immediate attention and, ultimately, to the Secretary of Commerce and Labor, Charles Nagel. Nagel and Keefe warned Hampton that "influential interests" would try to prevent a strict enforcement of the law at the Port of Galveston. Nevertheless, they assured Hampton that he would receive the full support of the Department of Commerce and Labor and of the Bureau of Immigration and Naturalization in his efforts to institute a campaign of enforcement.[23]

In order to provide the grounds for a change in poilcy, Keefe authorized Hampton to initiate an investigation of the Jewish Immigrants' Information Bureau to determine whether it was encouraging immigration through assurances of employment and, if so, whether these assurances were being carried out. Hampton wrote to various immigration officers throughout the West, asking them to assist in the investigation by interviewing local representatives of the JIIB as well as the immigrants whom they allegedly had assisted.[24] At the end of May, another ship arrived at Galveston, carrying 169 Jewish immigrants.[25] Many of these immigrants were included in the scope of the investigation. Each immigrant inspector was assigned a number of cities and given a list of Jewish immigrants who had been sent from Galveston to these cities. Altogether 107 immigrants were to be sought out[26] in some twenty cities, in the states of Illinois, Minnesota, Iowa, Nebraska, Kansas, Missouri, Louisiana, and Texas.

Without waiting for the results of the investigation, Commissioner-General Keefe issued a circular letter addressed to "Commissioners of Immigration and Inspectors in Charge at all Ports of Entry." This letter signaled a toughening attitude on the part of the Bureau of Immigration and Naturalization toward the Galveston Jewish immigrants, though the latter were not specifically mentioned. According to the new policy initiated by this letter, each arriving immigrant had to establish immediately, "clearly and beyond a doubt," that he would not become a burden on society:

> Has the alien an occupation? Is his physical condition such that he can be reasonably expected to labor at it? Has he a particular destination? Is it to a district in which he can reasonably expect to obtain early employment at his occupation? Has he funds sufficient to tide him over till work can be secured? Is he or she destined to a party who is or can be held legally responsible for his or her support (in case of a woman or minor child)? How were the funds secured for passage?
>
> Unless these and several other related questions which will readily suggest themselves can be substantially resolved in the alien's favor, the Bureau conceives that the alien has not established beyond a doubt the right to enter and the case should go to the Board [of Special Inquiry].[27]

Keefe's letter was issued on June 21, 1910, and its repercussions were swift and effective. On June 23, the S.S. *Hanover* arrived at Galveston, carrying 280 Jews. In accordance with the strict policy now in force, the immigrant inspectors at Galveston held 130 of these immigrants for the Board of Special Inquiry. The board admitted forty-seven of them and excluded the rest, mainly on the grounds that they were likely to become public charges. Henry Berman, the JIIB's manager in Galveston, cabled the following comments to his headquarters in New York:

> A habeas corpus proceeding would hold the Board of Inquiry Sessions up in a ridiculous light. Appeals taken by me should be in Washington Thursday or Friday. Believe Hampton and the newly elected inspectors entirely incompetent. Their removal is dictated by necessities of port immigration. Hampton in particular, who made the trouble, will always be a problem from our standpoint.[28]

As duly required, the appeals were filed at the office of the secretary of Commerce and Labor.

Charles Nagel was secretary of Commerce and Labor during the entire Taft Administration (March 1909-March 1913). As a former corporation lawyer and a conservative Republican, Nagel may have been inclined to favor the continuation of a liberal policy of immigration. Furthermore, he was a member of the Republican National Committee[29] and, more importantly, he was Taft's most loyal political supporter among the members of the Cabinet.[30] As such, Nagel might have been responsive to the lobbying efforts of Schiff and other leaders of American Jewry, many of whom were Taft supporters and prominent members of the Republican Party. As it happened, however, Nagel chose precisely this time to go on an extended trip to Alaska, leaving Assistant Secretary Benjamin S. Cable as Acting Secretary.[31] Unlike Nagel, Cable was not a member of any political party and, thus, he was not particularly sensitive to the pressures of lobbying groups. Moreover, Cable had special reason to be particularly unsympathetic to the overtures of Jacob H. Schiff, as his background reveals.

Before going to Washington, Benjamin S. Cable had spent ten years as an attorney for the Chicago, Rock Island, and Pacific Railway Company, known as the Rock Island Lines. Besides his professional connection, Benjamin S. Cable also had a strong sentimental attachment to this railroad—his father, Ransom R. Cable, had been its president, general manager, and, finally, chairman of its executive committee and of its board of directors. The senior Cable, who had dedicated a fifty-year professional career to the running of this sprawling midwestern railroad, had been the man chiefly responsible for its remarkable growth and for its sound financial condition. Rock Island was his home, and its railroad was his life.[32]

The Rock Island's main competitor was the mighty Union Pacific Railroad Company, headed by Edward H. Harriman, who represented a new, unpopular breed of railroad builder. In contrast to Cable, Harriman controlled his empire of western railways from an office building in New York City's financial center. Harriman established himself as America's leading rail magnate by the relentless acquisition and reorganization of roads all over the West, relying upon seemingly endless supplies of capital. In the process, he earned himself a reputation for insatiable greed and unmatched ruthlessness. Harriman's chief financial backing came from the second largest investment banking house on Wall Street—Kuhn, Loeb and Company. This company was headed by Jacob H. Schiff.

For some time, the Rock Island had been engaged in a desperate struggle with the Union Pacific for control of the strategically located Chicago and Alton Railway Company, known as the Alton Line. With Schiff's help, Harriman had reorganized the Alton Line in 1899 at considerable expense, but the Rock Island Company had later managed to obtain a controlling interest in the line by surprise tactics on Wall Street. As a compromise, a joint voting trust was established, and it was decided that the Alton Line was to be managed by both the Rock Island and the Union Pacific, on an alternate basis. Schiff's firm continued to serve as fiscal agent for the Alton Line.[33]

In 1906–1907, the Interstate Commerce Commission conducted an investigation of the Harriman lines, focusing most of its attention on the reorganization of the Alton Line which had taken place at the turn of the century. To the great consternation of Schiff, Harriman, and their associates, words such as "crippling," "looting," and "scuttling" were used by hostile critics, in describing the transaction. In its report, the commission voiced the opinion that the reorganization of the Alton Line had resulted in unreasonably large profits for Harriman, Schiff, and other insiders, thus draining the railroad of its resources. Although the commission found no basis for prosecution, it characterized the transaction as "indefensible financing." Needless to say, Schiff and his colleagues took offense at the characterization and viewed the commission report as unfair and unbalanced. For their part, the Rock Island interests took the position that they had been kept ignorant of the true nature of the Alton reorganization and had, thus, been tricked into acquiring a formerly sound railroad which had been shamelessly gutted. The commission's investigation gave the Rock Island interests a pretext to maneuver the Union Pacific into giving up all interest in the Alton Line, in 1907.[34]

The Rock Island's acquisition of the Alton Line had taken place as part of a general company policy of expansionism, which had begun with its acquisition of the Saint Louis and San Francisco Railroad Company, known as the Frisco Line. The Frisco acquisition had been a serious blunder, for the railroad was managed by a band of unscrupulous speculators. Furthermore, by acquiring the Frisco and Alton lines, the Rock Island Company had vastly overreached itself and ended up in a financially unsound position. Finally, by encouraging the impression that it had been hoodwinked, and by brazenly maneuvering the Union Pacific into giving up its Alton interests in 1907, the Rock Island Company had unwisely offended Schiff, who was the leading investment banker for the American railroad industry.

In 1908 it became generally known on Wall Street that the Rock Island had turned to Kuhn, Loeb and Company for aid, asking the prosperous firm to participate in the financing of the faltering Frisco Line. Schiff saw no reason to go out of his way to help, and he rejected the request. At the end of 1909, the Rock Island

Company was finally forced to sell its Frisco holdings. Again, Schiff and his firm declined to participate in the purchase, thus leaving the Rock Island no choice but to sell the Frisco at a severe loss, to the same unscrupulous speculators who had been milking it dry for years. This was a grave blow to the Rock Island Company, touching off a long, downward trend in its financial condition.[35]

The ill-advised decisions of the Rock Island Railroad had not been made by the aging Ransom R. Cable, but, rather, by a New York syndicate composed of callous manipulators, who had taken control of the company's board of directors in recent years. After half a century of dedicated service, Cable saw everything he had built up in Rock Island being destroyed in the smoke-filled rooms of New York office buildings. Painfully aware that he could do nothing to stop this disastrous trend, Ransom R. Cable died at the end of 1909. (Harriman had died two months before.) Earlier in the year, Cable's son, Benjamin, resigned his position as an attorney for the Rock Island Company in order to assume the position of assistant U.S. secretary of Commerce and Labor. Benjamin S. Cable brought with him, no doubt, bitter feelings about the callous, calculating methods of New York financiers and, perhaps, a special grudge against Jacob H. Schiff.

In its efforts to persuade Acting Secretary Cable to admit the Jewish immigrants who had been excluded on June 23, 1910, Schiff's Galveston Committee enlisted the help of William S. Bennet, a Republican congressman from New York. An influential member of the Committee on Immigration and Naturalization of the House of Representatives, Bennet also served on the United States Immigration Commission.[36] Bennet was one of the leading congressional advocates of a liberal immigration policy. Together with David M. Bressler, Congressman Bennet visited Cable in Washington, during the second week in July, on behalf of the Jewish immigrants in Galveston who were being threatened with deportation. In a meeting which lasted the greater part of a day, Bennet and Bressler attempted to convince Cable that, far from being "likely to become public charges," these immigrants would be well taken care of by the Jewish Immigrants' Information Bureau. Cable said he would think the matter over.[37]

On July 14, 1910, Acting Secretary Benjamin S. Cable wrote a formal letter to Congressman Bennet, advising him of his decision concerning the eighty-two excluded immigrants whose cases were being appealed. In his letter to Bennet, Cable made it clear that he was not merely dealing with one small group of immigrants, but with the entire operations of the Jewish Immigrants' Information Bureau. Technically, Cable pointed out, the immigrants were being excluded mainly on the grounds that they were "likely to become public charges." While this in itself was sufficient grounds, Cable made it a point to add an additional basis for exclusion. All of the immigrants, Cable wrote, had been "induced or solicited to immigrate to this country by offers of employment." Furthermore, they had been assisted and encouraged to do so through advertisements printed and published in foreign countries. Since this was against the law, Cable hinted that the JIIB itself might be subject to prosecution for illegal activity.[38]

Cable felt that, by right, all of the excluded immigrants should have been deported. However, since, as he wrote to Bennet, "it would not be fair, or humane, to suddenly adopt a practice of excluding all of those people in view of what has been allowed," Cable sustained the appeals of forty-eight immigrants, thus professing to assume a magnanimous attitude. His professed magnanimity, however, did not extend to the remaining thirty-four immigrants who, he felt, were most likely to become public charges and would have been rejected, in any case, at other U.S. ports. In the case of these immigrants, Cable confirmed the decision in favor of deportation.

In justification of the decision to deport, the Department of Commerce and Labor prepared a statement listing salient facts about most of the affected immigrants. The statement stressed the poor physical appearance of the rejected ones, the fact that they had arrived with little or no money, the absence of relatives or friends in the United States who would be able to help them, and the evidence that they had been assisted by the ITO's Jewish Emigration Society. The following examples, selected from the list, are typical of those who were to be sent back to their homes in Europe.

ABRAHAM DUBINSKI, was 37 years old; had wife and four children in Russia; possessed but $4; could give address of no relative or friend in the United States; passage paid by Society.

ISUCHER HANDELMAN, aged 30; wife and two children in Russia; had $3; certified for flat chest and poor muscular development; observed by board to be of extremely poor physical appearance; no relatives or friends in the U.S.

SCHIE KASMANN, aged 23; wife in Russia; had no money; of poor physical appearance; no relatives or friends in this country.

KOPEL KAFUTJANSKI, and son, aged 42 and 17; elder had wife and seven children in Russia; had no money; elder appeared much older than age claimed; no relatives in U.S., but a friend in Kansas City; in boy's case lack of friends and funds considered.

CHAIM SCHUSTER, aged 29; had wife and five children in Russia; had no money; no friends or relatives in the U.S. (although it was later claimed that he had a brother-in-law in New York and a cousin in Washington); assisted by Society.[39]

In his letter to Congressman Bennet dated July 14, Cable warned that his administration would deal still more strictly with subsequent groups of immigrants. He alluded to the investigations then being conducted by various immigrant inspectors throughout the West, under the direction of Galveston Inspector in Charge Alfred Hampton. Perhaps Cable wished to give the impression that these investigations had produced damaging evidence. Such evidence, however, was not forthcoming at this time. At the time of the writing of this letter, only a few of the inspectors had completed their investigations, and their reports demonstrated no evidence of illegal activity by the representatives of the Jewish Immigrants' Information Bureau.[40] One immigrant inspector, for example, who investigated JIIB activities in Fort Worth and Dallas, summarized his findings as follows:

> After my careful and thorough investigation concerning the above aliens, it is my opinion that there has been no aid or assistance given to the said aliens prior to their entrance to the United States. After going into the details of each alien I was unable to obtain any evidence that they were aided or assisted until after their arrival at Galveston.[41]

Another immigrant inspector, who was assigned to contact five recent arrivals at Beaumont and Houston, Texas, was equally unable to obtain any evidence of wrongdoing. Two of the immigrants could not speak English, so he could not communicate with them. A third immigrant could not be disturbed at the time because he was sleeping during the day, since he worked nights as an engine tender on the Southern Pacific Railway. A fourth immigrant could not be located. As for the fifth, "he would not work at any other trade but as a carpenter, and as there was no work of this kind in [Houston] that he could get, he was returned to the Society in Galveston, which sent him to some other city." The inspector's report contained evidence only of his frustration at being unable to conduct successful interviews with any of the immigrants.[42]

An immigrant inspector in New Orleans reported the arrival from Galveston of a sole Jewish immigrant, who had asked to be placed in his profession, as a locksmith. When the Jewish community there proved itself unable to provide a position for him, the immigrant left to join some friends in Chicago. After interviewing one of the officials of the Jewish community, the inspector concluded that their purpose was "to furnish work and care for such immigrants as so come to the United States, rather than to induce others to migrate."[43].

In contrast, an immigrant inspector based in Saint Louis, who conducted investigations in Iowa, Nebraska, Kansas, and Missouri, was quite suspicious of the operations of the Galveston Movement, both in Europe and in the United States. Thoroughly dedicated to his assignment, the inspector, Samuel L. Whitfield, left no stone unturned in his attempt to prove that the JIIB as well as Jewish communities throughout the West, in cooperation with the ITO in Europe, were violating U.S. law in their systematic organization of Jewish immigration. In spite of his persistent efforts, however, Whitfield was unable to come up with any concrete evidence to that effect. A careful reading of Whitfield's reports from Des Moines, for example, where he began his tour, shows that they contained little more than insinuations:

> I learn that one R.M——is the head of a Jewish organization here, and that their organization as well as all similar bodies receive $19 a head for all Jewish immigrants who[m] they can persuade to come to the United States via Galveston destined to the Western states instead of entering via New York and remaining in the East. While Mr. M——is the head of the organization, he does not take an active part in the work, but turns it over to [Solomon] L——and gets his part of the premium amounts and then holds up the poor immigrant for part of his wages.
>
> I spent most of the day trying to obtain a Jewish interpreter but without success. There are some Polish people here but they are ignorant and unable to speak English. I was obliged to hire a real Jew, and as a consequence I am not satisfied that I obtained all the facts. I obtained statements from two of the aliens who came to Solomon L——. They both denied that [Solomon] L——secured part of their wages; but stated that after they made up their minds to come to this country, they were shipped to Galveston instead of New York to save money, and upon arrival here they were taken care of by Jewish charities.[44]

One immigrant, Yudel Spivak, related to Whitfield that he had been cheated out of part of his salary, but it was hard to tell whether or not Solomon L——was implicated: "Solomon L——got me a position with Lev——on a building on East Walnut Street, near the Capitol . . . Lev——told me that I was to get $1.50 a day . . . When I went to get my pay he wanted to give me $1.25, but I refused and then I went to Solomon L——and he told me to sue Lev——for my wages. Then Lev——was sued in the court, and Solomon L——told the court that he had hired me out to Lev——for $1.25 a day." Strictly speaking, Spivak's testimony did not implicate Solomon L——, for the latter had merely brought him to his meeting with his employer. Thus, it is possible that Solomon L——was misinformed as to the salary which Spivak claimed had been promised to him. This fine distinction, however, was lost on the immigrant, who had placed his confidence in the representative of the Jewish community. In Spivak's mind, Solomon L—— seemed, somehow, to be involved in the swindle, as he told Whitfield, "Lev——promised me $1.50 a day, and Solomon L———took me to Lev——."[45]

While Spivak was understandably upset about the problems with his salary, he must have realized that the organized Jewish community had helped him considerably. Having arrived penniless in Galveston, he had been given a ticket to Des Moines, had been met at the train station by Solomon L——, and had been provided with free room and board, for ten days, until a job had been found for him. When he had an accident and was laid up for two weeks, the local Jewish committee paid his doctor bills as well as his room and board, until he was able to resume work. While Spivak must have appreciated the help, Whitfield only looked upon it as further evidence that organized charities were illegally promoting and sponsoring immigration.[46]

Sensing, perhaps, that Whitfield did not entirely approve of Solomon L——'s activities, another immigrant was reluctant to admit having found employment with the latter, and did so only after being sternly warned, as shown in the transcript of his examination:

Q. To whom did you come?
A. When I arrived here a rabbi of the church [sic] met me at the depot and took me and kept me overnight, and the next day he turned me over to Solomon L——.

Q. Then did Solomon L——secure a position for you?
A. No, I found my own job at Valley Junction at my trade.

Q. Did you work on the building at Seventh and Walnut Streets for Lev——?

A. No, I went there but could not speak English and they would not give me a job.

Q. Did Solomon L—— ever secure a job for you?
A. I went to [Solomon] L——to ask him for work, but he said he did not have any for me. (Alien cautioned as to the penalty for perjury).

Q. Did not Solomon L——put you to work upon your arrival here?
A. Yes, [Solomon] L——took me to a place and got me a job and I worked there for fourteen days.

Q. What place was that?
A. Valley Junction repair shops.

Q. How much wages did you receive there?
A. Sixteen cents an hour for ten hours.

Q. How much of your wages did you pay to Solomon L——?
A. [Solomon] L—— paid a week's board for me; he did not get any of my wages.

Q. What are you doing now?
A. I am not doing anything now, I am going to look for another job.

Q. Are you going to [Solomon] L——for work?
A. Yes, he promised to get it for me.

Q. How long have you known Solomon L——?
A. Since my arrival here.[47]

Another immigrant, at first reluctant to admit that he had found employment with Solomon L——, complained to Whitfield that he had been beaten out of his salary at the Valley Junction repair shops. Only after Whitfield's insistent interrogation did the immigrant admit "I think Solomon L——went [to Valley Junction] and got me the job with the Rock Island Railroad shops." The examiner continued:

Q. Did you receive the full wages of your three weeks' work?
A. No, I only got $9.60.

Q. Why did they not pay you the full amount?
A. They still owe me $23.20.

Q. What reason did they give you for holding that back?

A. The cashier there told me that they paid on the 17th and as long as I was not there to get my money they sent it back to Chicago [headquarters].

Q. When you collected the $9.60 did they make you give up all your time cards?

A. No, I never had any time cards, and I have nothing to show for the time I worked there.[48]

While Solomon L——may not have been to blame for the immigrants' troubles, he could, perhaps, have assumed more direct responsibility in protecting his charges from being hurt by their own naiveté or by conscious exploitation. There were those, however, who accused Solomon L——of much worse, as Whitfield reported:

The society at Des Moines is known as the Federation Jewish Charity . . . While Solomon L——, to whom the five Russian Jews were destined, is not an officer in this society, he is delegated by the society to look after all Russian immigrants and see that they are placed in boarding houses and employment obtained for them. Solomon L——, who was formerly a pawnbroker, insurance agent, and police officer, I [was] informed by a number of reputable Jews and others in this city yesterday, is a man of bad reputation and takes advantage of his connection with the Jewish society, to hold up the unfortunate immigrants for part of their wages after securing employment for them. I was also informed that while he was a police officer, he was let out because of his bad record. I beg to call your attention to the affadavit made by [Mr.] B——which was submitted with my report of several days ago. Mr. B—— states that he has known Solomon L——about 20 years, and that he is known to him as a man of bad reputation who fleeces immigrants out of part of their wages, after securing employment for them, and that he is not a fit person to be connected with any immigrant society. Mr. S. Engleman, the president of the society, stated that it was known to him that [Solomon] L——took money from the immigrants and that he secured jobs for several immigrants from Galveston about three months ago, on Lev——'s building, 7th and East Walnut Sts., Des Moines, and that while Lev——was furnishing the men to the contractor, for $2.25 a day, he was only paying the immigrants $1.50 a day. Later there was considerable trouble caused by this transaction and after being threatened with a law suit, Lev——refunded a part of the wages retained by him.[49]

Why Engleman chose to complain to a U.S. immigration inspector about acitivity within Engleman's own society is problematic. It would have been more logical for Engleman, as president of the society, to have drawn his own conclusions and to have taken appropriate action on his own. As it was, he lent support to Whitfield's allegations against the society's representative and, by extension, against the society's activities. Engleman's statement, however, was rather mild compared to those made by other honorable citizens of Des Moines. Whitfield continued his report with a statement by a local police officer, a neighbor of Solomon L——'s, who said that the latter had been indicted and charged with having started several fires for the purpose of collecting insurance, and that he had also been arrested for running a gambling game at his home. According to this statement, Solomon L——had been freed on the latter charge because he was "a man with considerable political influence," and the arresting officer had almost been dismissed from the police force.

With this unflattering impression of activity in Des Moines, Whitfield left for Sioux City. There, too, his attempts to communicate with the immigrants were hampered by his lack of an unbiased interpreter of Yiddish. The first Jew in Sioux City to whom Whitfield offered a job as interpreter was honest enough to tell him that "he would not take the job if the investigation would in any way hurt his countrymen." Another Jew whom he approached accepted the job, but Whitfield was convinced that this man was "biased to a certain extent in his interpretation, judging from some remarks he made when he had finished the work."[50]

It is hard to know to what extent Whitfield's suspicions were well founded and to what extent they were figments of his imagination, stemming from the frustrating feeling that he was working in the dark. Transcripts of examinations which he conducted in Sioux City show no evidence of wrongdoing, as demonstrated in the following excerpt:

Q. Did you pay any part of your wages to the man who met you at the train or the Jewish Society?
A. No.

Q. Who paid your board bill?
A. I did.

Q. You understood did you that when you left the old country you would be taken care of by the Jewish Society and given employment.
A. No, they said there that we should not depend on the company at all and I was sure I would find work.[51]

Hampered by his inability to speak the language of the immigrants, Whitfield set out to obtain a broader perspective by questioning citizens at large. Largely from the latter, he learned that the local society, known as the United Hebrew Charity Association, had appointed a man named K——to be its "relief agent" with the task of looking after and caring for the new Jewish immigrants. The gossip that Whitfield picked up led him to regard K——as a man of dubious reputation.

In his report, Whitfield stated that K——was a grocer and steamship agent, had failed twice in business, and at one of the bankruptcies had settled for 20¢ on the dollar. In addition, there had been several suspicious fires on his business premises and the insurance companies would no longer grant him coverage. K—— carried with him a bad reputation and was not trusted within the community. From the Cudahy Packing Company, Whitfield elicited the information that K——was a "go-between" for the employment of "green" Jews within their plant. According to the company's superintendent, K——worked hand in hand with a local lawyer of dubious character to pass through false injury claims for Russian Jewish employees. Another lawyer with whom K——was associated and who, like K——, was also engaged in finding employment for Jewish immigrants, had once garnished the wages of one of the immigrants. "I believe," Whitfield concluded, "that K——, through these attorneys, is no doubt taking advantage of his connection with the Jewish charities, to rob the Jewish immigrants of part of their wages."[52]

Whitfield next visited Council Bluffs, Iowa, where he interviewed a 28-year-old carpenter who had arrived two months before. This immigrant was put in the charge of a Sam F——, who had gotten him a job with a contracting firm.[53] Unimpressed by his interview with the young carpenter, Whitfield undertook to investigate this Sam F——, and even employed the services of a private detective. In the end, Whitfield came up with the following report:

> The Jewish society here is known as the Council Bluffs Relief Association; . . . Sec'y., S[am] F——. This organization is affiliated with the Jewish society known as "The I.O.B.B." [Independent Order B'nai B'rith] and with the Jewish immigration society of Galveston. S[am] F——is a pawnbroker, is well-to-do, and a leader among Orthodox Jews. I was informed by a reputable business man at Council Bluffs, that [Sam] F——is a man of questionable character and that to my informant's personal knowledge, [Sam] F——, on two occasions, issued fake pawn tickets on diamonds, in order to dispose of the stones at

double their value. A Council Bluffs city detective, told me he had known S[am] F——well for a long time, that he is connected with a local Jewish charity, and that [Sam] F——informed him that he took care of the poor Russian Jews, boarding and securing positions for them, and that as soon as they were able, they would pay back to the society, the amount expended in their behalf.[54]

For Whitfield, Sam F——'s allegedly dishonest business practices cast a shadow upon his communal activities and, by extension, upon organized Jewish immigrant work in Council Bluffs. It was no accident, he felt, that, in each of the three cities in Iowa which he visited, men of questionable character were entrusted with the task of placing the newly arrived immigrants. After having examined a dozen immigrants, Whitfield had still not been able to prove that these agents were violating the law, but now he intended to change all that. After numerous requests by Whitfield, the Bureau of Immigration and Naturalization had just authorized him to engage the services of a professionally competent non-Jewish interpreter from Saint Louis, who apparently spoke a highly Teutonic version of the Judeo-German jargon.[55] Confident that he would now arrive at the true facts, the immigrant inspector set out for Omaha, Nebraska, where he joined forces with Jack Dick, his interpreter.

In Omaha, one of the first immigrants to be interviewed by Whitfield and Dick was a seventeen-year-old boy who had originally been sent to Cedar Rapids, Iowa. In that city, the representative of the Jewish committee had found him a position in a packing house paying $10.50 a week. It was a job which turned his stomach—pickling pigs' feet. He promptly quit. After just three days, alone in a strange city, the resourceful lad had then managed to find a job on his own for $12 a week, carrying grain from the cars to the machine in a flour mill. Thus, the job he secured for himself in Cedar Rapids, without too much effort, was better than the one provided for him by the ostensibly "well-connected" Jewish representative. Even at his new job, the teenager felt that he was being underpaid, for other men were getting more money for doing similar work. Finally, he left Cedar Rapids for Omaha, a larger city, where he found a job working in a lumber yard. Although he was receiving only $1.75 per day, here he felt that he had the opportunity to learn a trade which would give him satisfaction.[56]

The Jewish immigrant mentioned above was typical of others in his inclination to look out for himself and his reluctance to be totally dependent on the agent of the Jewish society to which he had been sent. At least as often as not, the jobs provided by these agents turned out to be disappointing, and many immigrants felt that they could do better by fending for themselves. Justifiably or not, the immigrants sometimes suspected that their welfare was not always of the utmost importance to some of these local agents. Whitfield found a basis for this suspicion in his examination of the Jewish immigrants in Omaha. Almost to a man, no one in Omaha had anything good to say about the person who was supposed to be catering to the needs of the Jewish immigrants.

An immigrant named Chaim Shapiro, who had been a farmer in Russia, recalled that while he was in Galveston he was offered a job working on a farm in Texas at $25 a month. "I wanted to accept it," he remembered regretfully, "but Mr. Berman told me that he knew better than I did, and would send me to a better place, and then he put me on the train and sent me to Omaha." In Omaha, the immigrant was met by Charles E——, the representative of the local Jewish society, who took him to the Swift Packing Co., where he was employed at scalding pigs, for 19¢ an hour. Two days later, after Shapiro had burnt himself on the job, he went to see E——and asked him to find him another job. While he was speaking to E——, some workers for the city were cleaning the street where E——'s house was located. E——told the immigrant to ask the foreman for work. He said he had "pull" with the foreman and would use his influence so that the immigrant would have steady work. As a result, Shapiro became a street cleaner, working for two dollars a day.

After two days at this work, Shapiro quit, as he related to Whitfield:

The last day I worked was Saturday, and I saw everybody being paid off in evelopes, and as I did not get mine, I asked the foreman for it, and he told me he didn't make out my pay and to go to the office, that he would pay me there. I did not go to the office then, but a week later I applied for my money and they told me my wages were paid to some other man. Then I went to Mr. E——and he made out an order and told me to sign it, and that he would get my money. About ten days ago I went to Mr. E——'s house, but he was out, and Mrs. E——told me, "Mr. E——has your money." I went several times to E——'s house, but they always told me he was out. A short time ago I met Mr. E——and asked him for my money, as I had already spent over a dollar car fare in order to get it, and he replied, "I have no money now, but I will bring it to you next Sunday or Monday, but he never brought it."[57]

E——obtained still another job for Shapiro, as a porter in a hotel, but the immigrant was no more satisfied with this job than he had been with the others:

> E——told me I was to get $25 a month. I worked at that hotel two days and three hours, and then I quit because they wanted me to scrub the toilet. When I applied for my wages, they would only pay me a check for $1.35 and I objected to the amount and the man told me I should work the full month and I would get my full pay, but I told him that he was giving me different work from what I understood I was to do at first, and I did not intend to be taken advantage of, so he told me to go and refused to give me the rest of my wages.

Afterwards, Shapiro found a job on his own, working as a laborer for $1.75 a day.[58]

E——could hardly be blamed for finding jobs which did not quite meet their expectations, but the immigrants were justifiably indignant at his withholding their wages. It soon developed that Chaim Shapiro's story was not unique. An immigrant named David Weiner, alias Itzchok Bassarabsky,—he had changed his name to escape from the Russian army—had also been placed by E——in a job cleaning the city streets for two dollars a day. He quit after one day. "E——got the money," Weiner recalled. "Several times I called him on the telephone and he would not answer, and other times I went to his house and they always told me he was not at home. I signed a voucher for the money and E——collected it, because I could not, on account of [my] working."[59]

Weiner then worked ten hours a day in the Evans Laundry, operating a machine. He earned, however, only $7 a week, while he suspected that others were making $10, $12, and even $15 for the same type of work. Weiner was not one who allowed himself to be easily exploited. After two weeks, he asked for a raise, and when he was turned down, he quit. Then, E—— found him a job as a dishwasher in a restaurant, for $30 a month. He felt himself abused, however, by the Jewish foreman, and he quit after one day. Whitfield asked him if he had ever been paid for that day's work, and Weiner answered:

> No, I went to him for it, and he told me that some white jacket was lost, also a key to my locker, and they gave me 25¢ for my work, and said the rest was to pay for the lost articles. Then I asked E———to collect the money for me, and he said he would, but never gave it to me. Afterwards, Mr. E——got me a job in a restaurant on 18th St., at $30.00 a month. I was to work 10 hours a day, but they wanted

me to work 11 and I refused. The next day I went to collect my money and they threw me out. Then I went to E——and told him about it, and he promised to collect the money, but I have not seen him since. That was two weeks ago. Then I went to Desbrow Furniture Co., and secured my own job at $9.00 a week, as laborer. I worked there 11 days, and received my money. The work slacked and I was laid off, then I went back to the Evans laundry and secured a position myself, at $8.00 a week, and worked only 8 hours a day, and I expect soon to get a raise.[60]

Another immigrant, while he had no personal allegations against E——, related to Inspector Whitfield what he had heard:

Several Jewish immigrants told me that a man, also a Jewish immigrant, whose name I do not know, deposited $15.00 with him to send home to his wife, who was starving in Russia, and that Mr. E——kept the money here for three months. Afterwards, that man went to him and said, "I have given you money to send to my wife, and I received two or three letters from her saying she did not receive it at all, and that she is starving. Why did you not send it?" Then Mr. E—— admitted that he did not sent it, but gave no reason. The man threatened to notify the Jewish committee at Galveston, if he did not send the money, and then he said he would send it at once. I believe the man did write to the committee [at] Galveston, complaining about the matter . . .

I also heard that [E——] used to place men in hotels to work. The price for that work in this town is $30.00 a month and board, and Mr. E——used to give them only $25.00 and kept the rest. Several green immigrants told me E——had treated them in that way. I do not remember their names.[61]

The above charges were hard to prove, but it was obvious that E——was not very well liked by the immigrants of whom he was in charge. One of them, a jewelry maker by trade, was provided by E——with a job polishing metals in a small factory, where he was paid $4.50 for a week's work, as he recalled:

I could not make my living at $4.50 a week, and applied to E—— for another job. Then he secured me another job of the same kind of work, for $6.00 . . ., and I worked there four weeks. The pay was too small and I quit . . . I went to E——and told him to get me another job, that I could not make my living at $6.00 a week. He kept me at his house all day, and he wanted me to help him move and promised me one dollar, and the next day I also worked for him for one dollar, and he promised to pay me but he did not.[62]

It soon became clear that E——owed money to other people in Omaha. The JIIB had the same financial arrangement with E——

—as it had with its agents in other cities. The agent was allowed ten dollars for the maintenance of each immigrant or twenty-five dollars for each family.[63] In Omaha, E——divided the immigrants between two boarding houses, which were run by two Jewish women, who used the income to support their families. E—— promised to pay these women four dollars per week for each immigrant. Whitfield visited these boarding houses and found that, according to the landladies, E——had not maintained his share of the bargain. "He has owed me $36.50 for the last two and [a] half months," one woman told Whitfield," but just this morning he gave me a check on the Corn Exchange Bank for $25. I have had to telephone and go to him several times asking for my money as I am a poor woman and need it, and he finally gave me $25 . . . I believe that the only reason E——paid me was because [one of the immigrants] told him the officers would find out about his owing me money."[64] The other woman, who said E——owed her $42, told Whitfield, "I have gone to him many times and he hides himself and whenever I do find him he promises to pay me later on, but has never kept his promise."[65]

Of all the relationships which E——had with various enterprises in Omaha, the one which proved to be the most embarrassing was with a large Jewish-owned department store called J.L. Brandeis and Sons. The management of this store was willing to provide jobs for Jewish immigrants, and, naturally, E——eagerly availed himself of the opportunity to send immigrants there. Whitfield was told, however, that E——had been using the good will of the Brandeis management to peddle his own influence as a dispenser of patronage. An immigrant named Lawrinowich recalled that three days after he had arrived in Omaha E——'s son came to the boarding house looking for another immigrant, to take him to the Brandeis store for a job. Since the other immigrant was not there at the time, the new immigrant convinced E——'s son to take him instead, as he recalled:

When I reached the Brandeis store, I met Mr. E——there, and he asked me, "What are you doing here?" and I said I wanted a job and he said, "This is not for you, because you cannot speak English," and I said, "So far as English is concerned, I have been in England and know quite a little English, and I know they would not put me on a sales counter, but I can do lots of other work." E——told me to go back home, but the foreman of the store overheard the conversation and saw that I was willing to work, and he said, "That is all right, you can work here," and then he placed me at work for $9 a week. I worked there for three weeks.

Lawrinowich had no further dealings with E——. "Perhaps he was sore at me because I wanted to go to work only three days after I arrived here," he guessed. "I know he would not pay for my baggage, and I had to borrow from the landlady . . . to pay for it."[66]

Whitfield suspected that E——had been upset because he had expected to collect a commission from the previous immigrant. To the prodding questions of the immigrant inspector, Lawrinowich related an incident about a boy named Katz, who, he said, had promised E——$10 if he would get him a job. E——told Katz that he would use his influence to get him a job at the Brandeis store, but Katz waited two or three weeks and was impatient to work. According to Lawrinowich, Katz finally applied there on his own and got a job as a porter:

> After Katz had worked at Brandeis' about two-and-a-half months, E——
> —came to the store and demanded the $10 from the boy, saying he got him the job, but the boy refused to pay and they got into an argument. The foreman or headporter heard the talk and asked what it was all about, and when he learned of it, he told E——that, hereafter, any applicants which E——might bring to the store, he would not accept them nor give them employment.[67]

Whitfield visited the store, where W. H. Thomas, Brandeis' employment secretary, added his own accusations that E——had been grafting money from his employees. The employer's action in severing relations with E——was triggered, however, by another incident, which the immigrant inspector included in his report:

> Mr. Thomas also informed me that E——came to him one day with a number of immigrants and wanted him to put them to work, but he informed him that he had no opening for them and E——then said, "That is all right; I will fix you up," indicating that there was money in it for Thomas. Mr. Thomas was highly indignant and informed E——he was employing men for the Brandeis' store, and not to suit E——or the Jewish society, and he ordered E——out of the store, and reported the matter to Mr. Arthur Brandeis. He also told E——that he would not employ any more men from the Jewish society recommended by him.[68]

Actually, E——had been accused before of collecting commissions from the immigrants, but he had been cleared of those charges by an internal investigation which had been conducted by the Jewish society at Omaha. As a government inspector, however, Whitfield had the authority to take sworn statements from the immigrants. Thus, his examinations were more thorough, and they inevitably turned up more damaging evidence. The Jewish society was forced to face the probability that there was substance to these charges, and it removed E——from his position, replacing him with someone else. If the Jewish society thought that Whitfield would be impressed by this action, however, it was mistaken. In his summary report of his investigation in Omaha, the immigrant inspector reported:

> I learned that Mr. Jacob L——, E——'s successor, is known as a common gambler, making his headquarters in the Budweiser Saloon, which is the headquarters for gamblers and disreputable people. I do not believe that this man is any more fit for the position than his predecessor, E——. Secretary Zimman [of the Jewish society] informed me that it was hard for him to get a good man, and he admitted that [Jacob] L——was addicted to gambling.[69]

Satisfied that they had obtained a fair account of activities there, S. L. Whitfield and Jack Dick, his interpreter, traveled from Omaha to Lincoln, Nebraska, where they took statements from three Jewish immigrants of recent arrival. One of them was an eighteen-year-old carpenter who had found work in a planing mill. Other men doing the same work at the mill were receiving 25¢ or even 35¢ an hour, he explained, but "because I am a greenhorn I only get 20¢."[70] Aside from the low wages being paid to the newcomers, which Whitfield found to be a fact of life wherever he traveled, the immigrant inspector discovered nothing particularly amiss.

Whitfield and Dick next visited Leavenworth, Kansas, where they learned that the main person in charge of receiving the Jewish immigrants was a long-time furniture dealer named Jacob Heit. Unlike agents in other cities they had visited, Heit had a fine reputation. They interviewed a man who had arrived two months before. The newcomer recalled that he had carried with him a letter to Heit, who subsequently took care of him for two weeks. During this time, he approached Heit for a loan of $5 to send to his wife whom he had left penniless. Although the immigrant had been under the impression that such loans would be forthcoming, Heit answered him, "You are too 'green' yet to send money home; wait until you work yourself in, then you can send your own money." True to his word, after two weeks Heit got him a job painting bridges at $9 a week, out of which the immigrant was paying $4 a week room and board. He received his pay in full and was supporting himself. Thus, despite his initial disappointment, the immigrant now was able, presumably, to send money home to his wife.[71]

The immigrant inspector and his interpreter concluded their investigation in Kansas City, Missouri, which was, perhaps, the most important receiving center for Jewish immigrants from Galveston. Here, the agent who received the immigrants was certainly far from being an uninterested moonlighter. Jacob Billikopf, superintendent of the Federation of Jewish Charities in Kansas City, was highly regarded in the community at large as an expert in the budding field of social work. The fact that he took upon himself direct responsibility for the placing and caring of immigrants was a sign of the great importance which he attached to the project. He himself had come from Russia as a poor boy at the age of fourteen. Now, as a respected member of the establishment, Billikopf was anxious to demonstrate the opportunities which America presented to Jewish immigrants, and he considered it as part of his job to help them in getting settled.

Perhaps Billikopf should have assigned someone the exclusive task of handling these immigrants, for he could scarcely have had time to see to their daily needs while he devoted himself to his many communal responsibilities. A "former member of the Jewish Charities" told Whitfield that many immigrants had come to him for assistance, complaining that Billikopf had refused to help them or, at best, had provided them with very low-paying jobs. Actually, Billikopf did no worse than agents assigned to help Jewish immigrants in other cities. In fact, immigrants who had been disappointed in other cities often gravitated to Kansas City. Some of them fared no better there, but others finally received their first decent jobs.

A thirty-two-year-old butcher from Warsaw had read the ITO advertisement in the Yiddish newspapers which stated, he recalled, that men in his trade were earning $9 a week. Leaving his wife and children at home, he embarked for Galveston where, upon arrival, he was sent off to Fort Worth, Texas. Here, he was given a job in a packing house, piling oxen on a rack. The work, though, was too hard for him, so he quit after two days, receiving $1.90, as he recalled:

> I was idle two months and got tired of Fort Worth. Then I walked 190 miles to Oklahoma City where I got a job in the packing house and made $8.80 in eight days. Then I quit because of the small pay

and came to Kansas City and Mr. Billikopf sent me here to the Pier Brass Works where I have been every since . . . I have been working here two weeks as machine helper at $1.75 a day.[72]

Although this immigrant was not working at his trade, he was finally receiving the salary which he said he had been promised, thanks to Billikopf's efforts. After his experience in other cities, then, he must have felt that he had done the right thing by coming to Kansas City.

Billikopf took great pains to advertise the successful aspects of his operations in Kansas City. Many years later, Billikopf recalled that he used to have group photographs taken of the immigrants and would send these pictures to Jacob H. Schiff in New York:

In accordance with [Schiff's] wishes, I would note at the bottom of the photograph the name of the individual, his occupation, his job, and his starting wage. Six months later, another photograph of his group would go to Mr. Schiff. The second photograph was accompanied by detailed information as to the economic, physical and cultural progress of the individuals . . .

The contrasts were amazing. If these photographs could now be published in parallel columns . . . in the first column would appear groups of haggard, emaciated, frightened creatures, who, if they could speak out, would utter no word of English and confess ignorance of industrial conditions and opportunities. The second column would show men and women, bright-eyed, intelligent, with the air of well-being which is characteristic only of those whose present and future is assured.[73]

The disillusioned former member of the Jewish Charities who was interviewed by Whitfield had an entirely different view, however, of Billikopf and his activities, which the immigrant inspector included in his report:

This gentleman . . . told me that he had often caught Mr. Billikopf in falsehoods and misrepresentations regarding the handling of immigrants; that he was using every possible means to push himself, and believed him to be a man without principle; and that whenever Billikopf does anything for charity he promptly has it published in the newspapers; that on one occasion he saw a picture of a number of immigrants with Billikopf in the center with the amount of wages made by each man given thereon, which figures were greatly exaggerated, and that Billikopf forwarded said photograph to Mr. Jacob H. Schiff.[74]

It would not be unusual for a man of Billikopf's standing to pick up enemies and detractors; thus, the above statement need not necessarily be taken at face value. At the same time, however, it is certainly possible that Billikopf's press releases–and his reports to Schiff–presented a rosier picture than might have been called for by a strict adherence to the unblemished details. He claimed, for example, that eighty-five percent of the immigrants handled by the Jewish Immigrants' Information Bureau "remained in the cities and towns to which they were sent in the first instance."[75] This figure was obviously exaggerated. When Whitfield arrived in Kansas City with a list of nineteen immigrants who had recently been sent there by the JIIB, he found that eight had already left for Chicago, Saint Joseph, and other places. Only after much effort did Whitfield succeed in locating and in examining the remaining eleven immigrants.[76]

The Jewish immigrants who had been sent to Kansas City by the JIIB were part of a larger community of Jewish immigrants who had arrived there through various channels. As in other cities, these people did not lack for things to complain about, nor did they restrain themselves from doing so. Whitfield's informant in Kansas City reported having attended a banquet of Jewish immigrants, where one of them made a speech containing remarks to the effect that "the German Jews brought us to this country and secured poor jobs for us and fed us on dry bread, and gave us bones to lick." These remarks, he said, were greatly applauded by the other immigrants.[77]

It is plain that the keen disappointment felt by many of the immigrants with the wages and conditions of their jobs was due, at least partially, to their recollection of happy promises made in the pamphlets and advertisements circulated by the ITO in Russia. For example, a thirty-one-year old furrier, who had left a wife and five children in Russia, said that he recalled having seen an advertisement sponsored by the ITO which stated that furriers were making $14 a week. Upon arrival in Kansas City, however, he found that, if such jobs existed at all, they were not the types of jobs he was being offered, as he related in response to questions put to him by the immigrant inspector:

Q. Did the committee secure employment for you?
A. Yes, at the Empire Cap Co. at $4 a week operating a machine for making caps. I worked there two weeks . . . The work was slack and they laid me off.

Q. What did you do then?

A. Mr. Billikopf sent me with a man to the packing house. I worked there 4½ days at $7.50 a week carrying skins.

Q. Why did you quit there?
A. The work was too heavy for me. After that Mr. Billikopf sent me to another cap factory and they told me I should receive $7 the first week and $8.00 after that. I have not worked there a week yet.[78]

A forty-one-year-old carpenter, who had left behind a wife and eight children, said that the ITO's agent in his town had told him that men in his trade were earning from $12 to $20 a week in the American West. Borrowing 50 rubles from his son and 30 rubles from his sister, he had embarked for Galveston.

Once there, he was sent to Leavenworth, Kansas, where he was met by the representative of the Jewish society, Jacob Heit, who placed him in Mrs. Ellis' boarding house, where he remained for two and a half weeks. Then, Heit got him a job as a helper in a carriage factory at $7.50 a week, where he worked for two months. He found the job too hard, however, and it was not in his line of work, so he quit and looked for another job. This time, he did not even bother to ask Heit for help, for there were "other green ones coming and they did not have work for them." Unable to find work, he next tried his luck in Kansas City where, however, he was no more successful.

On a street in Kansas City, at three o'clock in the afternoon, the unemployed carpenter happened to meet Whitfield's interpreter, Jack Dick, with whom he struck up a conversation. The interpreter asked if the immigrant were satisfied with the treatment he had received from the representatives of the Jewish organizations. "No," the man grumbled, "I am broke now and have not had anything to eat today, and have no work, which they promised me before I came to this country." As the despondent immigrant had only five cents in his pocket, Dick took pity on him and bought him a square meal. Afterwards, he related the story to Whitfield, and a report of the incident eventually reached the U.S. Immigration Bureau in Washington, where it furnished proof that the Jewish Immigrants' Information Bureau was bringing in aliens who were likely to become public charges.[79]

One of the complaints voiced frequently by the immigrants was that they were being grossly underpaid, compared to others who were working at similar jobs. Two new arrivals related the following typical experiences, in response to the questions of the immigrant inspector:

Q. Did Mr. Billikopf . . . obtain employment for you?
A. Yes, he sent me to Mr. Mendlesohn, a tailor, and I worked for him for four weeks at $8 a week. I quit because the foreman abused me.

Q. What did the other men receive for similar work?
A. $10 and $12 a week. I only received $8 because I was a greenhorn.[80]

Q. When you arrived here did Mr. Billikopf take care of you and give you employment?
A. Yes, [he] boarded me for a week [and] put me to work in the Grand Pants Co. as a baster at $5 a week. I am still working there.

Q. What do the others receive for their work?
A. One boy gets $13 for the same work I am doing . . .

Q. Have you given Mr. Billikopf any part of your wages?
A. No.[81]

As he had been suspicious of agents in other Jewish communities, Whitfield had his doubts about the agent in Kansas City. He suspected that the low wages of the immigrants might be the net result of commissions which they or their employers paid to Billikopf.[82] His suspicions, however, were pointed in the wrong direction. The natural proclivity of employers to take advantage of "green" immigrants by paying them less money needed no encouragement from any outside force. Exploitation of new immigrants was a fact of life over which neither Billikopf nor agents in other cities had any control. In a way, though, it made their jobs easier. The superintendent of the Associated Jewish Societies in Minneapolis, who was responsible for placing Jewish immigrants from Galveston, acknowledged this when he was interviewed by an immigrant inspector:

I never get a job for anybody until they come [to Minneapolis]. When I get them the job, I tell the employers to pay what they are worth. I never had much trouble in finding a job for these men as the factories are more than anxious to get ahold of a green man because they work cheap.[83]

The examinations which were conducted by the U.S. immigrant inspectors during June and July, 1910, merely exposed a fact that had long been accepted in these communities, that salaries of newly arrived immigrants were invariably low. This was true whether the jobs were secured for them by the representatives of the local Jewish societies or by the immigrants themselves. For example, an immigrant working in a furniture factory in Omaha had complained that the $9 a week he had been receiving at the job found for him by E——, the local agent, was less than others were getting for the same work. After four weeks he was laid off, and this time found his own job at a mattress factory. Again, he was being paid $9 a week, which he still considered unfair.[84]

The initial salaries of the newly arrived immigrants, then, were comparatively low, but this could not be blamed on the representatives of the local societies. It is more than likely that the above immigrant eventually earned more money, if not at the mattress factory, then somewhere else. Perhaps he later moved to another city. The important thing was that he had gotten off to a somewhat reasonable start in an alien environment and had soon reached the point where he was able to fend for himself. In this respect, he was typical of most of the Jewish immigrants from Galveston who were examined by the U.S. immigrant inspectors in June and July, 1910. Most of the inspectors viewed the service that the Jewish communities were providing as an innocent and worthwhile charitable venture, designed to facilitate the acclimation of the immigrants to their new surroundings.

Samuel L. Whitfield, the most thorough of the investigators, did not agree with the above view. Even at the beginning of his investigation he had already been convinced that the jobs which were provided for the immigrants by the agents of the Jewish communities constituted the final link in a chain of evidence proving that the Jewish organizations were violating the contract labor laws. Whitfield's charges were backed by his superior, James R. Dunn, Inspector in Charge of Immigration for the region based at Saint Louis, Missouri. The critical opinion share by Whitfield and Dunn was not based on information which differed from the information gathered by other inspectors; it was simply a different way of viewing the same facts.

In rejecting the appeals of thirty-four of the Jewish immigrants who had arrived at Galveston on June 23, 1910, Acting Secretary Benjamin S. Cable showed that he preferred Whitfield's point of view to the one held by most of the other immigrant inspectors. The deportations, then, were ultimately based on subjective, rather than substantiative grounds. In fact, most of the inspectors, including Whitfield, had not yet completed their investigations by the time Cable ordered the immigrants to be deported.

The members of the Galveston Committee sensed that the Department of Commerce and Labor had a weak case against the immigrants. Therefore, they called upon Acting Secretary Cable to grant a rehearing of the appeals of these immigrants in the hope that, by sheer weight of logic, they could convince him to reverse his own decision and allow the immigrants to remain. In support of their request for a rehearing of the appeals, David M. Bressler, Nathan Bijur, and Max J. Kohler, all lawyers and all members of the Galveston Committee (actually, Kohler did not officially join the Committee until two months later) submitted detailed written statements in defense of the operations of the Jewish Immigrants' Information Bureau.

In his statement of facts, Bressler challenged Cable's premise that Jewish immigrants were being induced to come to America. They were forced to leave Russia because of intolerable conditions, and would, in any case, have found their way to the United States, Bressler said. He pointed out that the American government ought to have been applauding the Galveston Movement, since it was helping to solve an American problem, viz., the distribution of immigrants. The previous Inspector in Charge of Immigration at Galveston, E.B. Holman, had performed his task admirably, Bressler said, excluding immigrants who failed to meet the physical requirements for admission. Why, then, this sudden campaign of "enforcement"? Also, Cable had charged that the work secured for the immigrants by the JIIB was temporary and frequently changing, and that they were sometimes out of work. Bressler pointed out that this was generally true of most new immigrants during their initial periods of adjustment. Compared to most immigrants, Bressler felt that the JIIB immigrants were relatively very well adjusted. Besides all this, Bressler made special mention of the fact that about one-third of the Jewish immigrants arriving at Galveston were coming to join relatives already living in the West. These immigrants were not sponsored by the JIIB.[85]

The Jewish Immigrants' Information Bureau—and the immigrants themselves—were being accused of violating the Immigration Act of February 20, 1907, which had gone into effect on July 1, 1907, the day that the first group of Jewish immigrants had arrived at Galveston. The relevant provisions of this act were the contract labor laws of sections two, four, and six. Section two prohibited immigrants who had "been induced or solicited to migrate to this country by offers or promises of employment or in consequence of agreements, oral, written or printed, express or implied, to perform labor in this country of any kind, skilled, or unskilled." Section four made it a misdemeanor "to prepay the transportation or in any way to assist or encourage the importation or migration of any contract or contract laborers into the United States." Section six made it a "violation of section four of this act to assist or encourage the importation or migration of any alien by promise of employment through advertisements printed and published in any foreign country."[86]

In detailed legal memoranda, Nathan Bijur and Max J. Kohler demonstrated that the Galveston Movement was not acting in violation of the above laws. Since Jewish immigration was largely the result of Russian oppression, the immigrants were being neither "induced" nor "solicited." Each immigrant paid for his own passage; thus, there was no "prepayment of transportation." While it was true that advertisements were printed in foreign newspapers, these did not contain concrete offers of employment. Rather, they merely directed the attention of prospective immigrants to the availability of the Galveston alternative, as opposed to the immensely popular New York route.

Kohler's memorandum was especially convincing, as he cited several past decisions which would seem to have supported the legality of immigration similar to that of the Galveston Movement. For example, he recalled the recently raised issue as to whether the Territory of Hawaii was permitted to arrange for transportation of intended immigrants, and to advertise the advantages of its industrial conditions, without any specific offer or promise of employment. On this question, George W. Wickersham, Attorney General during the Taft Administration, had supported the activities of the Territory of Hawaii, stating that the law "could very properly be construed to prohibit only an offer or promise of employment which is of such definite character that an acceptance thereof would constitute a contract." Wickersham had continued:

> Certainly a representation to an alien or aliens as to the resources of a locality, of the industrial conditions there existing, by which representation, the alien is induced to migrate to the United States, does not fall within the prohibition of the statute. A broader meaning is not suggested by the sixth section of the act, which makes it unlawful to assist or encourage the importation or migration of any alien by promise of employment through advertisements printed or published in any foreign country. This, like similar phrases in section 2, is

directed against a promise which specially designates the particular job or work or employment for which the alien's labor is desired.

Summing up, Attorney General Wickersham had generalized as follows:

> Any plan which has in view a distribution of the alien immigrants among the rural population and to procure their services in the development of industries in which labor is deficient, and thus remove them from competition with American laborers in those vocations which are overcrowded, is in entire accord with the spirit of our immigrations laws.[87]

Armed with these, as well as other equally convincing arguments, several members of the Galveston Committee called upon Acting Secretary Cable on Thursday, July 21, 1910, urging him to consider a rehearing of the appeals of the thirty-four Jewish immigrants who were threatened with deportation. They left Cable's office with the impression that no deportation would take place until Cable would render a final judgment as to the merits of the arguments presented to him. Max J. Kohler formally submitted his memorandum on July 23, and Nathan Bijur submitted his on July 25.[88] They now waited for a decision to be made by the acting secretary of Commerce and Labor.

Jacob H. Schiff had a special arrangement with the Western Union Company entitling him to unlimited usage of their telegraph service, and he permitted the JIIB to share this privilege with him. In order to take advantage of this arrangement properly, all telegrams sent out by Bressler's office were signed "Jacob H. Schiff," and all those meant for Bressler's office were addressed to Schiff, whose office forwarded them to the headquarters of the Jewish Immigrants' Information Bureau. On Wednesday morning, July 27, 1910, Schiff's office received a telegram from Henry Berman, the JIIB's manager at Galveston, informing him that twenty-nine of the immigrants whose appeals Cable had originally rejected were to be deported that very day, on the North German-Lloyd Steamship *Frankfurt*, bound for Bremen, which was scheduled to leave Galveston at four o'clock in the afternoon.

At 11:55 A.M., Schiff (or Bressler, using Schiff's name) wired the following message back to Berman:

> Secretary Cable has given assurances that no one would be deported pending decision of the rehearing which took place twenty-first. We

had Secretary Cable on the telephone today and he assured Congressman Bennet that no deportation would take place until after decision is rendered. Take steps immediately with Hampton. Show him this telegram and if he is doubtful ask him to wire for instructions to Cable and to quote my telegram. We will pay any expense necessary to accomplish this. If the immigrants go back it will be in violation of the promise made by Secretary Cable.

As instructed, Berman showed the telegram to Inspector in Charge Hampton.[89]

It was now about 1:00 P.M., or approximately three hours before the scheduled sailing of the S.S. *Frankfurt*. As Hampton later recalled, he felt himself "in rather an embarrassing position, as it was most natural to believe that a telegram signed by Jacob H. Schiff would be worthy of credence, and furthermore that instructions to detain the aliens in question might have been issued by the bureau and have been missent or otherwise miscarried." He immediately wired the Bureau of Immigration and Naturalization at Washington as follows:

Jacob Schiff wires Berman, Secretary has granted rehearing cases twenty-nine Hebrews arrived steamship *Hanover* and ordered deported. Nothing received by this office, ship sails four o'clock, now one, will be deported unless otherwise advised.[90]

Hampton then arranged with the general agent of the North German-Lloyd Company that he would delay the sailing of the S.S. *Frankfurt* until six o'clock, if necessary, to allow sufficient time in which to receive a reply from Washington.

At 4:00 p.m., however, Hampton received the following telegram from the Bureau of Immigration and Naturalization:

No rehearing cases twenty-nine Hebrew[s], your telegram today. Deport.[91]

The aliens, therefore, were promptly put aboard the ship and deported. At 4:53 p.m., after the aliens had been deported, Schiff (or Bressler, using Schiff's name) cabled Berman that "we have spoken to Cable over the telephone an hour ago and he figured that he would not countermand order for deportation by outgoing ship."

In a subsequent letter to the commissioner general of Immigration, Hampton expressed deep distrust of the methods employed by the JIIB which, he felt, had tried to bluff him into postponing the deportation at least until the sailing of the next ship, about a month later. "To say the least," Hampton complained, "it appears rather strange that only a few hours prior to the hour fixed for the sailing of the North German-Lloyd Steamship *Frankfurt* on July 27, a telegram should be received of the nature of the one quoted . . . and signed Jacob H. Schiff."[92]

Hampton would have been still angrier had he known that an old, previously admitted immigrant had substituted himself for one of the twenty-nine rejected ones. The old immigrant, who had been ill, wanted to return to Russia, and he agreed to travel back under the name of the deported immigrant.[93] The exchange of identities never became known to the authorities, and by this ruse a rejected immigrant managed to avoid deportation. This was hardly a victory, however, which could be gloated over by the representatives of the Jewish Immigrants' Information Bureau. Clearly, the latter organization had lost the opening round in its battle with the restrictionists at the U.S. Bureau of Immigration and Naturalization.

CHAPTER 5

The Battle of the Bureaus

The activity surrounding the deportation action created a warlike atmosphere in the U.S. Immigration and Naturalization Bureau as well as in the Jewish Immigrants' Information Bureau. The deportation of July 27, 1910, had largely been instigated by the Inspector in Charge of the U.S. Immigration Service at Galveston, Alfred Hampton. The latter may not have initially realized the extent of the crisis which was bound to ensue from his actions. Be that as it may, Hampton now found himself in a difficult position, pressured, as he was, from different directions, by two opposing forces. While Hampton's superiors in Washington now began pressing him for further deportations, the JIIB was using every method at its disposal to prevent such deportations from taking place. It was in Hampton's power merely to detain immigrants for examination by a Board of Special Inquiry, which would make the actual decisions concerning deportation. Thus, while Hampton was held responsible by his superiors for the adoption of the new, tough policy, he was really bound by the decisions of the board, over which he had little control.

The S.S. *Frankfurt*, which carried the deportees of the forty-first Jewish immigrant party back to Bremen, had arrived at Galveston three days earlier, bringing the forty-second party with a record number of 291 Jewish immigrants. The new arrivals had first stopped over in Philadelphia, where they had been alerted to the government crackdown on organized Jewish immigration in Galveston. With great trepidation, the immigrants had proceeded to

Galveston, where about half were held over for hearings by the Board of Special Inquiry.[1]

The chairman of the Board of Special Inquiry in Galveston, Inspector M. Arthur Coykendall, thoroughly interviewed each immigrant, through the assistance of interpreters. These examinations revealed desperate last-minute efforts on board ship to provide the Jewish immigrants with addresses of "friends" or "relatives" in the United States who, it was claimed, would take personal interest in their welfare. These were meant to convince the U.S. authorities that the immigrants were coming on their own, rather than as part of an organized project, and also that they were not likely to become public charges, since they had "relatives" or "friends" who were prepared to look after them until they could become self-supporting.

Transcripts of the examinations show that these hasty, sloppy efforts to manufacture American acquaintances while on board ship were easily exposed by Coykendall and his fellow inspectors in Galveston. The immigrants revealed to Coykendall that, after the ship left Philadelphia, the ship's purser had distributed about seventy addresses to as many immigrants. They showed Coykendall the slips of paper which they had been handed, and they were forced to admit that they had never before heard of the individuals whose names appeared thereon. Coykendall's examination of immigrant Nachman Kesselman elicited a typical admission of this practice:

Q. Do you know F. Goldstein in Beaumont, Texas? (This address shown on the manifest on the line with that of the alien's name.)
A. He is a distant relative, but I was told that one must have an address, so I have the address to Galveston.

Q. Did you ever see me before?
A. Yes.

Q. Did you see me on the wharf?
A. Yes.

Q. Do you remember me asking you down on the wharf if you were going to this man, Goldstein, in Beaumont?
A. Yes.

Q. Do you remember telling me at that time that you had never heard of this man, Goldstein, before — did not know him?

A. The truth is, I do not know him, but they were talking on board that one needs an address and I have taken the address of Goldstein in Beaumont.

Q. Where did you get this address of Goldstein in Beaumont?
A. On board.

Q. Who gave it to you?
A. The Dolmetcher (purser).

Q. When did he give it to you? . . .
A. After the boat left Philadelphia.

Q. Did you ask him to supply you with an address, or did he come and tell you that he had given you this address on the manifest?
A. He called out "anyone that has no addresses," so most of the immigrants came to him and I also, and he gave us the addresses. I do not know that he gave it to me, but he sent it down to me.

Q. Have you the slip of paper that the purser sent down to you with Goldstein's address on it?
A. (Alien presents slip of paper reading "Mr. F. Goldstein, 526 Orleans St., Beaumont, Texas.)

Q. What man on the ship handed you this slip of paper?
A. The man that was sent down by the Dolmetcher.

Q. Do you know what his official position is?
A. He is an assistant rabbi. . . .

Q. The Dolmetcher told you, did he, that you would not be permitted to land without an address?
A. Yes, but I have an address of a good friend in Galveston.

Q. Where did you get this address of your good friend in Galveston?
A. When I went down Sunday I saw him from a distance and I recognized him and he recognized me and gave me this address. If I had had this address before, I would not have been given this address in Beaumont.[2]

The name of Kesselmann's "good friend" was also invoked by Abraham Fridman, another arriving immigrant. While Kesselmann had said his friend's name was "It[z]chok Colisey", Fridman referred to the latter as "Ike Karesen". Under Coykendall's persistent questioning, Fridman related that after the ship had docked he and Kesselmann had recognized Karesen from afar, and the latter then sent them fruit with one of the sailors. Hidden among the fruit was a slip of paper with Karesen's name and address. When Coykendall subsequently called Karesen for questioning, the latter denied having sent the fruit, but he declared his intention to help Kesselman and Fridman, both of whom, he confirmed, were old friends.[3]

As in his examination of other protégés of the JIIB, Inspector Coykendall called upon Henry Berman to testify as to what help he could offer the newcomers. The JIIB manager replied that he would send Kesselmann to Dallas and Fridman to Minneapolis, and that each would be provided with transportation, provisions, and funds necessary for his maintenance until work would be found by the local representative in each city. In the end, the Board of Special Inquiry ruled that Kesselmann and Fridman be admitted and forwarded to the destinations specified by Berman. Their avowed friendship with Karesen played no positive part in the decision to admit them. These friendships, if that is what they were, were no doubt viewed with skepticism, in light of the general practice of manufacturing acquaintances.

The Board of Special Inquiry was quite disturbed by what it considered to be the transparent efforts of the immigrants to distort the truth, apparently with the connivance of the North German-Lloyd Shipping Co. and the Jewish Immigrants' Information Bureau. Board Chairman Coykendall pointed out that supplying the aliens with addresses of dubious "relatives" and "friends" shortly before landing and altering the ship's passenger manifest to conform with this information, was against the law. Coykendall found Kesselmann's testimony to be especially intriguing, particularly in regard to the "assistant rabbi" who had handed him the American address while on board ship. When Coykendall informed Berman that he wished to secure a statement from the rabbi, the latter immediately returned to Europe on the return voyage of the same ship, despite his original declared intention of staying to investigate the immigration question. Coykendall concluded that the rabbi "was in possession of information concerning Jewish immigration into America which would materially strengthen our position and that he was acting upon the advice of the JIIB when he cut short his visit and hurriedly returned home."[4]

Interviews with other immigrants raised further questions. Inexplicably, two unrelated immigrants obtained the address of one Morris Edelman of Saint Louis, though Edelman's identity was a mystery to each of them. Despite its reservations about the methods used to gain admittance, the Board of Special Inquiry voted to admit these[5] and, indeed, all but twelve of the new arrivals, largely on the strength of Berman's promise that the JIIB would look after them until they found work. Thus, the clumsy efforts to supply the immigrants with addresses, while entirely understandable in view of the unfortunate experience of the previous party, were proven to be entirely unnecessary. In the end, only one immigrant was actually deported on the grounds that he was likely to become a public charge, and seven others because they were medically certified for trachoma.[6]

One of the immigrants who was admitted at this time was Tewja Breidberg, now calling himself Tobias Braitford, who had brought his eight-year-old sister with him to Galveston three months earlier, and had been forced by the immigration authorities to accompany her back to Europe. This time, Breidberg arrived alone and was admitted, after a thorough examination.[7]

Most of the immigrants were men who, if married, intended to send for their families later on. For example, a thirty-three-year-old farm laborer from the Kiev region had left behind a wife and four small children. His wife's mother had sold her house to give him money for the voyage. The man's plight—and that of his dependents—was depicted in his response to questions put to him by the immigrant inspectors:

Q. What arrangements have you made for the support of your wife and children in Russia until such time as you are able to send them money?
A. I left her without money.

Q. How do you expect them to live?
A. She will sell her clothes to buy something to eat. . . .

Q. Have you been supporting your mother-in-law in Russia?
A. Yes.

Q. Is it your intention to bring her to America when you bring your wife and children?
A. Yes.[8]

In the end, out of 291 Jewish immigrants arriving on July 24 on the S.S. *Frankfurt*, only eight were deported, seven of them for trachoma, as mentioned above. Thus, almost all of the immigrants constituting the forty-second party were admitted, despite the conviction held by the members of the Board of Special Inquiry that these indigent aliens were being assisted by organized Jewish charity.

The board felt that it was being generous in its actions, as evidenced by its finding in the case of a typical immigrant:

> The alien before the board is of robust healthy appearance, and has displayed more than the average intelligence in his reply to questions, and although he has testified that he borrowed the money in Russia with which to purchase his ticket to America, and that the Russian Jewish Society sold him the ticket for ten rubles less than the usual amount charged; also that he arrived in Galveston in a destitute condition and is immediately dependent upon the assistance of the Jewish Immigration Society for maintenance and assistance in securing employment, and transportation to such place of employment—we feel that his case is so similar to that of the other aliens applying for admission at this port . . . that we do not feel justified in excluding him. He is therefore unanimously admitted, and it is recommended that a copy of the minutes of the board in this case be transmitted to the Bureau in Washington for their information.[9]

When Cable read the minutes of the Board of Special Inquiry, he was furious. The acting secretary of Commerce and Labor was convinced that the board's latest findings constituted a shameful dereliction of duty, and he fired off an angry memorandum to the commissioner general of Immigration:

> I think you should send some additional instructions to Mr. Hampton as to our interpretation of the law. It looks as if he and the board, upon their own responsibility, were practically going back to the old system of admitting destitute Russian Hebrews of whom the Jewish Immigrants' Information Bureau offers to take charge. As already explained, in my opinion the methods of the Jewish societies in this matter are unlawful, and of this they have been fully informed.[10]

Commissioner General of Immigration Daniel J. Keefe was on vacation at this time, and his duties were being performed by his assistant, F. H. Larned. As acting commissioner-general, Larned passed Cable's remarks on to Hampton, adding a few harsh words of his own:

> The Bureau cannot refrain from here expressing its surprise and disappointment at the outcome of these cases . . . So clearly does it seem to the Bureau was the intended and future policy outlined . . . that it can scarcely conceive how you could by any possibility have misconstrued or misunderstood it, yet . . . it is forced to the conclusion that you did misconstrue or misunderstand . . . for it is loath to believe that you, or the officers under your jurisdiction, would refuse to be guided thereby.[11]

Inspector in Charge Hampton was dismayed to receive this letter of rebuke from Acting Commissioner General Larned, for it placed his very career in jeopardy. He felt called upon to answer with a spirited defense, in which he reminded Larned that it was he, Hampton, who had originally and persistently raised the issue of the legality of the JIIB and had initiated the investigation into its activities. Cable himself, in his letter to Bennet of July 14, had written that "it would not be fair, or humane, to suddenly adopt a practice of excluding all of these people in view of what has been allowed for perhaps a year or more." Thus, Hampton maintained, his actions were in complete keeping with Cable's professed strategy of initial leniency and gradual enforcement. Besides, he recalled, the S.S. *Frankfurt* had left Bremen fourteen days before Cable's letter to Bennet. These immigrants, therefore, had had no advance warning of the new policy which was to be initiated. Hampton assured Larned that "in a short time the enforcement of the immigration laws at this port would be as strict as at any of the more important ports."[12] These persuasive arguments convinced Larned to withdraw his harsh criticism of Hampton.[13]

The S. S. *Hanover*, bearing eighty-six Jewish immigrants, arrived at Galveston August 19, three days before the arrival of Larned's harshly critical letter of Hampton. The JIIB had learned from its experience with the forty-second party that it was unnecessary—and embarrassing—to provide immigrants with dubious addresses in the United States. In their examinations by the inspectors, most stated, truthfully, that they had no friends or relatives in the United States to whom they were destined. Furthermore, the immigrants of the forty-third party did not carry ITO identification cards, which, in the past, had been taken by the inspectors as evidence that the aliens were part of an organized immigration scheme. The members of this group were fortunate. Although twenty-seven of them were held over for questioning by the Board of Special Inquiry, none were deported.[14]

Despite the lenient attitude of the Galveston immigrant inspectors toward the latest group of Jewish immigrants, Hampton now began to adopt a new policy which demonstrated his suspicious feelings about the activities of the Jewish Immigrants' Information Bureau. Up until this time, the special deputy collector of Customs at Galveston had permitted JIIB manager Henry Berman, as a courtesy, to board the ship and enter the inspection quarters while immigrants were being examined. Hampton now directed the Customs collectors to deny Berman access to these areas until after the inspectors first had a chance to examine the arriving aliens.[15]

At the conclusion of the examination, Berman was then usually called in. His appearance at this point was often of crucial importance, as is demonstrated by the following excerpt taken from the transcript of a typical examination:

Alien sworn and examined by Inspector Coykendall.

My name is Schevie Lipkin, 27 years old. I am traveling with my wife Rifke Lipkin, 28 years old. We are Russian Hebrews. I am a hat-maker and my wife is a tailoress; we can both read and write; have no children; our last residence was at Iletz, Russia; paid my own passage and that of my wife; have no ticket to destination, but we are going to my nephew at Saint Paul, B. S. Aronowitz, 272 Fairfield St., have no other friends or relatives in America; have never been in the United States before; have no work promised; I have $22.00 (shows it).

Q. You have not enough money in your possession to purchase railroad tickets to Saint Paul; do you intend to telephone your nephew for money, or what will you do?

A. We will not telephone, but we will work at something else awhile until we can earn enough money to go to Saint Paul.

Q. What other kind of work can you do besides tailoress and hat-maker?

A. I would take any kind of work.

At this point, Berman was called in. He stated that the couple was already listed with the JIIB and that arrangements were being made to send them to Omaha, Nebraska, where they would be looked after and provided with suitable work. Since $22 would more than cover their transportation there, and since Omaha was directly on the way to Saint Paul, the Lipkins readily agreed to go. The Board of Special Inquiry then issued the following finding:

Both these aliens present a different appearance from the average Russian Hebrew immigrant: they are dressed cleanly, they have the appearance of strong, healthy, well-to-do middle class. They have enough money to live on until such time as they may be able to secure work in Omaha, to which point the JIIB have stated they would send them, and the board does not believe that after these aliens have once established themselves in positions, that there is the slightest likelihood of their becoming public charges, and therefore vote to admit.[16]

Other transcripts show the suspicious attitude of the U.S. officials towards the immigrants, ultimately outweighed, however, by their apparent decision to be lenient at this time:

> My name is Peisach Josmann, I am 28 years old, married, have a wife and no children in Russia; Hebrew; can read and write; traveling alone, hat-maker, paid my own passage; I am going to Galveston; I have no address; I have $8.00, have never been in the United States before; no work promised (alien shows the $8.00).
>
> Q. Yesterday, you had only $4.00. Where did you get the other $4.00?
> A. I said yesterday I had 8 rubles, I did not know how to tell American money, and so I said I had 8 rubles when I had $8.00.
>
> Q. Did you change any money for anybody since you were examined yesterday?
> A. No.
>
> Q. Did anybody pay you any money that they owed you?
> A. No.
>
> Q. Is this the same money you had yesterday?
> A. Yes, Sir.

After drilling Josmann with further questions, Coykendall adjourned the session. When the board was reconvened the following morning, Coykendall called Josmann once again and asked him when he had first made up his mind to come to Galveston. Apparently flustered by the question, the alien answered, "I never had any intention of coming to the United States." Josmann's answer was damaging, implying, as it did, that the Jewish organizations had induced his immigration to the United States, rather than having merely changed his port of entry to Galveston. Coykendall then asked Josmann if he could think of any reason why he should not be deported back to Russia. "I do not like Russia," Josmann answered, "and there is nothing for me to do there."

After Coykendall had finished interrogating the alien, he called in Berman. The JIIB manager stated that he would send Josmann to Oklahoma City, a trip that would cost less than $8. In that city, the local committee would look after Josmann and would be sure to find him a job soon after his arrival. Relying heavily on Berman's statement, the board finally ruled that Josmann be admitted.[17]

Another Jewish immigrant arriving on the same ship apparently had no formal connection with the Galveston Movement, but he nevertheless aroused the suspicions of the immigration officials and was interrogated by Inspector Coykendall:

> My name is Nissan Fradkin, I am 23 years old, Russian Hebrew, single, peddler, traveling alone, read and write, paid my own passage. I am going to Galveston to my brother-in-law, J. Agranowitz; I have no money, I have no other relatives or friends in America; I have never been in the United States before; I have no work promised.

Q. How long has your brother-in-law been in the U.S.?
A. About seven or eight months.

Q. What is his business here?
A. He works in a hardware store.

Q. Is your sister, his wife, here with him?
A. No, she is in Russia.

Q. Do you expect him to assist you in securing employment, and maintaining you until you secure such employment?
A. I do not know.

Q. How do you expect to maintain yourself without funds until you can secure employment unless he does assist you?
A. I think my brother-in-law will help me.

Q. Have you any other occupation besides that of a peddler?
A. No.

Q. Have you ever worked at anything else?
A. No. . . .

Q. When you purchased your ticket in the steamship company's office were you asked any questions?
A. They asked me no questions.

Q. Are you positive about that?
A. No, they did not ask me anything.

Q. Did they not ask you where you were going?
A. Yes, they asked me that.

Q. Did they ask you anything else?
A. No.

Q. Didn't they ask you your name and age?
A. Yes.

Q. Did they ask you whether you had any friends or relatives in the United States?
A. No.

Q. Do you know a man by the name of Alfred Holt?
A. No.

Q. Did you tell the agent of the steamship company that you were going to your friend Alfred Holt in Galveston?
A. No.

Alfred Holt was the Galveston agent of the North German-Lloyd Steamship Co. On the passenger manifests of arriving ships, Holt's name appeared incongruously as the "friend" to whom hundreds of immigrants were going. Fradkin was one of many immigrants who were forced to admit to the examiners that they had never heard of Alfred Holt, and that the latter's name had been inserted without their knowledge. It would have been more logical to have inserted the name of Fradkin's brother-in-law, whom he was really destined to join.

Fradkin told the Board of Special Inquiry that he had come to Galveston on his own, rather than through the auspices of the Jewish Emigration Society. Perhaps because of this, Berman was not called upon to testify. Instead, Fradkin's brother-in-law was called, and the latter declared his intention to look after Fradkin and see to it that he would get a job. Fradkin had neither money nor skills, but the board nevertheless voted unanimously to admit him. In doing so, the board relied heavily on the testimony of Fradkin's brother-in-law and on the fact that Fradkin himself was "of a good physical appearance and impresses us as well able to perform any kind of manual labor that he is called upon to do."[18]

Despite the rigorous interrogation, the members of the Board of Special Inquiry could find no reason to exclude any of the immigrants. Hampton found it necessary to explain to his superiors in Washington that this was "an exceptionally fine lot of Hebrews." "Apparently," he wrote, "they had been very carefully selected, for there was no sickness among them and there was only one man forty-five years of age, one forty-two years of age, and two forty years of age, the remainder, outside [of] a comparatively few women and children, being strong, vigorous young men."[19]

One of the immigrants, a 37-year-old blacksmith named David Schuschan, arrived with his wife and five children and was destined for Kansas City, where his wife's uncle lived. The Board of Special Inquiry allowed the family in, with the comment that

from an examination of the muscles of this man's arm we find that his statement of being a blacksmith is corroborated by the fact that the muscles of his arm are very large and well developed. He has ample money to provide for his family and purchase transportation to his relatives at Kansas City at which point we believe that his relatives will be able to secure work for him. He has been acccustomed to hard work, and if he could not obtain employment at his original occupation, we do not believe that he would hesitate to perform other manual labor. He impresses the board in addition as being intelligent and well able to support himself, and family.[20]

In the same group of immigrants, a 22-year-old butcher was certified by the doctors as having a "flat chest and poor muscular development, affecting his ability to earn a living." The Board of Special Inquiry could easily have ordered him to be deported, yet it passed him, with the following comment:

Although this alien is certified by the doctor as having flat chest and poor muscular development, we do not fully agree that it is of such a nature that it would affect his ability to earn a living as he has the appearance of being of very good physical build and seems to us to be well able to maintain himself after he has once established himself in a position; he has $25, and although he has no friends or relatives we believe he will have no difficulty in inducing some of his own race to assist him in the securing of a position.[21]

The thorough interviews conducted by the Board of Special Inquiry with the Jewish immigrants of the forty-third party did not lead to any deportations. The transcripts of these interviews, however, as well as interviews with other groups of immigrants, were forwarded to the U.S. Bureau of Immigration and Naturalization in Washington, where they were used to build a case against the Galveston Movement. The controversy was beginning to attract the attention of important people in and out of government. In defense of its policy, the Department of Commerce and Labor was now able to give a clear and fairly accurate account of the workings of the Galveston Movement, relying heavily on information which the inspectors had gleaned from the immigrants.

When originally signing up for the trip to Galveston, each emigrant had paid the ITO's Jewish Emigration Society 85 rubles, in exchange for which he received three documents. These documents were to be presented respectively to the ITO's agent on the German side of the Russian border, to the *Hilfsverein* representative in Bremen, and to the JIIB manager in Galveston. Presentation of the documents entitled the emigrant to railroad transportion across Germany, food and lodging in Bremen, the trans-Atlantic steamship journey (including the $4 immigrant head tax levied by the United States government), food and lodging in Galveston, railroad transportation and subsistence en route to the final destination, and food and lodging there until work could be found. According to the Department's reckoning, the 85 rubles paid by the emigrant was really sufficient to cover only the railroad ticket to Bremen and the steamship ticket to Galveston, and even these two tickets were probably obtained for them at reduced prices. Thus, the food and lodging in Bremen, Galveston and the city of final destination, and the railroad transportation and subsistence en route to that destination, had, in effect, been supplied free of charge. It was the contention of the Department of Commerce and Labor that this subsidy was in violation of the Immigration Act of 1907, which barred immigrants whose ticket or passage was paid for by persons other than themselves.[22]

While Henry Berman was matching wits with U.S. immigration officials, he found, to his great consternation, that he also had to face opposition from an unexpected source — from his fellow Jews in Galveston. The Reform Jews, largely of German descent, who were members of Rabbi Henry Cohen's Congregation B'nai Israel, wholeheartedly supported the Jewish Immigrants' Information Bureau and its leadership. The Orthodox, however, were divided into two groups. The Russians, whose synagogue was known as the Young Men's Hebrew Association, were mostly in favor of the Galveston Movement. On the other hand, many of the Galicians, who belonged to the recently established Bikur Cholim Society synagogue,[23] were opposed to the JIIB staff and to its manager, Henry Berman, whom they accused of having an "irreligious attitude."[24] This opposition group was headed by Mr. J. Lippman, a former employee of the Jewish Immigrants' Information Bureau.[25]

Lippman had been one of Morris D. Waldman's assistants at the founding of the JIIB, and had been present at the landing of the very first group of Jewish immigrants on July 1, 1907. He may not have expected to succeed Waldman as manager, but he certainly had hoped, at least, to continue on as an assistant to the succeeding managers. Instead, sometime after Henry Berman had been brought to Galveston, Lippman had been dismissed. Now, when the government was instituting deportation proceedings against the Jewish immigrants at Galveston, Lippman regarded this as proof of poor management on the part of the JIIB, and he did not hesitate in making his views known to Bressler. Lippman reminded Bressler:

I warned you. Understand the fellows are hated. . . . Whom did you make rulers over our own poor people? I am still a friend of the poor Russians and I expect to care for them again as I practiced three years vollunteerly [sic] but I [would] like to see you keeping it up and not go down. Believe me such would never [have] happened with me. Taking Bureau men off and leaving the others proved the [cause] of trouble. Such others as the impoliteness of your inexperienced men, fresh and sassy . . . helped the destroying [sic] of the movement.[26]

Determined to prove the incompetence of Berman and his staff, Lippman had, for some time, been gathering facts which emphasized the mistakes of the Jewish Immigrants' Information Bureau. He even collected an assortment of pamphlets, circulars and advertisements issued by the Jewish Territorial Organization in Europe, designed to recruit potential Jewish immigrants for the Galveston Movement. This literature was potentially harmful, because it could be used in an attempt to show that the Galveston Movement was illegally inducing or soliciting immigration to the United States. Lippman's purpose in gathering these facts and documents together was unclear, but he may have been planning to use them for an exposé in the Yiddish press at some future date. In the meantime, Lippman was spreading harmful gossip about the Galveston Movement, and he gathered to himself a large number of supporters, mostly Orthodox members of the Galician-Jewish community in Galveston.[27]

Most of the Jews in Galveston supported the Galveston Movement, and they harbored deep suspicions about Lippman and his clique who, they surmised, probably feared a large settlement of Jewish business competitors in Galveston. They suspected Lippman's group of passing on negative information and harmful documents to the U.S. immigration authorities, thus instigating the latter to initiate deportation proceedings against Jewish immigrants arriving in Galveston. Many of the deported immigrants learned of these accusations, and they reported them to the ITO representatives who greeted them upon their return to Bremen. Zangwill relayed these accusations to Bressler, who wrote to Berman, asking him to undertake an investigation of the matter.

In keeping with his characteristically direct manner, Berman confronted Lippman and two of his cronies with the charges which had been leveled against them. They heatedly denied these charges, protesting that they would never do anything which would put their fellow Jews in danger.[28] Berman was impressed by the sincerity of their denials, and he concluded that the charges against the Lippman faction were without any basis in fact. The truth was that the information used in the deportation proceedings had been gathered by the inspectors sent out by the Bureau of Immigration and Naturalization. In fact, much of the documentary evidence, which consisted largely of ITO advertisements and circulars printed in Europe, had been handed over to the authorities by the immigrants themselves, during interrogation proceedings.[29] The mere fact that such ugly charges were raised, however, points up the deep division that existed in the Jewish immigrant community of Galveston over the issue of the Galveston Movement.

The issue of the Galveston Movement was being discussed, at this time, by the members of the Jewish immigrant community of New York, as well. Two influential Jewish newspapers, the *Yiddishes Taggeblatt* and the *Morgen Journal*, chose this time to editorialize against the Galveston Movement and everything for which it stood. The Jewish masses, they declared, should immigrate to places where they are naturally inclined to settle, rather than be "led" or "transported" to destinations chosen for them by the German Jewish leaders.[30] Schiff prepared an answer to these editorials, but he was advised by the other members of the Galveston Committee not to send it, for it would serve the purpose of continuing the controversy, rather than containing it.[31] As it was, Jewish newspapers in Europe had picked up the story of the deportation crisis, and many potential immigrants were being scared away.[32]

All this time, Schiff's Galveston Committee was working quietly to influence the Department of Commerce and Labor to change its hostile stance. At all costs, the committee tried to avoid publicity about the deportations, since this would discourage additional Jewish immigrants from coming to Galveston. On August 21, 1910, however, the following article, presumably leaked by the Department of Commerce and Labor, appeared in the *New York Times*:

> *Bar Jews at Galveston*
> *Federal Government Asserts That Law Has*
> *Not Been Enforced There*

Washington, Aug. 20. The entry of Russian Jew immigrants at the port of Galveston, Texas, will be regulated more closely in the future. Department of Commerce and Labor officials reached this decision after an investigation which convinced the immigration authorities that the laws had been loosely enforced there and led to the discharge of one Inspector . . .

While the department disavows any interest of discriminating against that class of immigrants, Assistant Secretary Cable is determined that the immigration standards at Galveston shall come up to those required at all other ports. He is convinced that admission at Galveston has been too easy, and that this fact, known in Europe, has stimulated immigration to the port.[33]

For the publicity-shy Schiff, probably the most distasteful part of the above article was that it included a reference to "The Jewish Immigrants' Information Bureau, popularly known as the Jacob H. Schiff Society." After reading the article, Schiff promptly wrote Cable an angry letter, in which he recalled that the Galveston Movement had been established as a response to a suggestion made by the late Commissioner General of Immigration, Franklin Pierce Sargent. From the beginning, Schiff asserted, the JIIB and the ITO had consistently remained faithful to their original goal, which was to divert Jewish immigration from New York to Galveston and to encourage the dispersion of the immigrants throughout the West. Schiff accused the Department of Commerce and Labor of having since changed its attitude for no apparent reason and of now being bent on a new policy of destroying the Galveston Movement. Schiff sent a copy of this letter to the President for, as he wrote, "the administration of President Taft will be held responsible by a considerable section of the American people."[34]

If Schiff expected Cable to modify his stance, he was disappointed. In reply, Cable coyly invited Schiff to a legal battle, stating, "If the decisions that I make in these cases are contrary to law the courts would probably set me right upon proper application to them."[35]

Aware that his previous letter may not have reached Taft's personal attention, Schiff wrote to the President's secretary, Charles D. Norton, enclosing a copy of Cable's letter, and asking Norton to bring up the subject to President Taft in person. In his letter to Norton, Schiff called for Cable's resignation as the only means of restoring confidence in the Administration. He concluded with a politely-worded political warning:

We have in other respects experienced keen disappointment because of the non-fulfillment thus far of platform pledges and personal promises made during the last presidential campaign, and if I now write so unreservedly it is partly because I do not wish to see the President, whose loyal supporter I have been ever since he was nominated, placed into a false position, or lose the good will of the important section of the American people for whom I venture to speak in this.[36]

Schiff's hint of political repercussions was well timed, for the mid-term Congressional elections were fast approaching. Taft was especially anxious about the situation in New York, where a governor was to be elected. It was common knowledge that the Republican position in that state needed strengthening.[37] Furthermore, this was a time when Taft's breach with Theodore Roosevelt was taking on public proportions, and Republicans were already choosing sides between the two men. Norton, Taft's secretary, was especially interested in eliminating Rooosevelt as a factor in national politics.[38] Thus, Schiff's veiled threat to Norton that he might withdraw his support from Taft must have been taken seriously at the White House.

At this time, Israel Zangwill also wanted to personally address the American authorities, on behalf of the Jewish Territorial Organization. Schiff, however, wisely counseled Zangwill not to do this, noting that an approach to the United States government by the head of a foreign organization would undoubtedly backfire.[39] Zangwill was so pessimistic about the outcome that he felt he had little to lose by such action, but he abided by Schiff's wishes in the matter. Zangwill's pessimism was further indicated by his wish to suspend further immigration efforts until the situation would be resolved.[40] Schiff, however, feared that such a move would be seen by the government as a sign of weakness. He, therefore, insisted that the immigrants continue to come, albeit in much smaller groups.[41]

The JIIB asked the ITO to refrain from actions which tended to arouse the suspicions of the American government. For instance, the ITO's Kiev-based Jewish Emigration Society ran advertisements in the European Yiddish press which the government interpreted as inducing immigration to the United States. The JIIB suggested that future advertisements merely state that those intending to immigrate to America would do well to consider the advantages of settling in the western states, as compared with the East Coast, and that further details could be gotten by applying to the nearest branch of the Jewish Emigration Society. The Jewish Territorial Organization reworded its advertisements and incorporated other modifications in its recruiting methods, along the lines suggested by the Jewish Immigrants' Information Bureau. Most important, it agreed to continue symbolic immigration efforts as a sign of the resolve of the Galveston Movement not to be bullied by the U.S. Department of Commerce and Labor.[42]

In late September 1910, Cable sent word, through Simon Wolf, that he was willing to meet with a representative of the Jewish Immigrants' Information Bureau. Wolf, ever willing to make peace, enthusiastically passed this news on to the members of the Galveston Committee. Schiff, in no conciliatory mood, was inclined to ignore the invitation, but he was persuaded by the other members of the committee that Max J. Kohler should be sent to see Cable.[43] Kohler was chosen because of his thorough research into the legal aspects of the Galveston case. Kohler met with Cable on October 3, 1910, in a meeting at which Wolf was also present.

Thoroughly prepared, Kohler presented a brilliant case in favor of the legality of the Galveston Movement.[44] Once again, he cited Attorney General Wickersham's opinion on the Hawaii case as proof that the Galveston Movement was not violating the contract labor laws.[45] In addition, Kohler now maintained that the Galveston Jewish immigrants could not possibly be considered "likely to become public charges." In demonstrating this, Kohler challenged the instructions originally issued by Commissioner of Immigration William Williams of New York and Commissioner General of Immigration Daniel J. Keefe, which had permitted aid to an immigrant only by those legally responsible for him (such as a man's duty to his wife and minor children).[46] Kohler forcefully maintained that assistance proffered to an alien even by persons not legally obligated to support him must be positively taken into account. Despite the forcefulness of Kohler's arguments, the immigration authorities were considered to be vested with nonreviewable authority to interpret the law, by reason of a federal statute making their determinations binding on the courts. (Ultimately, however, Kohler secured a ruling from the United States Supreme Court that "nonreviewable" meant nonreviewability on the facts, and did not give the immigration authorities jurisdiction to make final determination on fundamental questions of law. Moreover, the Court ruled in Kohler's favor, that assistance proffered to an alien by persons not legally obligated to support him must be taken into account, in determining whether the alien is not to be considered indigent.)[47]

After listening once again to Kohler's arguments, Cable agreed to submit to the solicitor of the Department of Commerce and Labor, and subsequently to the attorney general, a statement of facts based on the records of the twenty-seven rejected immigrants of the S.S. *Hanover*—even though, of course, they had long since been deported—and to ask for an opinion as to the legality of the Galveston Movement. This was welcomed by the Galveston Committee as a sign that the Department of Commerce and Labor was preparing to change its stand regarding the Galveston operations.[48]

On October 18, 1910, President Taft visited the immigration station at Ellis Island in New York. Taft used the occasion to state that he would like to see immigration distributed among many ports, rather than concentrated in New York. An article which appeared the following day on the front page of the *New York Times* put it this way:

Taft Wants More Ports to Get Aliens

Ports on the Atlantic side like New Orleans, Charleston, South Carolina, and Galveston, where labor is badly needed, have been making individual efforts to divert the tide of immigration, and the President expressed the opinion that the Government should assist in this enterprise rather than encourage an increase in arrivals here.[49]

Since the elections were now barely three weeks away, the members of the Galveston Committee hastened to interpret Taft's statement as a public pledge to support the Galveston Movement, and they presumably leaked the following story, which appeared a few days later in the *New York Times*:

Think Taft Will Aid Immigration Plan . . .

As a result of President Taft's visit to Ellis Island a few days ago and his pronouncement in favor of encouraging the diverting of immigration from New York to other ports, a strong impact has been given to the project, supported by several leading Jews of this city, to divert to the Gulf cities and the territory of the West, Southwest, and Northwest the stream of Jewish immigration from Russia and the East . . . The pronouncement of President Taft in favor of the movement is taken by the members of the organization to show that the Government will now facilitate, insofar as it can by liberal interpretation of the law and an attitude of encouragement, the work of the organization in diverting the flow of immigration to Galveston and the territory it gives upon.[50]

Despite Taft's efforts, the Republicans fared very badly in the November elections, both throughout the country and in New York. Representative William S. Bennet, the JIIB's most ardent supporter in Congress, suffered defeat along with most of his fellow

Republicans. This occurred despite the fact that he had managed to attract the support of a certain number of Jewish Democrats who were familiar with his work on behalf of a liberal immigration policy. (Bressler, a Democrat, had sent out a letter to his acquaintances, urging them to support Bennet.[51])

Now that the elections were over, the Galveston Committee expected the Taft Administration to fulfill its pledge to revise its attitude toward the Galveston Movement. On December 11, 1910, the Jewish Immigrants' Information Bureau was granted a hearing before Attorney General Wickersham, Secretary of Commerce and Labor Nagel, and Assistant Secretary Cable. Representing the JIIB were Jacob H. Schiff, Max J. Kohler, David M. Bressler, and Abram I. Elkus. Two days before the hearing, the S.S. *Cassel* had arrived at Galveston, carrying a small group of Jewish immigrants. The members of the Galveston Committee were shocked to learn that twenty-one of these immigrants had been excluded on the grounds that they were "likely to become public charges." Schiff's sense of shock, however, was mixed with one of grim satisfaction, for he now had a clear-cut case on which to test the government's good faith.[52]

Kohler, who by this time had come to be considered the legal spokesman for the JIIB and its immigrants, made the opening argument at the hearing. As usual, he gave a very thorough presentation of the evidence which pointed to the legality of the Galveston Movement. It was Schiff's task to sum up. Annoyed at the technicalities which were being discussed at the hearing, Schiff rose, shook his finger at Nagel, and emphatically declared: "You act as if my organization and I were on trial. You, Mr. Secretary, and your department are on trial!"[53] Schiff then gave an impassioned plea on behalf of the Galveston Movement, relating its history and the fact that it had always endeavored to remain within the law. Instead of being suppressed by the government, the project should be supported by it, Schiff said. He warned that if the government persisted in its hostile attitude, it would have to bear full responsibility for the closing of the Jewish Immigrants' Information Bureau. This was a heavy responsibility to take, Schiff stated, in light of President Taft's pre-election pledge to support the distribution of immigration.[54]

When Schiff had finished, Secretary Nagel made a show of being terribly offended, because of the aggressive manner in which Schiff had spoken. Attorney General Wickersham quietly took Schiff aside and advised him not to antagonize Nagel and Cable. He promised

Schiff that he would do what he could to assist him. Finally, Nagel calmed down and allowed himself to be mollified. Nagel explained to Schiff that all he wanted to do was to act according to the law, and if he found that he could legally help the Galveston Movement, then he would do so. As a demonstration of Nagel's good intentions, the twenty-one detained immigrants at Galveston were eventually released.[55]

On January 18, 1911, the Union of American Hebrew Congregations held a convention at New York City. As chairman of the Board of Delegates on Civil Rights of the UAHC, Simon Wolf had invited Secretary of Commerce and Labor Charles Nagel to address the convention on the subject of immigration. It had required a certain amount of tact on Wolf's part to secure the secretary's acceptance of the invitation. After Nagel's address, which took place at the morning session, Schiff invited him to lunch. As they were dining, Schiff asked the secretary whether he now considered the Galveston Movement illegal in any respect, to which Nagel answered unreservedly that he did not. Schiff considered Nagel's answer highly significant, for it was the first time that the latter had been willing to make such a statement. Obviously, Attorney General Wickersham had advised Nagel that the Galveston Movement was operating within the limits of the law.[56] Schiff sent a friendly letter to the attorney general, warmly thanking him for "the position you found yourself able to take in regard to these matters."[57] Thus, the Galveston Committee had succeeded in reversing the hostile attitude of the Department of Commerce and Labor towards the Galveston Movement.

There was an ironic postscript. The Jewish immigrants who arrived at Galveston in February 1911 had been instructed to strictly deny any association with either the ITO or the JIIB. Thus, when questioned at the port of Galveston, they now, for the first time, professed their utter ignorance of anything connected with the Galveston Movement, much to the consternation and annoyance of Hampton and his team of inspectors. Bressler promptly wrote to the ITO, advising it that such a denial of the facts on the part of the immigrants was not only unnecessary and embarrassing, but harmful as well.[58]

By the end of 1910, about 2,500 Jewish immigrants had come to Galveston. All provinces of the Pale were represented, some more heavily than others. About one-quarter of the immigrants came from the region of Kiev, where the ITO's Jewish Emigration Society was based.[59] Interestingly, however, only a very small number of immigrants came from the city of Kiev itself, or from other large cities. Most of them came from small towns, where poverty was greatest. The town which contributed the most number of immigrants was Chodorkov, or Hoderkew, in the Kiev region. Out of a total Jewish population of only 2,000, as many as 127 Jews from Chodorkov had emigrated to Galveston between 1907 and 1910. They had been greatly encouraged to come, by glowing reports which had been sent by their former fellow townsmen who had gone in previous groups.[60]

In some cases, Jews coming to Galveston declined to commit themselves to the future planned for them by the representatives of the JIIB and decided, for various reasons, to strike off on their own. Among these was Nahum Shlomo Kaluzny, who later Americanized his first name to Nathan. Aged twenty-nine, Kaluzny came from the city of Davidgorodok, in the region of Minsk, where he had worked as a blacksmith. His first wife had died after bearing him a daughter, and he had then married his step-sister, Dobruschka, who bore him two additional children. In 1910, Kaluzny decided to emigrate to the United States.[61]

The Jewish Emigration Society's agent in Davidgorodok was a druggist named Betzel Dutch, or Judowitz.[62] This agent reportedly offered a most convincing argument to dissuade emigrants from entering America through New York or other Eastern ports: "Why do you go that way? We will save you money if you are sent by the Jewish committee, via Galveston." The emigrants each deposited 84 rubles with the druggist, who forwarded their money to Kiev and provided them with all the documents they would need for the trip.[63] As Kaluzny was to recall many years later, his principal reason for choosing the Galveston route was to save money.

Kaluzny left his family in Russia, promising to send for them once he would be permanently settled in America. Together with 168 other Jewish immigrants, he arrived May 30, 1910, and was undoubtedly among those questioned by the team of immigration officers headed by Alfred Hampton, Inspector in Charge of the U.S. Immigration Service at Galveston. On the passenger manifest of the S.S. *Frankfurt*, Kaluzny's final destination was given as Saint Joseph, Missouri, which meant that the Jewish Immigrants' Information Bureau had arranged a place for him in that city. The Jewish immigrants arriving in this group were probably held over in Galveston for questioning. If so, Kaluzny had the opportunity to grow accustomed to Galveston, and, perhaps, for that reason he never made it to Saint Joseph.

Many years later, Kaluzny would relate to his grandson how he got his first job in America. As previously mentioned, the Port of Galveston served as a large terminus for railroad lines from all over the West. While in Galveston, Kaluzny went to the railroad station looking for work. Under the watchful eye of the foreman, a Polish immigrant was loading a train, pushing a wheelbarrow up a ramp. The load proved too heavy for the unfortunate laborer, and the wheelbarrow tipped over, spilling its contents. The foreman then turned to Kaluzny, who was five feet tall, and asked him, doubtfully, "Do you think you can do it?" In a flash, Kaluzny reloaded the wheelbarrow and shot up the ramp. "O.K.," said the foreman, "you got yourself a job!"

Kaluzny liked Galveston; it was a nice, clean city, as he recalled. He felt very much at home there, attending one of the Orthodox synagogues—probably the Young Men's Hebrew Association, which was frequented mainly by Russian Jews. Yet, when his cousin in New York sent him a letter inviting him to join him, Kaluzny could not resist the attraction of the great metropolis. New York City, his cousin wrote, has Jews as well as jobs. After a year and a half of satisfaction in Galveston, Kaluzny left for an uncertain future in New York. We shall hear more of him later.[64]

Although many others, like Kaluzny, eventually drifted to New York and other Eastern cities, most of the Galveston immigrants established themselves in the West. A statistical analysis of Jewish immigrants who arrived at Galveston through the end of 1910, compared with early twentieth century American Jewish immigration in general, shows that Galveston was then attracting a more suitable class of immigrant—one for whom it was relatively easier to find employment. To begin with, about 84 percent of the Jewish immigrants arriving at Galveston were men, who were more easily employable than women. Among American Jewish immigrants in general, only 57 percent were men. Second, about 90 percent of the Galveston Jewish immigrants were between the ages of fourteen and forty-five, and virtually none were older. (The Galveston Movement did not accept immigrants over forty-five.) Among all Jewish immigrants arriving in America, only 70 percent were between fourteen and forty-five.[65] Finally, only about 13 percent of the Galveston Jewish immigrants were illiterate, while the proportion of illiteracy among the American Jewish immigrants in general was approximately 28 percent.[66]

By this time, the Galveston Jewish immigrants had been distributed among more than a hundred cities in some twenty-five states.

Four of these states—Texas, Missouri, Iowa, and Minnesota—had taken in nearly two-thirds of the total number of immigrants.[67] The Jewish communities in those four states were apparently better prepared to accept the newcomers. Now that the government had changed its hostile attitude toward the Galveston Movement, many Jewish communities throughout the West prepared themselves, once again, to welcome more of their brethren from Eastern Europe.

CHAPTER 6

1911: A Weakened Movement Resumes Operations

The deportations of 1910 presented the Galveston Movement with the worst crisis of its existence, a setback from which it never fully recovered. While the legal battles were being fought, shipments of immigrants were severely curtailed. In January 1911, upon the favorable resolution of the crisis, the Jewish Immigrants' Information Bureau requested that the Jewish Territorial Organization resume the direction of immigrants to Galveston. The formal request for renewed shipments came from Jacob H. Schiff and was addressed to Israel Zangwill. In his letter, though, Schiff stipulated that the ITO would have to keep emigration "within the limits and regulations, as from time to time communicated to you by Mr. Bressler's office."[1] In the years to come, these "limits and regulations" would prove to be sources of friction between Bressler's JIIB headquarters in New York and Zangwill's ITO headquarters in London. They reflected Bressler's desire to prevent a recurrence of the near-disastrous deportation crisis in which the very existence of the JIIB had been placed in jeopardy.

Like Bressler, the United States immigrant inspectors in Galveston also wished to avoid another showdown. At the same time, however, they did not wish to appear lax in the eyes of their superiors in Washington. A new examining physician proved to be a more lenient man than the one whom he had recently replaced and, as a result, many men of doubtful physical strength were admitted. Such was the case of the forty-eighth party of immigrants, arriving March 5, 1911, about 20 percent of whom were in their late thirties and forties. Although all but one were admitted, the local inspectors, including Inspector in Charge Hampton, took Henry Berman aside and warned him, in a friendly manner, that next time they would not be so lenient. The message, of course, was immediately transmitted through Bressler to Zangwill and eventually reached the ears of Dr. Jochelmann in Kiev and his subordinates throughout the Pale. From now on, the ITO was asked to send only young, able-bodied men. This was no small request. To be sure, succeeding parties of immigrants often did not meet these strict standards which were demanded by Bressler.[2]

From 1911 until the end of the Galveston Movement, the JIIB scrupulously avoided, as a matter of policy, any activity that could possibly displease the United States immigration authorities. An offer by Dr. Jochelmann, for instance, to help out especially impoverished emigrants by supplying them with shoes and other simple necessities was vetoed by Bressler on the grounds that it might be interpreted as assisting immigration to the United States which, of course, was illegal.[3] At the same time, Bressler instructed the ITO not to send over any emigrant who did not have with him at least ten dollars, so as to avoid deportation on grounds of pauperism. In imposing this rule, Bressler was being more strict than United States law, which did not define pauperism in terms of a fixed amount. Ten dollars was not an insignificant amount for the destitute refugees to possess.[4]

A proposal to safeguard the money of the emigrants during the ocean voyage was put forward by Samuel F. Bloch, who, in 1911, was appointed secretary of the Bremen-based Emigrants' Dispatch Committee. Bloch proposed that the emigrants' money be entrusted to the ship's purser for safekeeping until arrival in Galveston, when it would then be returned. Even this seemingly routine procedure was rejected by Bressler, on the grounds that the U.S. immigration authorities might falsely suspect the steamship company of somehow subsidizing the emigrants' fare.[5]

Other equally innocent schemes put forward by Bloch, in order to facilitate financial transactions, were overruled by the overly cautious Bressler. For instance, the JIIB had long been concerned with the problem of immigrants with pre-fixed destinations, that is, those who, rather than be assigned to any community, were joining relatives who had already settled in the West (usually through the Galveston Movement). Early in the Movement, Schiff had decided, over Zangwill's objection, that these reunion cases would have to provide their own railroad transportation, though on the usual reduced charity rate worked out with the railroad companies. The JIIB, however, was constantly confronted by arriving immigrants with pre-fixed destination who, willfully or not, neglected to bring sufficient money for the trip inland. In these cases, the JIIB notified their American relatives of the predicament and warned that deportation was imminent unless money was sent for transportation. The fare usually arrived shortly, but in the meantime the JIIB was obliged to undergo the additional expense of maintaining the immigrants comfortably in its Galveston quarters.

To circumvent this problem, Bloch proposed that emigrants with prefixed destinations be required to pay the cost of their anticipated railroad fares to his committee in Bremen. Bloch would then send, with each ship, a large check to cover the railroad tickets of all the immigrants with prefixed destinations. Upon the advice of Henry Berman, Bressler overruled the plan on the grounds that it would unnecessarily arouse the attention of the United States inspector in charge of immigration at Galveston. Inspector Hampton had never liked the idea of a reduced railroad rate for any JIIB immigrant, let alone those joining relatives, whose credentials for a charity rate were even more open to question. Hampton was convinced that if any immigrant received preferred treatment in any way, this would be enough to constitute assisted immigration, which was against the law. The less Hampton knew about the intricacies of the Galveston Movement, the better it would be, and it would be unwise to present for his scrutiny a check made out by a Jewish organization, accompanied by an itemized list of expenses of individual Jewish immigrants. Furthermore, as Berman wrote,

> If the Bureau gets a check for a lump sum from a foreign institution for a number of incoming Jewish immigrants, it will be very hard for Mr. Hampton to divest himself of the idea that in certain instances help has been extended the immigrant in Bremen.[6]

During the following year, 1912, Berman was to find himself increasingly troubled by the problem of reunion cases arriving without railroad fare. At the end of that year he finally approached Hampton on the question of whether the Bremen committee would be allowed to send a check covering the railroad fare of immigrants with pre-fixed destinations. Presumably, both Berman and Bressler were happily surprised when Hampton raised no objection to this scheme. Thus, over year later, their precautions in this matter were proved to have been unnecessary.[7]

In May 1912, Bloch brought Bressler's attention to the problem caused by the Galveston-bound emigrants who refused to pay for room and board at Bremen. He proposed that every emigrant, when originally signing up for Galveston, be required to pay a fixed additional charge, which would represent the cost of an average emigrant's stay in Bremen. As usual, Bressler's response was negative. "Averaging" the cost would be inherently favorable to some and discriminatory against others, precisely the sort of practice that would be ruled illegal by the authorities.[8]

Until 1911, dissatisfied immigrants who wanted to return were given an opportunity to work their way back on a ship. When the North German-Lloyd Company discontinued this practice, some of these immigrants threatened to turn themselves over to the authorities for deportation. The JIIB was so anxious to avoid the unfavorable publicity that deportation would bring, that it sometimes actually provided the money for a return trip out of its own funds.[9]

Among the immigrants who were particularly vulnerable to deportation were single girls unaccompanied by parents. For them, the only alternative to deportation was to find them immediate employment in Galveston and this, Bressler wrote to Zangwill, was out of the question, presumably because the JIIB had assured the Jewish community of Galveston that its presence would not become burdensome. Bressler directed that no single girls be sent unless accompanied by a parent. The ITO did its best to comply, for it understood the importance of avoiding deportations.

In general, those restrictions made by Bressler which had as their aim the avoidance of deportations were easily understood, accepted, and complied with by the ITO. Indeed, there were few deportations in 1911 among Jewish immigrants to Galveston. Some restrictions by Bressler, however, were intended not so much to avoid deportation as to promote the success of the Movement by preventing potential malcontents from coming to Galveston. It was this category of restrictions which proved to be a bone of contention between the JIIB and the ITO. Some of Bressler's restrictions were self-defeating, impossible to enforce, and therefore, as repeatedly pointed out by Zangwill, quite harmful to the success of the Movement. To be fair to Bressler, he was often following Schiff's wishes in the matter.

In order to discourage Galveston immigrants from abandoning the locations to which they were sent, Schiff stipulated that emigrants with relatives in New York or other Eastern centers of heavy

Jewish population should not be allowed to join the Galveston Movement, for fear that they might eventually work their way East. This stipulation was impossible to enforce, for it merely encouraged applicants to lie when it suited their purpose. Zangwill brought out the ludicrousness of the situation when he reminded Bressler of the JIIB's long-standing prohibition against immigrants with pre-fixed destinations. That is, immigrants who wished to join relatives in the West were not being given help by the JIIB on the grounds that the JIIB wished to reserve the right to determine ultimate destinations. Besides, it was considered the responsibility of those already established in the West to send for their own relatives. In effect, then, anyone with relatives in either the East or the West was barred from the Galveston Movement. This ruled out most European Jews, so they certainly could not be blamed for lying to the ITO in Europe about their relatives in America, despite Bressler's complaints about such falsehoods.[10]

Occasionally, an "immigrant" arrived who, despite his protestations to the contrary, was discovered to have lived in America before, perhaps for several years. This always provoked a harsh letter from Bressler, who demended to know why the ITO had permitted the Galveston Movement to be diverted from its purpose, which was to acquaint totally new immigrants with the New World. The ITO invariably replied that the "immigrant" had misrepresented himself to its European agents, who always tried their best to arrive at the truth. Bressler greeted this answer with skepticism, for he knew of Zangwill's view that immigrants who had returned to Europe should be given another chance to make a fresh start in America.[11] In one case, a phony "immigrant" was discovered to have lived in Buffalo, New York, for two and one-half years. He revealed that he had been told in Kiev by the ITO official who had enrolled him that, when he reached Galveston, he should not speak of the fact that he had been in America before.[12] It was easy to draw the conclusion that in other matters as well, ITO officials in Europe were instructing emigrants to evade the truth when talking to JIIB officials in Galveston.

The JIIB's decision to impose self-restrictions on immigration, and the ITO's objection to most of these restrictions, reflected a basic conflict in ideology between Schiff and Zangwill. The latter's purpose in founding the Jewish Territorial Organization was to create an autonomous territory which would be maintained and operated by a crosssection of Jewry and would be a haven for the great masses of displaced Jews, including the sick, the destitute, and the aged. By participating in the Galveston Movement, Zangwill demonstrated his willingness to forego the principle of autonomy for the time being. However, he maintained strenuous objections to any plan which would categorically exclude large segments of the Jewish people.

Schiff was ideologically opposed to the principle of autonomy on the grounds that it would leave all Jews open to charges of dual loyalty. As previously mentioned, he had confided that one of his purposes in originally inviting the participation of the ITO in the Galveston Movement was to divert the organization from what he considered to be its dangerous principle of autonomy.[13] Schiff's main object, however, in creating the Galveston Movement was to prevent the enactment of legislation to restrict immigration. By seeing to it that immigrants were gainfully employed and successfully settled in less populous areas of the country, he and his friends had a better chance of convincing Congress and the government that it was in the national interest to continue a liberal immigration policy. If certain types of immigrants could not be settled easily in the West, Schiff was in favor of excluding them temporarily in the hope that eventually they, too, could be absorbed.

Nowhere was the ideological conflict brought out more clearly than in the question of whether or not to accept unsuitably skilled immigrants into the Galveston Movement. Jews who had been peddlers, shopkeepers, and clerks in the Old Country arrived in America without the funds necessary to begin anew. Zangwill's suggestion that they be given goods or capital to start their own enterprises was not accepted by Bressler and Schiff. They disagreed with Zangwill's and Jochelmann's view that immigrants of "the merchant and clerk type" would readily adjust themselves to America, despite Zangwill's reference to "old Mr. Guggenheim who began as a peddler and left a large family of millionaires."[14] For all practical purposes, Bressler considered these immigrants to be unskilled. It was difficult to find jobs for them unless these jobs were low-paying, menial in nature and, in addition, demanded hard physical work. The immigrants were little prepared for this type of employment, and they often refused such jobs or quit them after a short time. In the meantime, they wrote letters to their friends and relatives or, worse, to the newspapers, advertising their dissatisfaction and blaming it all on the Galveston Movement. Bressler wrote that enrollment of this class of emigrant should be severely restricted by the ITO. Time and again, he relayed Berman's constant complaint that too many merchants were being sent, very few of whom were fit for hard physical labor.[15]

What Berman and Bressler wanted were young men with trades that were in demand throughout the West: tailors, carpenters, butchers, blacksmiths, bakers, furriers, and the like. At the same time, they warned against sending men with skills which were not particularly in demand. Thus, while shoemakers were welcome, "shoe-upperers" were not.[16] Even glaziers and diamond polishers were ruled out.[17] Those who had been teachers were considered to be in the same category as the unskilled.[18] Since potential applicants were informed that Sabbath observance would be virtually impossible, it is safe to assume that many emigrants, though trained in the right skills, did not choose the Galveston route for fear of being forced to violate the Sabbath. In addition, there may have been concern about the anticipated lack of ritual slaughterers, circumcisers, rabbis, and other religious officials who were likewise not wanted by the JIIB.

Zangwill was philosophically opposed to such sweeping restrictions on the types of immigrants who would be allowed to proceed to Galveston. Only if all were encouraged to come—skilled and unskilled, young and old, religiously observant and nonobservant—would the Movement be a success, he felt. Bressler, however, argued that the success of the Movement, at that time, depended upon the careful selection of candidates who would easily be acclimated into the environments in which they would find themselves. In mid-1911, a series of incidents in Rock Island, Illinois, helped bolster Bressler's argument.

Rock Island and Moline, Illinois, and Davenport, Iowa—together they were known as the Tri-Cities—formed, along with neighboring towns, a moderate-sized metropolitan industrial center, supplying farm machinery and other necessities to the large agricultural area surrounding it. George Ellman, the JIIB's agent for the area, was regarded by Berman and Bressler as a competent administrator, though he was a somewhat controversial figure in the Jewish community of Rock Island. Formerly vice-president of the local Orthodox synagogue, Ellman had renounced his membership following a squabble among the leaders of the synagogue. After Ellman's resignation, one of these leaders had tried to oust him from his position as JIIB agent and, failing that, had then written a letter to Secretary of Commerce and Labor Nagel, accusing the JIIB of improper conduct. Eventually, the charges were proven false, and the scandal subsided.[19] Bressler and Berman demonstrated their continued faith in Ellman by sending him well over a hundred men from Galveston through the middle of 1911.[20]

During the spring and summer of 1911, several dissatisfied immigrants who had been sent to Rock Island expressed their negative opinions in letters which they addressed to Berman, to Dr. Jochelmann's Society in Kiev, to their friends and relatives in Eastern Europe and, most damaging of all, to Jewish newspaper editors throughout the world. The immigrants complained bitterly that there was no employment waiting for them when they arrived in Rock Island. The jobs which Ellman did provide for them, after a few weeks' wait, were of the most menial kind, demanding exhausting labor and paying near-starvation wages. Often, the jobs were located in far-flung towns, scattered throughout Iowa, distant from any Jewish community. When they complained to Ellman about their condition, he replied that that was the best he could do for them. A special meeting of representative Jews of the Tri-Cities failed to rectify the situation. In many cases, the immigrants abandoned all hope of gaining suitable employment in the Tri-City area and wandered off on their own seeking work in other cities, often ending up in Chicago, 180 miles away. In one tragic case, a young immigrant left Rock Island by train and arrived in a village fifty miles away where he bought a revolver for six dollars and shot himself to death. The letters blamed Ellman for his alleged indifference to their problems. One letter, which was addressed to Jewish Emigration Society in Kiev, accused Ellman of accepting more immigrants than he could place, simply because he wanted to insure the continuance of his salary.

Berman defended Ellman against the last accusation by pointing out that JIIB policy was to continue paying agents' salaries even during the lull in activity, in order not to lose them as contacts. In circumstances which would have caused another agent to call for a halt, Berman wrote, Ellman, perhaps too conscientious, continued to accept immigrants in the hope that he would be able to place them somehow. Ellman's vehement self-defense, in letters addressed to Bressler and in a trip to New York in August, tells the story of a thoroughly dedicated individual fighting against a cabal. Ellman contended that those immigrants who came in 1911 seemed to have drastically different ideas from those who had preceded them. Each party had a "leader" who, considering himself an "intellectual giant . . ., could not see [why he had] to work like a slave in a factory every day," which he could have done "in Russia as well." At the instigation of Ellman's long-standing enemies in Rock Island, these "leaders" organized letter-writing campaigns to Bressler and, Ellman charged, even threatened to write letters of complaint to the authorities in Washington. At a meeting of the "committee of the representative Jews of the Tri-Cities," continued Ellman, one of these people made "false statements, deliberately misrepresenting facts and deceiving every one at the meeting." Of these experiences, Ellman wrote: "It hurts me more than anything I have ever lived through in my fifty-three years of life."[21]

The Tri-City committee eventually exonerated Ellman of any wrongdoing and Bressler, after a conference with Ellman in New York, reaffirmed his confidence in him as a competent and dedicated worker. It was clear, however, that something had gone wrong in Rock Island. Berman offered a studied analysis of what had occurred, which placed the circumstances in their proper context. Berman pointed out that during the winter of 1910 and the spring of 1911, several Iowa and Kansas towns were in and out of industrial depression at various times. The uncertain economic conditions, changing almost from week to week, made it impossible for agents of the JIIB to know precisely when to call for more immigrants and when to call for less, or for none at all. Some, such as the representative in Des Moines, exercised the better part of valor by confessing their inability to accept a steady flow of immigrants.

> But in Rock Island, Mr. Ellman believed his influence with the industrial plants sufficient to allow him to accept the half-dozen or so men a month . . . And as all men will lapse in judgment occasionally, Mr. Ellman soon began to find himself with a number of unemployed men on his hands.

Although Ellman's committee supported them for a few weeks, the men grew restless because they were not earning money needed to send for their families. Furthermore, they often turned down menial jobs for which they considered themselves unfit, thus further exacerbating the situation. Berman recommended that the Rock Island agency be continued because Ellman, on Berman's instructions, had just completed a trip throughout Iowa and had succeeded not only in placing the remaining unemployed immigrants but also in securing a considerable number of requisitions for immigrants in the next group, which was due later in July.[22] By this time, however, the unfavorable publicity generated by the immigrants' letters had reached embarrassing proportions. Although nobody mentioned it out loud, Rock Island was an especially sensitive area because it happened to be the home town of Assistant Secretary of Commerce and Labor Benjamin S. Cable. In the end, Bressler was left with no choice but to close down the Rock Island agency.[23]

Actually, the JIIB had known all along that unfavorable conditions might hinder the placement of immigrants in positions of employment. At a meeting of the Galveston Committee held in New York on January 30, 1911, Bressler had pointed out "that industrial conditions throughout the country are very bad at this time, that most agencies cooperating with the Bureau had practically suspended cooperation for this reason, and that therefore it would be very unsafe at this time to authorize much larger shipments." Nevertheless, Bressler called, at that time, for an increase in the size of shipments and suggested that the maximum figure be one hundred immigrants per month. (Later in the year, he called for another increase to 125 per month.) Bressler's impatience to handle more immigrants was entirely understandable, for he had been pressured by Schiff to renew operations, after the deportation crisis of the previous year. His decision had been based upon the reasonable premise that the key to successful placement was higher quality, rather than lower quantity. In short, Bressler had thought that if the new shipments included only strong, able-bodied young men, then the JIIB agents would be able to place the newcomers without too much difficulty.[24] The crisis in Rock Island demonstrated that even these "high quality" immigrants were hard to place sometimes. Bressler thought, however, that an application of even stricter standards might finally eliminate the problem.

In light of the above, the Rock Island crisis served to reinforce the conviction of the JIIB leadership that it was necessary to maintain and even strengthen their stringent specifications on the quality of immigration. Berman recommended that the Galveston Movement no longer "accept unskilled men unless they agree to any work . . . which promises reasonable wages for an exchange of manual labor." Furthermore, Berman wrote, potential emigrants in Russia should be told in no uncertain terms that they might have to wait a while before receiving employment in the towns to which they would be sent.[25]

Even more so than Berman, Bressler remembered the lessons of Rock Island for a long time to come. In June 1912, about a year after the crisis, Berman suggested that the JIIB organize paid agencies in small towns for the exclusive reception of unskilled immigrants. Predictably, Zangwill welcomed the idea,[26] but Bressler, after conferring with Schiff, turned it down. He based his reasons

125

on the crisis of the previous year. In Rock Island, Bressler reminded Berman, unskilled immigrants gained employment mainly in two large manufacturing plants, where a considerable number found the work too hard.

> Others, after a short employment, were laid off for one reason or another, generally a decrease in the output of the plant . . . The result you recall. They drifted away, where we do not know, nor do we know what has become of them, except through the medium of a number of letters written to the Jewish newspapers of New York in which the work of our Bureau was savagely attacked.

Bressler feared "that agencies in still smaller towns for unskilled would only result in repeating the experience in Rock Island, and while it may be that I am unduly fearful, I still believe that we cannot use too much caution to guard against such an unfortunate mix-up as resulted in Rock Island."[27]

Dissatisfied and misfitted immigrants were not, of course, confined to Rock Island; they found their way to other communities as well. Time and again, but to no avail, Bressler stressed the importance of limiting the number of unskilled men. Unskilled immigrants soon learned that if they were to be assured acceptance into the Galveston Movement, they would have to lie about their occupations. This caused further complications, as can be readily imagined. A man with little or no experience in shoemaking would be sent to a community in need of a shoemaker, where it would soon be discovered that he knew nothing about this craft. Promptly fired, he became a likely source of future negative propaganda. Bressler forcefully expressed his wish that the European ITO agents demand complete candor on the part of the emigrants. Bressler's wish, however, was unrealistic. Both the agents and the emigrants knew that the United States immigration authorities were reluctant to admit unskilled immigrants, and they preferred being exposed to Bressler's wrath, rather than running the risk of deportation.[28]

Closing down the Rock Island agency eliminated one weak area, but the basic problem remained, for the ITO continued to send unskilled immigrants. These immigrants were distributed to cities which were unable to offer substantially more than that which had been offered by Rock Island. The agency in Oklahoma City, for example, was a frequent target for the criticism of dissatisfied immigrants, who aired their views in the press. It soon went the way of the Rock Island agency and was discontinued by the JIIB. Omaha, Nebraska, and Saint Paul, Minnesota, as well as other cities, encountered similar difficulties in their attempts to provide unskilled immigrants with employment. Rumblings of discontent were heard from these quarters as well. By October 1911, it had become clear both to the ITO and to the JIIB that changes were necessary for the success of the Movement. Each side, however, felt that it was the other who must make the changes.

On October 4, 1911, Zangwill sent Schiff a typical letter of complaint, written by a dissatisfied Galveston immigrant, which had been turned over to him by a friendly Yiddish newspaper editor. Zangwill enclosed his own comments, written in his usual, frank style:

> It seems too bad that the American part of the chain, hitherto so strong, should show the weakest links. I am at a loss to imagine whether your agents have been instructed to be too economical or whether some of them are merely inefficient.[29]

By coincidence, a few days before Zangwill's letter reached Schiff, Schiff had given his full approval to a letter from Bressler to Zangwill. The JIIB, far from being ready to accept fault for the current crisis, placed the blame squarely at the door of the ITO. It was clear, wrote Bressler, that the ITO was incapable of supplying Galveston with a suitable number of skilled immigrants. He reminded Zangwill that the Galveston Committee had "stated upon several occasions in official communications that we could handle 125 cases (excluding women and children in families) per shipment." (Shipments usually came about once a month.) On occasion, wrote Bressler, the JIIB had even stated that it "would not object to handling" 150, 175, or even 200 per shipment, providing that these immigrants would be highly skilled. Instead, complained Bressler, only 750 immigrants (presumably excluding women and children) were handled by the JIIB in Galveston during the first eight months of 1911. Of these, seventy-five were not sent by the ITO and 155 would have come anyway, since they were arriving to join relatives who had previously settled in the West. Thus, Bressler computed that the ITO had actually recruited only "520 persons, or an average of sixty-five immigrants per month."[30]

Bressler's analysis appears to have been less than generous. It is unclear whether the ITO understood that women and children were not to be counted in the requested minimum of 125 immigrants per shipment. By eliminating the women and children from consideration, Bressler reduced the arrival figures by about 25 percent. If all Jewish immigrants to Galveston were counted—male and female, children and adults—with no deductions being made for non-ITO cases nor for those with pre-fixed destinations, it would be seen that about one thousand arrived in January-August 1911.[31] This figure would yield the required average of 125 immigrants per month, for which Bressler had called.[32]

Whatever the justification for Bressler's criticism, it was clear that he had struck a sensitive nerve. Zangwill had just sent off his letter of October 4 to Schiff complaining about the "weak links" of the "American part of the chain." He was shocked to receive this letter from Bressler, which had crossed his in the mail, followed by a reply from Schiff supporting Bressler's viewpoint and declaring that the weak links were, actually, on the European side.[33] Unfortunately, an element of personal enmity developed between Zangwill and Bressler, and they traded accusations and counter-accusations in their subsequent correspondence. Zangwill, for instance, reminded Bressler of the latter's letter, written in August, imploring Zangwill to keep the number of immigrants to a minimum.[34] Bressler answered that the letter had been written not with a desire to decrease immigration but, rather, as a reply to Zangwill's oft-expressed wish "to inaugurate a policy of an unselected and uncontrolled stream of immigrants to Galveston."[35]

Wherever the blame lay, it was obvious to both the ITO and the JIIB that, after more than four years of effort, the Galveston Movement was not accomplishing what it had set out to do—namely, to significantly alter the trend of American Jewish immigration. It was mutually acknowledged that the main obstacles to the success of the Movement had arisen as a result of forces beyond the control of either side. These main obstacles were the United States economic depression of 1907–1909, the ITO's legal difficulties with the Russian government in 1908–1909, and the United States government deportation actions of 1910. Now that this last crisis was over, Bressler felt that 1911 should have been a year of singular success for the Galveston Movement. When the anticipated success failed to materialize, he blamed the ITO for not living up to its responsibilities in the arrangement and called for negotiations with the Paris-based Jewish Colonization Association (ICA) toward having that organization supplement ITO activities or, if need be, actually replace the ITO as European partner in the Galveston Movement. In defense, Zangwill declared that although the deportation crisis was over, the unfavorable publicity generated by it was still being felt. This, in addition to the letters of complaint from dissatisfied immigrants, persuaded many skilled artisans, who were already securely employed in Russia, and who could find work easily in New York, to steer clear of the longer and more arduous Galveston route. In the midst of these handicaps, said Zangwill, he had been obliged by Bressler to eliminate from consideration those candidates who, while unskilled, were unwilling or unable to engage in hard physical labor. If the ITO were left free to recruit from all members of the Jewish population in Russia, it would surely be able to send at least as many immigrants as the JIIB could possibly handle. However, wrote Zangwill, Bressler's demands for skilled tradesmen were so unreasonable, and his accusations so unwarranted, "that I am driven to Dr. Jochelmann's conclusion that there is now on the American side a willful pessimism as to our work."[36]

Happily, the dispute between the two sides was resolved amicably with a compromise put forward by Zangwill and accepted by Schiff. Instead of turning to the ICA which, Zangwill warned, would never be able to match the efforts of the ITO, the Galveston Movement should be allowed to continue its present operations for one more year. At that time, it would pause to take stock of what it had accomplished. By then, about five thousand persons would have arrived. Both the JIIB and the ITO could then boast, with some justification, that they had accomplished their goal of creating a stream of emigration to Galveston. At the end of 1912, the JIIB and the ITO could honorably decide to formally end the Galveston Movement. Succeeding waves of immigrants, who would come on their own, would have the Galveston Movement to thank for having established the conditions favorable to their success. Of course, if the JIIB still desired, at that time, to continue its work, and to invite the participation of the ICA, then the ITO would be prepared to gracefully cease its activities at the end of 1912.[37] (It was fairly well understood that the ITO and the ICA, who were bitter rivals, could not cooperate on the same project.) Although Zangwill did not state it, he no doubt hoped that in a year's time Schiff would be sufficiently impressed with the activities of the ITO as to refrain from turning to the ICA. For his part, Schiff, though skeptical of the ITO's possibilities for success, extended Zangwill the courtesy of a year's probation.[38] To the relief of both sides, the question of the ITO's resignation from the Galveston Movement was put off for a year.

During the year 1911, over 1,400 Jewish immigrants had come to Galveston, far more than in any preceding year. This amounted, however, to less than 2 percent of total Jewish immigration to the

United States in that year.[39] The year 1911 was the first in which the Galveston Movement had been able to proceed without interruption caused by outside interference. It was forced, for the first time, to identify its own shortcomings and to come up with the solutions that would strengthen its areas of weakness. The question remained whether these weaknesses could actually be corrected or whether they were, perhaps, inherent to the very premises of the Galveston Movement.

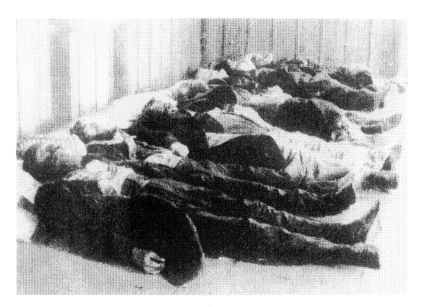

1. Casualties of the Kishinev pogrom of 1903.

2. Wounded casualties of the Kishinev pogrom of 1903.

3. Wilkomir, in the province of Rovno, one of the cities in which many Jewish families were burned out of their homes, in 1904.

RELIEF FOR SURVIVORS OF RUSSIAN MASSACRES.

OFFICIAL CALL FROM PRINCIPAL JEWISH ORGANIZA-
TIONS OF AMERICA.

The victims of the awful riots and massacres in Russia are not all numbered with the dead. The living, starving survivors who have lost their breadwinners and the maimed, mutely appeal to a pitying world for aid. Therefore each community is hereby requested to organize at once and without further notice, for the purpose of raising funds to aid these destitute living victims. Funds when collected may be forwarded to Mr. Jacob H. Schiff of New York, for proper distribution.

ADOLF KRAUS,
President Independent Order B'nai B'rith

SAMUEL WOOLNER,
President of Union of American Hebrew Congregations

MRS. HENRY SOLOMON,
President Council of Jewish Women

DR. H. PEREIRA MENDES,
President of Union of Orthodox Jewish Congregations in the United States and Canada

DR. JOSEPH STOLZ,
President of Central Conference of American Rabbis

DR. HARRY FRIEDENWALD,
President of Federation of American Zionists

MAX STERN,
Grand Master Independent Order B'rith Abraham

SAMUEL DORF,
Grand Master Order B'rith Abraham

ISAAC ANDERSON LOEB,
Grand Master District No. 2, Independent Order Free Sons of Israel

ABRAHAM ROSENBERG,
Grand Master Independent Order Sons of Benjamin.
Chicago, November 8, 1905.

---

4. Well before the inauguration of the Galveston Movement, Jacob H. Schiff was acknowledged as the financial leader of American Jewry, as is evidenced by this call, appearing in the *American Israelite*, Nov. 16, 1905.

5. Jacob Henry Schiff, founder and sponsor of the Galveston Movement.

6. Dr. Paul Nathan, secretary of the Hilfsverein der Deutschen Juden.

7. Israel Zangwill leaving the hall after his main speech to the Seventh Zionist Congress in Basle, July 30, 1905.

8. A Jewish Territorial Organization
membership card.

9. Dr. Max Emmanuel Mandelstamm, president of the ITO's Jewish Emigration Society, in Kiev.

10. David M. Bressler

11. Morris David Waldman, first manager of the
Jewish immigrants' Information Bureau at Galveston. (a later photograph).

רוסישע אידען פערפידרט צו שקלאפעריי אין אמעריקא.

געטריבען פון ניגערם, געצאָרסעם מיט חזיר, דיא בערד מיט נעיאָהד ארונטער געשאָרן.

א בריעף פון איינעם פון דיא קרבנות צום „פֿאָרווערטס".

צי פּים צו א האָלץסקלאַד, וואו מען האָט אונז געשטעלט האַקען האָלץ. אינזערע הענד זיינען נאַטירליך ניט געוויע געוואָהנט צו אזעלכע ארבייט, דאָבען אינד דיא ניגערם, אונזערע אויפּזאַבער, זיינער טריעבען מיט קאָנטשיקעס אין מיט רעוער. וויענען עסען איז שוין גאָר ניטאָ וואָס צו ריידען: מען האָט זיך מיט אונז געריגט הערפאַר, וואָס מיר זיינען איין אין מען האָט אינו דיא רוא געגעבען עסען דאָיר. עם האָט זיך אבער געמאַכט פּאַר אינזו א גליקליכע געלעגענהייט אין מיר זיינען אנטלאָפען, איבעראיענין בײ אונזערע פײנינער דיא באנאַט איז דיא טריתוב. דיא ניגערם האָבען אונו נאָבגע יאַכט, אבער מיר זיינען גרידריך געקומען אין לינהאָל, געראָבסאָ. פֿון יואַנען א אין דישער פֿעראיין האָט אונו אײנגעשיקט. קיין אָבאַה. פֿון דאָרט זיינען מיר געהן־ מען קיין שיקאַגאָ, אין פֿון דאָרט האָט מען אונו אבענעשיקט קיין ניו יאָרק. איך שרײב דאָם צו אייך, אים איהר זאָלט וויאַסען דיא ריסישע עמינראַנטען פֿון אזויגע מער דער.

משה אפּאטאָוסקי".

דער צווייטער אונטלאָפענער איז אי־ ציק מעלדמאַן. זיי בײדע געפֿינען זיך אין בכנסת אורחים, 229 איסט בראָדוויי.

קראָנקע פֿריי וואָרפֿט זיך אַראָפּ פֿון דך אין שטאָרבם.

א שווערעליכען טױט האָט זיך זיל׳ אלײן שבת נאַך האַלבע נאַכט געמאַכט דיא קראַנקע פֿרם. מערי מילשטיין, פֿון 831 איסט 103טע סטריט. זיא האָט זיך אַראָפּ־ געוואָרפֿען פֿון דעם דך פֿון דער 5 פֿאָ־ רינער געביידע אין איז אײנגעבראַכען געשטאַרבען.

Russian refugee who tells of cruelties inflicted by negro waiters in a Colorado lumber camp.

12. A letter of complaint by Galveston immigrant Moshe Opotowski, printed on the front page of the *Jewish Daily Forward*, December 2, 1907.

13. Dr. David S. Jochelmann, secretary and manager of the ITO's Jewish Emigration Society, based in Kiev.

14. Rabbi Dr. Henry Cohen of Galveston.

15. Jacob Billikopf, superintendent of the United Jewish Charities in Kansas City, Missouri, who actively participated in the settling of immigrants from Galveston.

ITO EMIGRANTS—BEFORE AND AFTER.

The photograph on the left represents a group of ITO emigrants on their Transatlantic sailing from Bremen and Bremen is. The second group represents a party of emigrants who arrived in Kansas City 18 August. They are all at present at work, earning from 9 to 15 dollars a week, and one of them is receiving as much as 21 dollars weekly.

16. Promotional literature prepared in 1907 by Jacob Billikopf of Kansas City.

ПРАВЛЕНІЕ
Еврейскаго
ЭМИГРАЦІОННАГО ОБЩЕСТВА
въ КІЕВѢ
Кузнечная, 34 кв.
Телефонъ 25-06

JÜDISCHE
EMIGRATIONS-GESELLSCHAFT
KIEW.
Kuznetznaja, 34, # 4.
Telephon 5-06

חברה היהודית
לעמיגראציע
יודישע עמיגראציאנס-געזעללשאפט
קיעוו.
קוזנעטשנא, 34, קעוו. 5,
טעלעפאן 25-06

Объявленіе.

(Для вывѣшиванія въ синагогахъ и другихъ обществен. мѣстахъ.)

"Еврейское Эмиграціонное Общество" въ Кіевѣ (Кузнечная 34. кв. 5.) извѣщаетъ. что оно продолжаетъ отправлять каждыя 3 недѣли партіи еврейскихъ эмигрантовъ въ юго-западные штаты Сѣверной Америки черезъ портъ

ГАЛЬВЕСТОНЪ,

гдѣ американскіе еврейскіе комитеты оказываютъ эмигрантамъ содѣйствіе при прінисканіи работы и устройствѣ на новыхъ мѣстахъ

За подробными свѣдѣніями объ условіяхъ эмиграціи въ Гальвестонъ можно обращаться ПИСЬМЕННО: къ Предсѣдателю Общества. Д-ру М. Е. МАНДЕЛЬШТАМУ. КІЕВЪ. АЛЕКСАНДРОВСКАЯ. 27. или ЛИЧНО къ мѣстному Уполномоченному "Еврейскаго Эмиграціоннаго Общества", Госп

по адресу

ежедневно отъ _____ до _____ час. дня и отъ _____ до _____ час. вечера.

Правленіе
Еврейскаго Эмиграціоннаго Общества
въ КІЕВѢ

Житомиръ. типографія Ш. Хоржанскаго.

מודעה

(צווי אויסצוהענגען אין די שילען, בתי מדרשים און אנדערע ערטער.)

די "יודישע עמיגראציאנס-געזעלשאפט" אין קיעוו (קוזנעטשנא 34, וואהנונג 5) מעלדעם, אז זי שיקט אויך יעצט, ווי ביז אהער, אלע 3 וואכען פארטיעס יודישע עמיגראנטען אין די דרום-מערב שטאטען פון אמעריקא דורך דעם פארט

גאלוועסטאן,

וואו די אמעריקאנער יודישע קאמיטעטען העלפען די עמיגראנטען געפינען ארבייט און זיך איינאָרדנען אויף די נייע ערטער.

וועגען אלע בעדינגונגען און גענויע ידיעות וועגען דער עמיגראציע קיין גאלוועסטאן, קען יעדערער אנפרעגען: שריפטליך ביי דעם פרעזעדענט פון דער געזעלשאפט. דאקטאר מאנדעלשטאם. קיעוו, אלעקסאנדראווסקא'יא 27. אדער פערזענליך ביי דעם היגען פאראטסטעהער פון דער יודישער עמיגראציאנס-געזעלשאפט ה'

היזט דעם אדרעם:

פון ____ ביז ____ אדער ביי טאג, און פון ____ ביז ____ אדער אין אוונד.

די פערוואלטונג
פון דער יודישער
עמיגראציאנס-געזעלשאפט
אין קיעוו.

דרוק ס. חוראזשאנסקי ק״י אליהו פינבערג בזשאמיר.

---

17. "Announcement, to be posted in synagogues, study houses, and elsewhere." This announcement, in Yiddish and Russian, said that groups were leaving for Galveston once every three weeks, and that those interested in further information could apply to Dr. Mandelstamm in Kiev or to the local representative of the Jewish Emigration Society whose name, address, and receiving hours were to be filled in at the bottom. The announcement was carefully worded so as to avoid any charge of inducing immigration to the United States.

I. T. O.

To show at the Gal-
veston Jewish
Immigrants Infor-
mation Bureau.

אי. טי. או.

צו ווייזן לעבײם גאַל-
וועסטאָן דזשועיש אימיגראַ-
נטס אינפאָרמאַציאָן ביוראָ!

(ה. ג.)

Mr. (Mrs) ....

....

is going to Galveston with the

.... party through our ....

.... Burea

מר. (מרס) ....

....

גייט קיין גאַלוועסטאָן מיט דער

.... פּאַרטי דורך אונזער ....

.... ביוראָ

(stamp: Russisch Emigrat Regulat Departm. / Centr-Bureau / Kleff. / I. T. O.)

18. ITO identification card carried by immigrants to Galveston.

 י. ט. א.

צענטר. עמיגראצ. ביורא

פֿאַר גאַנץ רוסלאַנד

אין קיעװ.

הויפֿט ‮ידיעות‬ װעגען עמיגראַצִיע

אין

גאַלװעסטאן

(שטאַט טעקסאַס)

נדפּס ע״י אליהו פֿײנבּערג בּזיטאָמיר.

Главнѣйшія свѣдѣнія объ эмиграціи въ Гальвестонъ

(шт. Тексасъ).

Изд. Центр. Эмиграціон. Бюро въ Кіевѣ.

19. Cover page of an 11-page pamphlet printed in Zhitomir in 1907 by the "ITO Central Emigration Bureau for all of Russia, in Kiev", entitled *Important Information about Emigration to Galveston (State of Texas)*.

אויך א פאבריק פון זײגערס . על-פא ס א (El Paso), אויף דער גרעניץ פון די
פעראײניגטע שטאטען און פון דער רעפובליק מעקסיקא , איז וויכטיג פאר
דעם האנדעל מיט פיה . אין דער שטאדט געפינען זיך גרויסע אײזענגיסערײען
און סינארען-פאבריקען . די אלע שטעדט האבען ײדישע געמײנדעס : אין וואקא—
די געמײנדע „אגודת יעקב' , אין על-פאסא—די געמײנדע „הר סיני" א. ז. וו

אין גאנץ מעקסאס געפינען זיך אונגעפעהר 20,000 ײדען , וועלכע
בעשעפטיגען זיך מערהסטענטהײלס מיט האנדעל .

י. ט. א.

צענט. עמיגראצ. ביורא.

פאר גאנץ רוסלאנד

אין קיעװ.

These cities and the whole state of Texas offer only
limited opportunities, and only for a small
minority of our people. The opportunities in
Kansas, Missouri, Iowa, and minnessota are
greater. We suggest that you do not emphasis
Texas but the states we have just mentioned.
Please say that Galveston is being used by us
only as a port of entry that none of the immigrants will remain here.

M. D. Waldman

20. Last page of a pamphlet printed in Zhitomir in 1907 by the "ITO Central
Emigration Bureau for all of Russia in Kiev", entitled *Important Information about
Emigration to Galveston (State of Texas).* Waldman added his comments at the
bottom of the page.

NAME (JULY 1st.)	OCCUPATION	Is he laboring?	Name of Concern With Whom He is Employed	Wages per Week	Is he employed at his Trade?	If He Left Town, When Did He Go?
SCHEFFER LEISER	Upper maker	Yes	Barton Bros, Shoe Concern	10.00	Yes	
FORT IN CHARZ, wife						
PURCARSKY CHAIM	Ass't Cutter					Left for Itjeorah
BARABAN WOLF (1)	Shop maker	Very	chw.rs & S.:abor or P.H.	0.00	Yes	Clo...
LEVIN JACOB	Cabinet maker	Yes	Ehelich & Sons	11.00	Yes	
MITCHELL SAMEZ (2)	Cabinet maker	Yes	Summons and Company	10.00	Yes	
FREED NUTA	Tailor	Yes	Grand Pants Company	10.00	Yes	
FREED SHILKIN (3)	Butler	Yes	"	15.00	Yes	
FREED SHILKIN (4)	Bricklayer	Yes	Lyons & Co. Hard. & Furn	13.00	No	
YAROV (5)	Ass't Bookbinder	quite	"iplirg Bros, Wire hat frame	2.00		
ISAAC WAXMAN (6)	Presser & Cook	Yes	In Restaurant at present	10.00	Yes	
ISRAEL ZAROUSKY	Gen. Laborer	Very	Rubenstein Junk Yd.	9.00		

Remarks: (1) Sent his family since here about $175.00 (2) brought his brother
to this country, 2/00/00 (3) sent his family over $100.00 Expects wife and
children after Pesach. Could not get employment in Kansas City at his
trade. S was employed at his trade until recently, will resume own work
soon. He is Bro in care of Mitchelle. — His wife and three children on
way to this country. He sent them over $100.00 7. saved over 100.

(Signed) J. Billikopf
Town _____
State _____

Please return this promptly to JEWISH IMMIGRANTS' INFORMATION BUREAU, Galveston, Texas.

21. Report sheet from Jacob Billikopf of Kansas City, Missouri, on progress of immigrants sent to him from Galveston.

22. A conference of the Jewish Territorial Organization, with Israel Zangwill standing in the center. The seated figure with the white beard is Israel Isidore Jasinowski, a renowned Warsaw lawyer and early Zionist leader who became a leading member of the ITO.

23. Israel Zangwill, founder and president of the Jewish Territorial Organization (ITO).

24. Galveston-bound emigrants in Bremen, with representatives of the Hilfsverein.

25. Boarding ship in Bremen for the voyage to Galveston.

26. Immigrants arriving at Galveston.

27. Ephraim Zalman (Charles) Hoffman, an immigrant who settled in Fort Worth after arriving at Galveston in 1913, posing for a photograph to send to the woman to whom he was engaged in Poland, showing that her image is in his mind as he looks at her picture. Two years after arrival, he married another woman.

28. W. H. Novit, a Jewish immigrant from Russia, selling bananas in Gatesville, Texas (c. 1912). Novit wrote to relatives, urging them to settle in various cities of Central Texas, where they, too, eventually engaged in the successful banana trade.

29. Sarah Bernstein and Ephraim Zalman (Charles) Hoffman, two immigrants who arrived separately in Galveston in 1913, met in Fort Worth, and got married in 1915.

30. Ephraim Zalman (Charles) Hoffman (left), an immigrant who arrived at Galveston in 1913, as half-owner of a fruit, vegetable, and grocery store in Fort Worth (c. 1913–20). Despite the apparent success, the business failed in 1922 and the Hoffmans moved to Comanche, Texas, two years later.

CHAPTER 7

1912: Difficulties in Recruitment

A shocking incident at the end of 1911 resulted in a readjustment of managerial responsibilities at the beginning of 1912. The incident had occurred October 15, 1911, when a freshly-arrived seventeen-year-old female immigrant, who was staying at the JIIB's immigrant quarters, was raped, after being induced to leave the premises. The assailant, who had free access to the quarters, was himself a formerly-arrived immigrant, now boarding at the private residence of JIIB assistant manager Louis Greenberg, where the assault took place. Although the crime was immediately made known to the JIBB's management, the latter made no attempt to report it, and it was only two days later that the perpetrator was turned over to the immigration authorities, at the victim's private initiative. Appalled at "the inexcusable carelessness shown on the part of the management," Inspector-in-Charge Hampton directed that "no Hebrew aliens detained by the Immigration Officers shall be placed in the JIIB for safe-keeping."[1] As a result, Rabbi Cohen, who in any case was deeply in debt, partly as a result of expenses related to the care of immigrants, quit the JIIB.[2] After a protest from Hampton, who greatly admired the rabbi,[3] and after appeals by Bressler[4] and Schiff,[5] Cohen withdrew his resignation.[6] Since JIIB manager Berman had an unfortunate way of alienating people with his tactless manner, it was decided that only a visit by Bressler would help resolve difficulties by placating Hampton and by giving Cohen support in his effort to improve supervision at the immigrant quarters.

In the latter part of December 1911, Bressler spent about a week in Galveston smoothing over the problems. At the following meeting of the Galveston Committee in New York, held in January, it was decided upon Bressler's recommendation to send Cohen six hundred dollars per annum to be used by Cohen at his discretion for such purposes as were "kindred to, but not actually within the scope of our Bureau's work."[7] The following month, Schiff authorized an additional check for $1,150 to Cohen, which was one-half of the latter's indebtedness, "on the ground that the debt was incurred by Doctor Cohen, as a member of the Galveston Committee, and because of his prominent connection therewith."[8] Cohen remained actively associated with the Galveston Movement until the end. As for Greenberg, though he was in no way blamed, and his work was appreciated, he was expediently asked to resign.

Bressler returned to New York in mid-January 1912, from his month-long journey to Galveston and the West. The immediate purpose of his trip had been to resolve the very difficult situation which had emerged in Galveston. Once that had been accomplished, he had made a tour of various cities to which JIIB immigrants were sent (and some which received immigrants from the Industrial Removal Office). Schiff wrote Zangwill of Bressler's report that there were "unsatisfactory business conditions now prevailing throughout." Nevertheless, Bressler was convinced "that there will be no difficulty in placing 150 to 200 people monthly, provided they are of the right kind."[9] At a meeting of the Galveston Committee held in New York on February 1, Berman presented a slightly less optimistic report which, again, Schiff communicated to Zangwill: "Notwithstanding the depression," wrote Schiff—although "depression" was really too strong a word—"there will be no difficulty to place from 125 to 200 proper immigrants a month."[10]

It is interesting to note that while Schiff, quoting Berman, brought Bressler's minimum figure down from 150 to 125, he did not bring the maximum limit down from 200 to 175. This was a tactic which favored the JIIB and kept the ITO on the defensive. It was quite clear that the ITO was having difficulty meeting even the minimum demands of the JIIB. By declaring that it was willing to accept as many as two hundred immigrants, the JIIB was always able to point out that the ITO's achievements were falling far below expectations. In his arguments with Zangwill over the number of immigrants, Bressler invariably made reference to the maximum figure, rather than the minimum figure.[11]

In addition to the quantitative goals that Bressler set, he also demanded that the ITO carefully select and investigate the immigrants with respect to their ages, skills, and physical ability. He stipulated "that not less than 75% of all selected be artisans of the kind which we may indicate from time to time." Of the remaining 25 percent, all "must be physically capable of performing manual labor."[12] Immigrants up to the age of forty should be accepted only when they possess desired skills. For men without trade, the age limit should be put at thirty.[13]

Zangwill had some demands of his own, which were designed to liberalize the selection of immigrants for Galveston. He conditioned his continued association with the Galveston Movement upon Bressler's acceptance of these demands. Bressler rejected all of them. First, Zangwill asked Bressler "not to object to previous residence in America when that residence has been in New York or another of the great Eastern towns. The very fact that these emigrants deliberately do not return to New York," Zangwill argued, "is the best advertisement for our work."[14] Bressler turned down this request because, as he wrote, "our experience with immigrants who have had previous residence in America has been exceedingly unfortunate. They are difficult to satisfy; they tend largely to drift Eastward; they make trouble for our representatives; and they make trouble for their employers."[15]

Zangwill also called for more leniency in the acceptance of women and children in the Galveston Movement.[16] Bressler replied:

If it is your idea to send girls to Galveston who are unaccompanied by their parents, and who have no destinations, you will encounter decided opposition on the part of the immigration authorities at that port. It must be obvious that we cannot afford in any way to run counter to the judgment of those passing upon the admissibility of immigrants at Galveston.[17]

Zangwill made yet another suggestion, designed to take into consideration the fraternal feelings of the immigrants and to facilitate their adjustment to new surroundings: When two or three friends from the same town in Europe wished to be assigned together to the same town in the United States, their wishes should be accommodated wherever possible.[18] Just as he rejected Zangwill's other attempts at liberalization, Bressler responded negatively to this suggestion as well. He wrote:

In the selection of destinations for its immigrants, Galveston can be guided only by its arrangements with the various towns with which it is cooperating. No promises can be made on the score of keeping the Russian batches intact. Just because the accompanying immigrants are unskilled, the likelihood of such batches remaining unbroken is lessened. Working at all times with an eye to the best interests of the newcomers, Galveston cannot be ruled by the dictates of sentiment. Whenever it is possible to keep friends together, it is done. Needless to say, relatives are never separated.[19]

Zangwill also had a number of additional complaints as to how the immigrants were being treated. He had heard that immigrants were not being provided with hot food at Galveston and that Berman was not answering letters of complaint from dissatisfied immigrants.[20] Bressler denied both charges. In response to the second charge, Bressler pointed out that Berman had "attached to his staff a man able to write Yiddish of the character required to meet the situation. You may rest assured," Bressler concluded, "that the feelings of disgruntled immigrants will always be met in a kind and conciliatory spirit."[21]

Although Bressler rejected all of his conditions for continued participation, Zangwill did not break off the ITO's association with the Galveston Movement. Without Galveston, the ITO would have no project with which to occupy itself and Dr. Jochelmann would have no place to send the emigrants who were being recruited by his agents throughout Eastern Europe. Despite the long, hard trip to Galveston, despite the relative lack of Judaism and Jewish culture in many Western cities, despite the unfavorable publicity surrounding the project, some Jews were still interested in trying their luck out West. For these people it was important to keep the Galveston Movement going. However, the ITO found it very difficult, at first, to increase its 1912 performance over that of the previous year. Its efforts to do so may have been retarded slightly by the unfavorable American business conditions, which reduced general immigration during the early part of 1912.[22] However, it is doubtful whether this minor economic decline had much effect on the volume of Jewish immigration, which generally responded "much more slowly and less completely to the pressure of unfavorable conditions" than non-Jewish immigration.[23] Furthermore, since the Galveston-bound emigrants were promised employment, there was no reason for them to consider as a factor the fluctuations of American business conditions.

Jewish immigration to Galveston during the first four months of 1912 was not overly impressive, averaging only about one hundred per month. The April group contained only forty-seven individuals, the low number being induced, apparently, by reluctance to travel during Passover. Berman continued to complain about the poor quality of the arrivals, quoting unfavorable comments by the United States immigration inspectors.[24] In one case, an unskilled 47-year-old widower arrived in Galveston with five children and would have been deported but for the intervention of the local JIIB officials, who guaranteed that these immigrants would not become public charges. Berman sent this family to Cleburne, Texas, in the hope that the father would be able to "eke out an existence in running a boarding house for our immigrants consigned to that community. Should he fail in this," Berman warned, "there will be little opportunity to find other work for him and his family."[25] In another case, an immigrant in danger of deportation because of poor physique was released on a five-hundred-dollar bond provided by a Jewish citizen of Galveston.[26] This was a procedure which was frequently employed in order to gain the admission of borderline cases.

The physical and vocational attributes of the immigrants did not improve during the rest of 1912, but the quantity accelerated dramatically after the Passover holiday. The next five ships each brought an average of over 150 immigrants, thus meeting the minimum goal initially proposed by Bressler. The volume of immigration reached a peak of 207 in July, which surpassed even the JIIB's called-for maximum of 200 per month. The fine July showing, however, was marred by the exclusion of six immigrants based on medical certificates provided by the physician in charge of the post who, Bressler assured Zangwill, "is one of the most kindly disposed we have ever had . . . [being] noted for his courtesy and helpfulness." Bressler reported that two of the cases would be appealed, but "the other cases make appeal useless, and we would merely antagonize the immigration service if we forced the issue." In his report to Zangwill, Bressler, characteristically, expressed no appreciation for the extraordinarily large party of immigrants, making only passing reference to that fact. His comments dealt solely with the unfavorable aspects of the group. Extolling the fairness of the marine surgeon who, it seemed, gave the immigrants the benefit of every doubt, Bressler concluded with Berman's words that the exclusions "really represent the very bad cases of the boat."[27]

Ever since the beginning of the year, Berman, in response to a request from Bloch, had been supplying the latter with a list of deportation cases and the reasons for those actions. Since almost all deported immigrants applied for aid when they arrived in Bremen, Bloch wanted to be sure of the merits of each case.[28] When Berman's report on the July deportees reached Bremen, Bloch questioned the rejection of one of them, a tall, strong, 24-year-old cab driver named Golbert, who had been excluded from Galveston on grounds of valvular disease of the heart. Bloch maintained that the unfavorable diagnosis must have been caused by psychological rather than medical factors:

> Intimidated, still under the impression and anguish our unfortunate persecuted Russian brothers conceive when in presence of 'authority', his heart went down to his heels, he became excited, nervous, his temperature rose, (hence, and as a consequence, the quick strengthened palpitation) and the doctor certified for heart disease.[29]

Berman replied:

> The Surgeon,—to whom I talked on the matter after the exclusion,—advised me that the valvular derangement was so decided, that the "hiss" on action was very pronounced. It is possible that Golbert may live to be an old man; it is also possible that he may, without warning, be stricken dead, or fall into invalidism which may pass into death at any time. In the opinion of the Surgeon, he was not the sort of man to be passed. Many people may be troubled as Golbert is,—without having the opportunity to have the sad fact revealed to them. Outward appearances are no final indication . . . I hope that Golbert will not have his delusion disturbed that his momentary excitement alone militated against his admission.[30]

"Poor physique" was a designation which was used to justify many cases of deportation in 1912. This was a description which could be applied to any ailment, whether serious or minor. Although Bressler insisted that the Galveston physician was completely objective, he acknowledged that the designation "poor physique" was vague enough to allow for subjective interpretation. Thus, he was active, along with others favoring a liberal immigration policy, in seeking to repeal the provision allowing for such a designation. Realizing, however, that "the temper of our Congress is anything but favorable to greater laxity in our immigration regulations," Bressler strongly urged Zangwill to adopt a far more diligent approach.[31] Berman was more specific. "It would be safest," he wrote, "for the ITO to reject any applicants who are thin, underweight, stooped, flat-chested, or present any other appearance which would centre the surgeon's attention upon them. The general rule should be: When in doubt, reject."[32] Zangwill passed along this dictum to Dr. Jochelmann. In addition, he asked Bloch to carry out a separate inspection in Bremen, sifting out and rejecting all dubious cases. However, Zangwill wrote, Bloch "is so soft-hearted that he kicks at 'playing the hangman.' I am pointing out to him how his kindness is really a greater cruelty. Of course," Zangwill concluded, repeating an explanation which Bressler and Berman had rejected before, "the Galveston surgeon has unfortunately so little to do that he has far more time than the New York examiners."[33]

In addition to the problem of deportations, Berman and Bressler continued to be plagued by the arrival of what they considered to be unskilled immigrants. In his report on the August group, Berman wrote:

> There were in the neighborhood of twenty-two unskilled amongst the immigrants of this group, two being teachers, one a diamond polisher, a number clerks , two being glaziers, etc. This would not be serious if the group sized up well physically. It did not, and was one of the poorest within the year. Very few of the unskilled were fit for physical labor, and several expressed condemnation of us when advised that they might have to do manual labor.[34]

Showing that he had not lost his sense of humor, Zangwill replied:

> We are conveying your warning against clerks. But diamond polishers can hardly be called "unskilled" even though there are no diamonds to polish, and glaziers, too, may be more in demand as your suffragette movement develops.[35]

During the fall, Jewish immigration to Galveston slackened off sharply. Reluctance to travel during the Jewish holiday season contributed, no doubt, to the reduction. There was, however, another reason why the immigration figures were especially low during September, October, and November 1912. At that time, the rival ICA organization initiated a campaign which resulted in the diversion of emigrants from the Galveston route. Ever since the days of Baron de Hirsch, the ICA had regarded Argentina as the land offering the best opportunity for Jewish settlement. Until now, it had been involved in settling Jewish farmers on the land. Aware that most Jews had little inclination for farming, they now established an employment agency in Buenos Aires and began recruiting Jews in Europe for the purpose of sending them there.

This campaign, of course, was designed to attract the same type of emigrants being recruited by the ITO for Galveston—young, skilled, able-bodied workers. In spite of the enormous difference in distance, a trip to Argentina took only a few days longer than a trip to Galveston, due to the inferiority of the Galveston-bound ships. In addition, a ticket to Argentina actually cost less than one to Galveston, and many potential Galveston immigrants were swayed to the Buenos Aires route.[36]

By the end of the year, Dr. Jochelmann's recruitment campaign regained its momentum. The ship arriving in December 1912 carried 198 Jewish immigrants, none of whom were excluded or deported. Although Berman pointed out "that there were several immigrants who should not have been accepted for Galveston," he conceded that "as a whole, the group rated high in physique." When interviewed by JIIB officials, several of the immigrants volunteered the information that they had decided to come on the basis of favorable reports by friends and relatives who had already been settled by the JIIB. One immigrant had two brothers in Nebraska, "one of whom had purchased land for farming purposes." Another immigrant, a weaver, wished to go to Des Moines, Iowa, because a friend who had been sent there "was doing well at that trade." A third immigrant "told of another previous removal who was doing finely in Davenport, Iowa." (It may be remembered that Davenport was one of the Tri-Cities, which had been a center of dissatisfaction during the previous year.)

Besides Iowa and Nebraska, December reunions took place also in Dallas and San Antonio, Texas, and in Wichita, Kansas. As usual, reunions also took place in Kansas City and Galveston, which, Berman wrote, "are habitual enough to be a matter of course." Unfortunately, as Berman pointed out, "our successful protégés make too much of a virtue of silence."[37] During the closing months of the year, a growing percentage of immigrants consisted of those who were coming to join relatives or friends who had been previously removed by the JIIB. The highest number of reunions, fifty-one, was achieved in December. This was considered a healthy sign, since it showed that previous removals were largely satisfied with conditions and were encouraging others to follow in their footsteps. In fact, some of these formerly destitute immigrants had by now become important members of local committees in charge of receiving new immigrants from Galveston.[38]

Among the new arrivals there were, inevitably, those who, once arrived in Galveston, shunned the good offices of the Jewish Immigrants' Information Bureau and preferred to strike off on their own. Typical of these, arriving in the December group, and listed somewhat pretentiously as a "merchant," was a nineteen-year-old boy named Leib (later, Louis) Haft, from the city of Uneczia in the province of Chernigov.* Leib Haft was one of seven children, the only one who came to America. He had left Russia in order to avoid serving in the army. Many years later, his sister, who was eight years old when her brother left, would recall the bitter tears of their mother, who wept for many days, because Leib had to steal across the border. One of the neighbors brought him *gribenes* (chicken cracklings) to take along as a treat. The Haft family was fined three hundred rubles for Leib's failure to report to the army. Leib Haft arrived in America with only ten dollars in his pocket, but he eventually earned enough money to reimburse his family for the expense they had incurred on his behalf.[39]

From Galveston, Haft was assigned by the JIIB to a small town in central Texas with the unlikely name of Dublin. It is not known how long he remained in Dublin, but Haft apparently became quickly disillusioned with the Galveston Movement, relating to his family many years later that he felt he had somehow been exploited. Haft was independent by nature, nonconformist in behavior, and hotly tempered when crossed. Soon after arrival, he cut off ties with the JIIB and set out to seek his fortune, visiting various locations throughout the West. In 1923, Haft received his U.S. citizenship papers in Galveston. Photographs taken during this period show him in mines and stores, and even alongside oil wells. His letters to his family in Russia showed that he was in good spirits; he wrote that he was doing well. Nevertheless, his family worried about him and imagined that he must have been leading a hard life, as his sister recalled many years later.

In his late thirties and still unmarried, Haft received a letter from his father, mentioning a *landsman* (fellow townsman from Europe) then living in Wilkes-Barre, Pennsylvania, who had an eligible daughter. His curiosity aroused, Haft set out for Pennsylvania. In 1932, the *landsman*'s daughter became Mrs. Leib Haft, and thus Haft finally settled in Wilkes-Barre, where he raised his family. While the facts in each case are unique, it may be assumed that there were other immigrants who, like Haft, settled down in one spot only after years of restless wandering.

* Today, Uneczia is in the Rusian Soviet Socialist Republic, while Chernigov is in the Ukranian S.S.R.

In late October 1912, Dr. Jochelmann came for a visit to America, his trip being subsidized by a grant from Schiff of one thousand dollars.[40] Jochelmann and Bressler took a tour of Galveston and eleven other cities, where they spent four weeks interviewing more than six hundred immigrants, in order to find out for themselves how these immigrants were faring. In each city, first a general meeting was held, in which discussion and criticism were invited. This was followed up by a private session with each individual immigrant. Virtually all of those interviewed were acquainted with Dr. Jochelmann's activities in Russia. This proved to be a significant asset in gaining their confidence and in inducing them to be frank and open in their statements.

Upon returning to New York, the two men attended a meeting of the Galveston Committee, where Bressler presented a report on the condition of the immigrants, with which Dr. Jochelmann concurred. While it contained some criticism, the report was generally quite favorable:

> With the exception of not more than ten, all the immigrants [interviewed] were employed in gainful occupation, earning anywhere from $9 to $30 a week. Quite a number were engaged in small business and earning considerably in excess of the maximum amount mentioned. Quite a number own their own homes, while still others own other real estate as well. Practically all of them have bank accounts. With very few exceptions, they expressed themselves deeply grateful to the Kiev Bureau, the Galveston office, and the respective local committees for what had been done for them, and as well contented with the progress made by them. Here and there a dissenting voice was heard on the score of expectations realized. In these instances, everybody in general was accused: Kiev, the local bureaus of the ITO, the Bremen Committee, the steamship company, Galveston, the local American committees, and the paid agents. The charges included everything, from misrepresentation on the part of the ITO Bureau to exploitation of them on the part of our paid agents. One or two persons went as far as to say that the Galveston Bureau was a business proposition pure and simple for the purpose of furnishing cheap labor to railroads and other industrial plants, particularly in times of labor disputes. It is a noteworthy fact, however, that the most bitter complaints came from men who were employed and doing very well indeed.[41]

One of the immigrants' complaints contained in the report was that the ITO agents in Russia had promised them much higher wages than they were actually given in America. Dr. Jochelmann categorically rejected this claim as having no basis in fact. Bressler reported:

140

In this connection, it is interesting to relate that some of the earlier immigrants who attended some of our meetings openly made the charge against the more recent immigrants that their own inflated ideas of their ability and the wages they were entitled to were responsible for most of the difficulties experienced by them during the first few weeks of their residence in this country.

Another complaint was that "the Bureau officials ignored the preferences expressed to be sent to certain stated cities. These complaints were taken up by Dr. Jochelmann and Mr. Bressler with Mr. Berman and fully and satisfactorily explained."

The arrival of Jochelmann and Bressler in Galveston was timed to coincide with that of the seventy-second party of immigrants which arrived, however, three days late, on November 10. Jochelmann and Bressler were impressed with the sense of fairness exhibited by the immigration physician and inspectors, and by the Board of Special Inquiry which reviewed the deportation cases. Bressler remained convinced "that the immigration officials are an able, conscientious set of men, performing their duties not only efficiently, but humanely as well." Jochelmann, however, noted that the physicians in Galveston had relatively few immigrants to examine, and thus had time to be a bit too thorough.[42]

During their trip, Jochelmann and Bressler heard complaints that some of the JIIB agents were incompetent, unconscientious, or unsympathetic. After considering the charges against the agent in Saint Paul, Minnesota, they recommended his dismissal. They would have done the same in Dallas, Texas, but the agent in question had already been replaced. In this connection, Bressler recalled the case of George Ellman, formerly stationed at Rock Island and subsequently at Memphis, Tennessee, who had since been relieved of his duties. With the exception of these three agents, however, he "found that the agents were generally competent, conscientious, sympathetic, and fulfilled the obligations imposed upon them." The local committees, which supervised the agents, "were found to be composed of the best men in their respective communities and were deeply imbued with the importance of the work, and with a fine spirit to aid it to the fullest extent of their ability."

The most serious complaints which Jochelmann and Bressler heard concerned travel conditions. The immigrants were overwhelmingly dissatisfied with the lodging and boarding facilities at Bremen. They bitterly complained about the long and arduous voyage over the Atlantic. Most alarming of all, they told stories of ill-treatment on board the ships of the North German-Lloyd

Steamship Company. A few expressed the sentiment that "the ill-treatment was largely due to the arrogant behavior and unreasonable demands of the immigrants themselves." However, the vast majority of the immigrants maintained that there was no excuse for the distressing behavior which the German crews displayed toward their Jewish passengers. Once settled, the immigrants usually sent for their families as soon as they could afford to do so. However, because of the extreme length and the degrading conditions of the Galveston voyage, most of them instructed their families to come through the Port of New York.

While an average trip from Bremen to New York or Philadelphia took less than two weeks, a trip to Galveston generally lasted about twenty-three or twenty-four days and sometimes even a few days longer. The extra length of time for the latter voyage was caused only partially by the greater distance covered. (This can be readily seen from the fact that the return voyage, the trip from Galveston to Bremen, which was meant to attract American businessmen and tourists traveling to Europe, required only eighteen days.[43]) Instead of traveling straight from Bremen to Galveston, the ship first made one stop, either at Baltimore or at Philadelphia. Often, some immigrants previously destined for Galveston would disembark at these ports, thus prematurely ending their agonizing voyage. The ship continued down the coastline into the Gulf of Mexico until it reached its final destination. Sometimes it traveled slowly deliberately in order to conserve coal, as it did with its very first party of Jewish immigrants in 1907.[44]

The location of the immigrant was, no doubt, an important factor in his deciding through which port his family was to come. An immigrant living in Texas, for example, would undoubtedly tell his family to take a ship to Galveston. An immigrant living in Minnesota, however, would be foolish if he did so, for the rail service alone took less time from New York than it did from Galveston.[45] Most JIIB immigrants, however, were located neither in Texas nor in Minnesota, but somewhere in between. For these people, the length of the ocean voyage was an important factor which they took into consideration when sending for their families.

Far more serious than the length of the voyage were the charges of bad food and of ill-treatment at the hands of the ship's crew. Such complaints had been made since the very beginning of the Galveston movement, producing nothing but empty promises by the North German-Lloyd Company that it would somehow try to correct the matter.[46] However, the complaints continued. One immigrant, for example, who had crossed the Atlantic in April 1910, had found that the normally hard conditions were especially complicated on that voyage due to the brutally insensitive attitude of the crew to the Jewish dietary requirements of the Passover holiday:

They gave us some stale meat, soup and rotten herrings. It was the Easter holidays and the cook just before those days gave the sailors the unleavened bread, and we did not have enough to eat during the holidays.[47]

A seventeen-year-old boy who had been on the same ship gave a more dramatic account of the voyage:

We received bad treatment by the sailors and if we complained to the Captain, we got the worst of it. One day three boys, Jossel, Solomon and David, were taken up on the bridge where the Captain was and they tied their hands behind their backs and kept them there for six or seven hours as a punishment because they complained about the treatment at the hands of the sailors, and they were not allowed to raise their eyes. Another day I wanted to get some hot water from the kitchen and I was in the way of a sailor and he hit me in the back with a broom stick and I was sore for a long time afterwards. The Cook would not give us enough to eat and the three boys complained to the Cook and he pushed them away from his door and went to the Captain and then the Captain had the boys tied and took their S.S. tickets away and told them he would send them back to Bremen. Some agent on the boat in Galveston had the boys discharged. We only got meat the first eight days and the meat, herrings and potatoes were rotten; the bread was stale and mouldy; after three days' fast of the Jewish-Easter Holidays Yankel Baer and Labe went to the Steward and complained that they were starving and wanted something to eat, but the Steward slapped Yankel in the face and he came down stairs again crying.[48]

Still another immigrant traveling on that ship added more grisly details in his account of the voyage:

On account of the bad food there was fighting between the immigrants and the sailors. They gave us potatoes, water and a small piece of meat which was rotten and the bread was wormy. We showed the bread to the Steward and he said you will eat worse bread in America. The Steward had considerable trouble with us because we objected to the food, so he told the sailors to bother us in the night time and they would not let us sleep; and the sailors fought with us. Jossel Brengel, an immigrant, was hit in the head with a bone by a drunken sailor. We stayed in the Port of Galveston for five days before they

143

would let us off, and he was so badly injured that they had to put him in the ship's hospital, and he was finally sent back to Bremen. The ship's officer called the U.S. Immigration officials' attention to him, and the man was refused landing.[49]

Other immigrants traveling on that vessel corroborated the reports of spoiled food and brutal treatment. One of them, who left the ship as soon as it landed, said that he learned from others who were kept aboard for a few days that a sailor later assaulted one of the women.[50]

Immigrants arriving in May 1910 had reported further incidents of inedible food, callous behavior, and physical brutality:

The food was bad but towards the last days when everybody refused to eat they gave us a little better meals. The bread was mouldy and stale. The first few days after we left Bremen the meat was good, but afterwards it was rotten and we could not eat it; the herrings were also rotten.[51]

The steward on the boat was a very bad man, and I begged him in Philadelphia to post a letter for me and gave him the stamp money, but he said "Today is my Sabbath." He, however, accepted letter[s] and money from about 50 Christian immigrants.[52]

Our quarters on the boat were so crowded we could not get sufficient air. In the evening, when we went on the upper deck, the seamen threw pails of water on us and drove us down again. A Jewish woman was sitting on the deck with her husband and he left her for a few minutes, and a sailor who swept the deck pushed and struck her and the woman was in a family way and she complained to the Captain about the treatment. I heard she did not get any satisfaction.[53]

The above incident had been reported by other Jewish immigrants traveling on that ship, and had caused quite a sensation among them. At that time, the JIIB had been chiefly concerned with its legal battles with the United States Bureau of Immigration and had found it difficult to concentrate on the problems of the immigrants. When active operations were resumed in 1911, however, the JIIB was able to give its attention to recently intensified reports of mistreatment on board ships carrying its immigrants to Galveston. In July 1910, for example, an expectant mother had miscarried during the voyage after she had been refused admittance into the ship's hospital. Subsequently, her husband brought suit against the Lloyd Company, although he offered to settle for a $250 compensation out of court. The case dragged on, seemingly without hope of being resolved. Berman and Bressler brought the matter to the attention of the ITO, which took it up directly with Lloyd headquarters in Bremen. It was over a year after the original incident when the couple, at last, received a check for $50 which they reluctantly agreed to accept as "full compensation."[54]

At the time that the above matter was finally being resolved, the *Jewish Daily Forward* received the following letter, which was signed by forty-four immigrants who had left Bremen on June 29 and arrived in Galveston July 21, 1911:

> We, Galveston immigrants of the 53rd Party, having left Bremen June 16th [according to the "Old Style" Julian calendar, which was used in Czarist Russia] on the S.S. *Hanover*, hereby deem it our moral duty to publish a strong protest against the unusual, inhuman treatment accorded to us Jewish immigrants by the officers of the steamship company from the smallest to the biggest.
>
> It will not be exaggerated to express ourselves that we were treated worse than cattle. Not alone were we insulted with remarks such as "dirty and piggish Jew," but many of us actually felt fist blows from the sailors and officers. When the heat is intense and we must leave our cabins to go on deck to cool off, the sailors purposely pour water at us. The food is also not of the very best kind. The bread is stale and with worms inside. It happened that a rat was found in one of the rolls and when it was taken to the captain, he said, "Such things can happen. Why all this fuss?" An instance as to the treatment we received from the higher officers is recorded as follows:
>
> An immigrant received a punch in the face from a sailor who passed by and the immigrant reported it to the captain. The captain instructed that the guilty sailor be brought before him. When the sailor came, the captain left.
>
> We could write more in regard to our ill-treatment, but we believe the facts we have published are sufficient.[55]

The letter was never published. The editor, realizing the harm such a document might do to the Galveston Movement, turned it over to Bressler in exchange for the latter's promise that he would act on the matter. Bressler forwarded the letter to Zangwill with the recommendation that Joseph Michaelowitz issue a full report about conditions on board steamers of the Bremen to Galveston line. Michaelowitz, Dr. Jochelmann's assistant in Kiev, had taken a Lloyd ship to Galveston earlier in the year and "had considerable to say of a score of intolerable conditions in the steerage."[56] Upon receiving Bressler's letter, Zangwill addressed a strong letter to the directors of the North German-Lloyd Steamship Company.[57] Bressler was soon gratified to learn that the Lloyd Company had "dealt

in a drastic manner with the chief delinquents of the S.S. *Hanover*."[58]
And Zangwill wrote to Schiff: "We have largely grappled with these
[complaints]—as you will perhaps have seen from the concessions
I recently extracted from the Norddeutsher Lloyd."[59]

The problem, however, did not go away. Rabbi Cohen, who
usually communicated with Berman or Bressler about matters concerning the JIIB, wrote directly to Schiff in early 1912 about the
poor steerage accommodations he had observed on the ships arriving at Galveston. Schiff relayed this report to Zangwill but,
unfortunately, conditions remained the same throughout the year.[60]
Apparently, the Lloyd Company, which engaged also in an "au-
tocratic financial policy," felt itself, in Zangwill's words, "immune
from competition," and it did not feel motivated to change its
ways.[61]

Then, in November, upon returning from their trip to the West,
Jochelmann and Bressler issued their report that most pioneering
immigrants, though having arrived through Galveston, instructed
relatives and friends to join them via New York. The JIIB viewed
this trend with concern, but it took solace in the fact that these
families were, after all, settling in the West. It considered these
people to be indirect products of the Galveston Movement. The
JIIB bemoaned only the fact that no accurate record could ever
be compiled of the number of "Galveston" reunions which were
actually achieved through New York and other eastern ports.[62]

The ITO viewed the trend more seriously. Over the years, the
ITO became increasingly aware that a growing proportion of its
"market" were those who were going to join relatives and friends
already settled in the West. If most of the reunion cases came in
through ports other than Galveston, then the ITO's recruitment
campaign was being largely undercut. The JIIB might claim to
have attracted these later settlers to the West, but the ITO could
scarcely claim to have sent them there, and it was still expected
to supply Galveston with the same numbers of immigrants, or even
more.

After discussing Bressler's and Jochelmann's report, the Galveston
Committee decided upon a plan that would help eliminate abuses
on board North German-Lloyd steamships. According to this proposal, the JIIB would hire a "commissioner" to accompany the
immigrants on their journey from Bremen to Galveston. He would
be appointed on a monthly basis, subject to the approval of the
Lloyd Company, and the JIIB would pay him one hundred dollars.
The Lloyd would provide him with free, first-class, round-trip

transportation, permit him to mingle freely with the Jewish steerage passengers, and authorize him to represent their interests with the ship's officers.[63] In anticipation of the Lloyd's approval, Bressler tentatively chose as "commissioner" an experienced American social worker with a college degree, who spoke both Yiddish and German.[64] The Lloyd, however, was far from enthusiastic about the proposal. Fearing that such a "commissioner" might become a thorn in it side, it insisted upon separate authorization for each trip. The JIIB accepted this stipulation, but still the Lloyd delayed its approval of the proposal, and negotiations were to drag on throughout 1913.[65]

As one party of immigrants after another landed, each with its own report of miserable conditions on board, it became clear that the Lloyd was doing little, if anything, to combat these conditions. During the summer of 1913, Dr. Jochelmann, who was normally quite diplomatic, finally lost patience with the intransigence of the steamship company. He granted an interview to a Russian newspaper in which he charged the North German-Lloyd Steamship Company with maltreatment of its passengers. The Lloyd used this incident as a pretext to refuse the request for a "commissioner" to accompany Jewish immigrants to Galveston. The steamship company further declared that it was unable to accede to any demands which were not strictly provided by the rules of the service. Lest the point not be understood, the Lloyd, in a letter to Schiff describing its experiences with Dr. Jochelmann and the ITO, ended with the words, "Friendly relations cannot be resumed." The Galveston Movement never got the "commissioner" it sought, and treatment of its immigrants during the Atlantic crossing remained as bad as ever.[66]

Thus, the Galveston Committee's attempt to improve conditions during the voyage failed. However, the committee, after hearing Bressler's and Jochelmann's report, did make one important change in policy which was designed to encourage immigrants who were already settled to send for their families through Galveston. Ever since the beginning of the Galveston Movement, Schiff had insisted that these settlers pay the railroad transportation for their families from Galveston to the points of reunion. The JIIB, of course, did pay the railroad fare for the original immigrants whom they assigned to various destinations. Yet, despite the urging of the ITO, Schiff had continually refused to finance the railroad fare of the families who later came to join these immigrants. He had explained his position as follows:

Aside from the considerable burden this would bring upon our funds, we should not encourage men to send for their families until it is certain that they can provide for them. If these men are not willing, or cannot afford to pay the inland transportation, they are probably not yet in a position to adequately support their families.[67]

Emigrating families who had not possessed prepaid railroad tickets or the funds with which to pay for such tickets had been advised by Jochelmann's organization to come via New York, since the immigration authorities at Galveston did not permit families without these funds or tickets to land at that port.[68]

When Bressler and Jochelmann returned from their trip in November 1912 with the news that most Galveston immigrants were sending for their families via New York and other eastern ports, Schiff was persuaded to compromise on his long-standing policy. Henceforth, he wrote, "we shall advance to any of the immigrants who have been placed by the Galveston Bureau, if they ask for this,—after they shall have been settled for a reasonable time,—one-half of the cost of transportation from Galveston, of their families for whom any immigrant may wish to send."[69] During the next few months, many immigrants arrived who, eager to take advantage of the half-rate subsidy, claimed kinship with persons living in whatever cities of the West they wished to settle. Alarmed by the sudden increase in expenses, Bressler sent a telegram to Dr. Jochelmann declaring that the JIIB had committed itself to subsidizing only the wives and children of heads of families who had previously been removed by the JIIB. Furthermore, added Bressler, it was to have been "clearly understood that careful discrimination would be practiced so as to limit the beneficiaries of the resolution only to such families as could not themselves pay the entire transportation."[70]

The limited subsidy granted by the JIIB was not sufficient to induce a reduction in the number of reunions taking place through the Eastern ports. Berman wrote that he had even come across cases where such reunions were effected through Quebec. He concluded that

there seems to be a tendency to avoid the lengthy Bremen-Galveston route; and not even the cheaper railroad fare we secure seems to offset its undesirability. Faster boats would go far towards increasing the reunions via Galveston, and towards a greater popularization of Galveston.[71]

Berman's wish was never fulfilled. The inferior steamships which the North German-Lloyd Company sent to Galveston remained slow, conditions on board these ships remained unsatisfactory, and most "Galveston" reunions continued to take place through ports other than Galveston.

It may be remembered that early in 1912 Berman and Schiff had called for a minimum average of 125 immigrants per month.[72] This wish was just barely fulfilled by the ITO, if we count all Jewish men, women, and children arriving in Galveston throughout the year. The maximum figure of 200 was approximated three times, including the fine December showing, which ended the year on a good note. Schiff, however, had more ambitious plans for 1913. He wrote Zangwill that the JIIB was now ready to place a minimum of 250 immigrants per month, and he challenged the ITO to meet that figure.[73] Schiff had long wished to invite the ITO's rival, ICA, to participate in the sending of immigrants to Galveston. He had threatened to do so if the ITO were not able to meet the minimum demands of the JIIB during 1912. Since the ITO proved that it was able to meet these demands without outside help, Schiff was once again restrained from initiating an invitation to the ICA. He doubted, however, whether the ITO alone would be able to meet his minimum demands for 1913, that is, the sending of 250 immigrants per month.

Just then, internal developments within the ITO cast grave doubts upon the future ability of that organization to participate at all in the Galveston Movement. When Dr. Jochelmann visited the United States toward the end of 1912, he expressed considerable dissatisfaction with the amount of financial backing which his Jewish Emigration Society in Kiev was receiving from Zangwill's ITO headquarters in London.[74] It soon became clear that the ITO was in the midst of a financial crisis. If Zangwill were to fail in his effort to raise fresh funds, he would be forced to close down Jochelmann's Jewish Emigration Society, thus effectively ending the ITO's participation in the Galveston Movement. Schiff was certainly concerned over the ITO's predicament, but at the same time he welcomed the chance to open a dialogue with the ICA.[75] Thus ended the year 1912. The ITO's future participation depended upon its ability to solve its financial difficulties. And the ICA was presented with a fresh opportunity to attach itself to the Galveston Movement.

CHAPTER 8

1913: The Rothschilds Withdraw, and a Hernia "Epidemic" Breaks Out

From its inception in 1907, the ITO's Emigration Regulation Department, which was in charge of Galveston Movement operations, was supported by a special fund which had been established by its treasurer, Mr. Leopold de Rothschild of London, and his brother Nathaniel, Lord Rothschild. The money from the Rothschild fund, which amounted to £20,000 (almost $100,000), was doled out to the Emigration Regulation Department from time to time whenever requested.[1] The department sent the bulk of this money, over the years, to Dr. Jochelmann's Jewish Emigration Society, which used it to run its office in Kiev and to pay the salaries of its agents, who were situated throughout the Russian Pale. By the end of 1912, about £16,000 was used up, leaving only enough money for about another year's operations.[2] Zangwill approached Leopold de Rothschild about the possibility of a new grant.

This was the second time in as many years that Zangwill had tried to convince Mr. de Rothschild to continue sponsorship. It will be recalled that at the end of 1911, Schiff had expressed his dissatisfaction with the ITO's recruitment campaign, but was persuaded by Zangwill to give the ITO another year in which to improve its performance.[3] At that time, Leopold de Rothschild had been in favor of giving Jochelmann a year's notice, raising the distinct possibility that the Jewish Territorial Organization would have to cease its Galveston recruitment operations at the end of 1912. Zangwill had assured Mr. de Rothschild that the ITO would improve its performance during 1912 to Schiff's satisfaction, and he persuaded the London Rothschilds to fulfill, at least, their original pledge of £20,000.[4]

Now, at the end of 1912, the £20,000 Rothschild fund was one year away from exhaustion. This time, the two Rothschild brothers of London informed Zangwill that they had no intention of issuing a new grant.[5] In this refusal they were joined by their French family relation, Baron Edmond de Rothschild, the patron of Jewish settlement in Palestine, whom Zangwill also approached for funds. In addition, Zangwill asked Jochelmann to approach the Russian-Jewish philanthropist Lev Brodski in Kiev, with a request for 100,000 rubles (a little over £10,000 or $50,000) and with an offer of the presidency of the Russian branch of the ITO's Emigration Regulation Department, as successor of the widely mourned Dr. Mandelstamm, who had passed away during the year. At first, Brodski seemed willing to accept the presidency as well as the obligation to raise the required sum. However, Brodski's private secretary, the Hebrew poet Judah Leib Levin, who was a leading Zionist, persuaded him that the Galveston Movement encouraged assimilation and that, besides, it was so insignificant as to be unworthy of Brodski's efforts.[6]

Even supporters of the ITO in Russia were, at this time, expressing dissatisfaction with the Galveston Movement, which many had long felt to be an alien cause. For example, a Russian-Jewish monthly which backed Territorialism, and was probably even subsidized by the ITO, carried an editorial severely criticizing the ITO for its participation in the Galveston Movement. The editor wrote that the ITOists had "diverted all their energy into a side-venture, and by changing the ITO into a 'Jewish Emigration Society' they had thrown out the baby with the bath water." He concluded that the Galveston Movement was "not an adornment of the ITO's flag."[7] Zangwill saw that the leading Jewish philanthropists of Europe refused to back the Galveston Movement. In desperation, he wrote Schiff a letter asking him if he would consider sponsoring the European end of the Galveston Movement in addition to its American operations.[8] This suggestion, however, was unanimously rejected by Schiff's Galveston Committee in New York, for it would be clearly illegal for an American individual or organization to recruit foreign immigrants. Instead, the Galveston Committee decided to open negotiations with the Jewish Colonization Association (ICA) toward having that organization assume control of the Galveston recruitment campaign. For the time being, the Galveston

Committee asked the ITO to continue its recruitment activities so that the anticipated transfer of authority could be accomplished without interrupting the flow of immigration.

The attempt to bring about a smooth working relationship between the rival ITO and ICA organizations was complicated by Zangwill's unfortunate tendency to become irritated at the slightest pretext. He was peeved, for instance, that Schiff had wasted no time in turning to the ICA. ("Mr. Schiff, taking advantage of a letter which I wrote to him . . . stating the position honestly . . . had already started proposing to the ICA to take up the work.") Zangwill, however, felt himself somewhat placated by the following flattering remarks which Schiff wrote to him:

We are very certain that you are as desirous as we are that this work shall suffer no interruption, and that you will offer the ICA every facility to step in and to continue the work. In no better way can you show your own unselfishness, which I have always appreciated.[9]

The same day that Schiff sent Zangwill the above letter, he also wrote the following words to Franz Philipson, vice-president of the ICA:

It is a great satisfaction to me to see from your letter that the ICA is still ready to take in hand the matter of emigration to Galveston. Strictly between ourselves, it has long been our wish here that the ICA should do so, but Zangwill has all through opposed so violently the proposal that the ITO should give up even a part of this work, that it was not practicable to include the ICA in the project. I enclose herewith in strict confidence copy of the correspondence which I have just had with Zangwill and from which you will see that he is now prepared to withdraw and to permit the ICA to go ahead. But as you probably already know, it is impossible to deal with Zangwill, and I therefore beg you in the interest of the cause to give special instructions to your office in Paris to make the thing as palatable as possible for him and particularly to avoid injuring his pride, because otherwise transference will not be easy.[10]

Happily, the 122 Jewish immigrants arriving at Galveston during the first week of 1913 "sized up excellently," according to Berman's report to Bressler. For example, one family of three came with $400 and were tailors by trade, although they expressed an interest in farming. They were sent to Omaha, Nebraska, where it was their intention to "work at their trade for the winter, and go nearby for farm work with the spring."[11] These were the types of immigrants that the JIIB considered most favorable: young, able-bodied men with trades who were anxious to work hard and who arrived with the means to estalish themselves successfully.

Unfortunately, the February party of 143 immigrants contained a large number of detained and deported cases. Ten of the arrivals were men forty years and over, and of these, seven were unskilled. An additional seven "immigrants" were discovered to have been in America before. Berman also learned that three emigrants who were sent by the ITO to Bremen were rejected there by the medical examiners.[12] These facts led Berman to conclude that the ITO was inexcusably lax in the selection of the members of this last group. Bressler wondered whether the ITO might be "growing careless and indifferent, in view of its expected withdrawal shortly." In the past, Bressler would not have hesitated to chastise Zangwill or Jochelmann for such a poor showing. This time, however, he restrained himself and even censored a critical comment from Berman's report before sending it to the ITO headquarters in London. Bressler explained his delicate position this way:

> From past experience, I know how thin-skinned they are about well-meant criticism, and since we are negotiating with them to continue the work until such time as we can make arrangements with another organization to relieve them of further responsibility for the work, I do not want to do anything which might be seized by them as a pretext for summary withdrawal, thus leaving the Galveston work suspended in mid-air.[13]

Although he was at least as sensitive about criticism as Zangwill was, Dr. Jochelmann had established a close working relationship with Bressler during their joint tour of the West in November 1912. Relying on the strength of this friendship, Bressler occasionally addressed to Jochelmann notes of tactful criticism, always tempering them with assurances of high personal regard. The March 1 party, which contained a number of unskilled men, some over forty years old, prompted one such note. Fortunately, the JIIB agencies in Omaha and Saint Paul were willing to accept these types of immigrants. The Rock Island agency, undoubtedly still remebering its bitter experiences of 1911, agreed to accept some unskilled men, but only those who were young. The other agencies were even stricter, insisting that the men be both young and skilled.[14]

In terms of sheer quantity, the ITO did very well in March 1913. In addition to the 142 immigrants arriving on March 1, another 190 landed on March 29.[15] In fact, the Russian ITO agents

had actually recruited even more emigrants for the March shipments, but seventeen of these recruits were rejected at Bremen—
one because he was under eighteen years old and the rest on
grounds of ill health. Zangwill maintained that this was no reason
to criticize the ITO's vigilance, for Bremen was the "second line
of defense" against unqualified emigrants. The important thing,
wrote Zangwill, was that these emigrants were stopped before
boarding the ships to Galveston.[16]

In his report on the March 29 group, Berman was enthusiastic
about "the high percentage of skilled immigrants . . . a percentage
higher than at any time in the history of the Bureau." Instead of
congratulating the ITO, however, Berman attributed the unprecedented influx of skilled immigrants to the unfortunate developments in Poland.[17] In that country, the anti-Semitic National Democratic Party was then leading a nationwide boycott of Jewish
businesses, a campaign which it had begun during the previous
year. As a result, many Polish-Jewish tradesmen sought relief in
emigration to the United States. During the spring of 1913, Jewish
immigrant parties arriving at Galveston contained a large percentage of skilled workers. This was a continued source of grati-
fication to the JIIB.[18] Whatever its true cause, the favorable trend
toward skilled immigrants helped maintain a friendly relationship
between the ITO and the JIIB even while the latter organization
was negotiating with the ITO's rival, ICA.

At first, the JIIB asked the ICA merely to supplement the ITO's
recruitment activities by contributing fresh funds for that purpose.
However, the ICA's Russian representatives reported that the ITO's
recruitment operation was wasteful and inefficient. During 1912,
the ITO had spent approximately 26,000 rubles on its Galveston
recruitment campaign. The Russian ICA agents estimated that they
could perform the same operation for 7,200 rubles per year. The
ITO, of course, denied this claim, and Bressler also thought that
the ICA's estimate was far too low.[19] During the spring of 1913,
when Schiff was vacationing in Europe, he attempted but failed to
reach a financial understanding between the ITO and the ICA for
joint sponsorship of the Galveston recruitment operations. Schiff
left the questions to be decided by the ITO and the ICA themselves.[20] The two European organizations negotiated with one another throughout the summer but were unable to agree on a
formula for joint sponsorship.

The leading officers of the ICA, meeting in Paris, were generally
willing to work out a compromise with the ITO. However, their

Russian representatives, meeting in Saint Petersburg, gave three reasons for their opposition to joint sponsorship. First, they pointed out that the ITO was still somewhat outlawed in Russia and was operating surreptitiously there by disguising its true identity. For the ICA to join forces with the ITO, then, would be for it to compromise its legal status with the Czarist government. Second, the Russian ICA representatives pointed out that many of their own projects were wanting for lack of funds. The ICA could hardly undertake a new financial commitment with another organization at a time when it could not meet its own obligations. The final reason for rejection was that the ICA wished to remain aloof from the Territorialist-Zionist controversy. The Russian ICA representatives warned that by allying itself with Zangwill's Territorialists, the ICA would lose its image as being above all political ideologies. In the end, the ICA directors voted to reject the idea of joint sponsorship. They declared their willingness to participate only if they were awarded sole control of the Galveston Movement's European recruitment program.[21]

The ICA directors announced their decision in October. By that time, the ITO had made a remarkable comeback. Though working on a limited budget, Jochelmann's agents managed to recruit twice as many immigrants during the first ten months of 1913 as they had during the corresponding period of the previous year. Of course, it should be noted that overall Jewish immigration to the United States was up by 55 percent during that period. Be that as it may, the Galveston increase was still quite impressive, even when compared with the general increase in Jewish immigration.[22]

Schiff was encouraged by the ITO's good showing, and disappointed by the ICA's inability or unwillingness to cooperate with the ITO. He asked Zangwill to continue the ITO's recruitment operations for at least another year, by which time about ten thousand Jewish immigrants would have entered the Port of Galveston. If, by the fall of 1914, the ITO were forced to discontinue its Galveston operations for lack of funds, Schiff would then invite the ICA to take over from the ITO.[23]   The extraordinary increase in Jewish immigration to Galveston during 1913 was most pronounced during the peak summer months of July and August, when well over a thousand arrived. While the JIIB, of course, was gratified by the quantity of immigrants, it complained about a deterioration in "quality." Berman was chagrined by "the large percentage of clerk-merchant type accepted for Galveston. Now that the Polish boycott is sending many immigrants to the ITO agents in Poland," he wrote, "it would seem that a selection in favor of skilled men should be possible."[24]

The issue of the unskilled Polish immigrants was complicated by the fact that, more than their Russian predecessors, they objected to working Saturdays. Berman was not impressed by the refusal of some Polish-Jewish immigrants to violate their religious principles. He wrote:

> With all due respect to their convictions, it must be pointed out that since they will go into industrial establishments, their failure to report for Saturday will bring about their discharge, and the firms who are extending aid to our agents will prove hostile to the further acceptance of our people.

Bressler emphasized this point in a letter to Zangwill:

> You know, of course, that could we control it, no man who wishes to keep the Sabbath would be barred on that account. But we simply have to accept conditions as they are . . . This point should be emphasized by your agents so that there can be no possible misunderstanding on this account, and an efficient agent can almost tell at a glance that certain types will not work on the Sabbath, and these should be absolutely discouraged from going to Galveston.[25]

Many Polish-Jewish immigrants, upon arriving in Galveston, were genuinely surprised to learn that they would be required to work on Saturday. One 34-year-old shoemaker, upon being informed of this, bought a full-priced ticket for the next ship to New York. Most, however, could hardly afford this luxury, and allowed themselves to be sent to places where Saturday work was expected. Of these, some set aside their religious scruples and began working on Saturdays. Others refused all Saturday work but, by doing so, became financial burdens on their Jewish communities, many of whose members, themselves, worked Saturdays. There was little sympathy expressed for these men of religious principle.[26] Three Jewish communities (in Cleburne, Texas; Rock Island, Illinois; Cedar Rapids, Iowa) requested Berman to send no more Polish immigrants "because of their exactions, faultfinding, and refusal to abide by the labor conditions upon which they come."[27]

Reluctantly, Zangwill agreed to instruct his agents in Poland to turn away Sabbath-observing applicants. Zangwill wrote:

> If emigrants who refuse to work on the Sabbath can get work by landing at New York, then obviously the attempt to divert them from

New York is neither practicable nor righteous. . . . But the whole tragedy of the Jewish question lies here, and nothing could more vividly illustrate the inadequacy of any solution other than the creation of an ITOland.[28]

Starting with the peak summer months of 1913, the Galveston Movement became involved in a new, unique problem: acute inguinal hernia. The group arriving on July 7 contained eight cases of hernia, all of which were deported later that month. An additional nine were deported for other medical reasons.[29] Among those who arrived on August 8, "the deportations were numerous, those for hernia outnumber[ing] other causes of rejection."[30] Of those who arrived August 30, "the number of men . . . deported [was] the largest for physical defects in the history of the [Jewish Immigrants' Information] Bureau. In the main, the cause of exclusion [was] inguinal hernia."[31] In the party arriving September 11, "the exclusions [were] again disquieting; and again deportations [were] in the majority of cases for hernia."[32] Of the group arriving September 28, Berman wrote, "the hernia exclusions continue; and each hernia exclusion means deportation."[33] There were five deportations for acute double inguinal hernia and two more for other medical reasons.[34] The ITO immigrants' party arriving October 10 contained eight cases of exclusion, seven of them for hernia. The JIIB appealed some of the cases, and in the end only three ITO immigrants were actually deported.[35] The November 25 group produced three deportations for medical reasons, only one of them for hernia.[36] The December 11 group, however, contained eight immigrants who were deported after a physical examination. Six of these were deported because they (or the heads of their families) had acute cases of inguinal hernia.[37] The immigration authorities took this action in spite of a strong appeal put foward by the JIIB on behalf of some of the rejected immigrants.[38]

Berman took a personal interest in every Jewish immigrant who was excluded at Galveston. He was often present when physical examinations were made, and he appealed every case in which there was some hope of reversal. The Department of Labor advised the Immigration Service at Galveston to treat relatives as a unit. Thus, if the Board of Special Inquiry excluded a particular immigrant on the ground that he had a hernia, all his accompanying relatives would be excluded along with him as a matter of routine. The JIIB would then appeal the cases of the accompanying relatives before the department, and these relatives would invariably be admitted. However, if the accompanying relatives were minors, they would be deported along with the affected immigrant.[39]

If Berman felt that the excluded immigrant had only a mild case of hernia, he would appeal that case. However, Berman reported that the physician in charge of the Port of Galveston was a sympathetic man and usually gave the immigrant the benefit of every doubt. Berman wrote:

> It is impossible for a man so skilled as Dr. Bahrenburg, of this port, to make a mistake in inguinal hernia; and in a long talk I had with him, he showed considerable concern that the doctors on the other side do not make a more thorough examination. He looks back with keen pleasure on Dr. Jochelmann's visit, and bespeaks his surprise that the various agents under Dr. Jochelmann are not following the latter's instructions. It does not appear to him that there can be any other reason for the large number of hernia. He is greatly interested in our work.[40]

Zangwill answered Bressler that Jochelmann was then being treated in a Berlin hospital for heart disease and had been there for a few weeks. His absence, therefore, may have caused a lapse in the diligence of ITO's recruiting agents in Russia.[41] "At the same time," Zangwill wrote, "I have never been able to believe in the naive good faith of your good-hearted Galveston doctor, or that an epidemic of hernia has suddenly broken out among our emigrants."[42] On the contrary, wrote Zangwill,

> I cannot help feeling . . . that your doctor has developed a morbid flair for hernia . . . I believe a doctor, like a patient, can find any disease he is looking for . . . Some cases deported for hernia did not even know they had it, so it could hardly be much of a disability in earning their livelihood. I have just consulted a London doctor who says that the only disability arising from hernia is the disability of wearing a truss, and if this is worn the emigrant would have no disadvantage in the struggle for existence. I do not believe, therefore, that inguinal hernia is the legitimate cause of exclusion at all.[43]

As the year 1913 drew to a close with no sign of a let-up in the rate of deportations, the American JIIB officials came to agree with Zangwill that there were other, hidden reasons behind the exclusions. As soon as Woodrow Wilson had become president in March 1913, he had signed a law creating a separate Department of Labor, where before there had been a Department of Commerce and Labor. Instead of leaving the Bureau of Immigration and Naturalization under the jurisdiction of the reorganized Commerce

Department, the law placed it under the jurisdiction of the new Labor Department. This left the Immigration Bureau* exposed to the pressures of the labor lobby, which was generally in favor of restricting immigration. During the latter half of the year, the number of deportations for hernia increased dramatically not only in Galveston, but in New York as well. In November, Schiff wrote to Zangwill, "It cannot be denied that there is an ill wind blowing as far as immigration is concerned, and that the restrictionists have the upper hand."[44]

In November 1913, members of the Galveston Committee began to lobby vigorously on behalf of the Galveston Movement and of immigration in general. Max J. Kohler sent a letter to the new secretary of Labor, William B. Wilson, urging him to adopt a more favorable policy.[45] At that time, Abram I. Elkus, a New York lawyer who was a member of the Galveston Committee, happened to be in Washington attending the argument of a case in the Supreme Court. At Schiff's suggestion, Elkus called upon Louis F. Post, a newly appointed assistant secretary of Labor, who was considered by the JIIB to be the most sympathetic man in the department. Long identified with progressive and humanitarian causes,[46] Post showed himself to be very interested not only in the Galveston Movement but in other Jewish immigrant organizations as well. Bressler followed up Elkus' visit by sending to Post various articles of propaganda concerning the Jewish Immigrants' Information Bureau, the Industrial Removal Office, the Baron de Hirsch Fund, and other Jewish organizations active on behalf of immigrants.[47] In December, when Schiff was in Washington, he arranged to see Post personally, but he was well aware that other officials of the Labor Department were not as favorably disposed toward immigration as Post was.

Just then, Zangwill received a letter which offered a unique perspective on the problem. Its author, a Jew, had been literary secretary to the Galveston, Harrisburg and San Antonio Railroad, which merged into the vast Southern Pacific network, and he later represented the railroad and several leading steamship companies in Europe. In his own words, he knew "the emigration business, Galveston, the whole South West of the States, etc., thoroughly, and [had] an *inside* knowledge of the currents and undercurrents that underlie the immigration policy of the United States." The

---

* The Bureau of Immigration and Naturalization was split into two bureaus. Both the Bureau of Immigration and the Bureau of Naturalization were placed under the jurisdiction of the Department of Labor.

writer asked that his name be withheld, and he begged Zangwill to keep the letter strictly confidential. While recognizing that this letter may reflect the frustrations of one private individual, we may still find it useful for what it tells about the general attitude of at least some United States immigration officials of the time.

The author of the letter wrote that "the whole attitude of the Galveston authorities [was] the outcome of 'Risches' [spitefulness], political considerations, and, last but not least, it is an attempt at blackmail." He explained his views this way:

> The very influential Trade Unions . . . hate the Jewish newcomer who lowers wages and the standard of life; this feeling is of special severity if Polish or Russian Jews are in question. (I myself had to change my name in the United States of America; the President of the Southern Pacific Railroad *told* me I had better, [since] a Jewish name would prejudice me and my task.) The immigration officers, the doctors, though nominally appointed by the Washington headquarters, are practically appointed by the political 'bosses', and so long as they are backed by powerful wirepullers behind the scene any complaint in Washington will do more harm than good . . . [because it] will simply be a feather in the Port Authorities' cap and call forth an increase of deportation.

In explanation of his charges of attempted blackmail, the author wrote:

> They [the United States immigration officials at Galveston] know that rich Jews are behind this Galveston scheme and, true to the spirit that controls official life in the States, they want "to be squared." I can and will not go into detail here, but the thing is being done in New York and in other ports. I shall be glad to lay the "facts" before you . . . Now I do not for a minute want you to believe that I suggest "bribery", although I frankly confess, compared with the terrible consequences of deportation, it would be the lesser evil. I have made exactly twenty-five double trips to America; I have seen dozens of deported Jews, pictures of dejection, misery and nameless despair which haunted me for years. In Hamburg, they are received by Hilfsverein "Bumbles" and transported through Germany like ferocious animals. And their fate when they get back to Russia?? . . . It is my opinion that complaints in Washington will lead to more stringent measures still; the Government's attention should be deviated instead of being called to Jewish immigration.[48]

In spite of this advice, the Galveston Committee resolved to continue its strenuous lobbying campaign in Washington. The committee members recalled that it was precisely these efforts which had convinced the government to reconsider its anti-Galveston stand in 1910. However, there was a difference. In 1910, when Taft had been president, Schiff and his Republican friends had had a considerable amount of influence with the administration. In 1913 the new Wilson Administration was composed of Democrats, many of whom, as labor supporters, had a restrictionist approach to immigration. Schiff, who had, ironically, broken a lifelong habit and voted for the Democratic candidate,[49] now found himself with few contacts left in Washington. Thus, he and his colleagues stood little change of effecting a change in government policy.

The unfortunate change in the government's attitude was especially disappointing, for it came at a time when the Galveston Movement was at the height of a boom. The ITO was able to report that it had sent 2,700 immigrants to Galveston in 1913, as compared with 1,500 during the year before.[50] In 1913, Jewish immigration to Galveston had reached its largest numbers. This was mainly due to the increased emigration of Jews from Poland, which was triggered by the boycott of Jewish businesses there. Naturally, Polish Jews not directly affected by the boycott also joined the general wave of emigration.

Let us now focus our attention upon two of the immigrants who arrived that year, one from Poland and the other from Russia. Eventually, their fates became intertwined, as we shall see.

Among those arriving in Galveston in 1913 was nineteen-year-old Ephraim Zalman Hoffman of Hrubishov, located in the region of Lublin, in Russian-controlled Poland. Hoffman's emigration was not prompted by economic circumstances, but rather, by problems of a more personal nature. As Hoffman was to tell the story years later, his mother had given birth to three healthy girls, but several males who were born died in infancy. His father, Hersh Baer, had been receiving spiritual guidance from a respected Hassidic rabbi, who comforted him with the assurance that he would have a son some day. A few days after the death of the rabbi, Hersh Baer's wife gave birth to a healthy boy, on March 7, 1894. Hersh Baer took this to be a sign that his son was born to assume the role of the late Hassidic rabbi. The baby was given the Hassidic rabbi's name, Ephraim Zalman, and he was dressed in white clothing as a sign of his special predestined status.[51]

By the time Ephraim Zalman was eighteen years old, Hersh Baer had already arranged for his son's marriage to an older woman in the community and had received the large sum of a thousand rubles as her dowry. Hersh Baer traveled often, throughout the area, as a salesman, dealing in furs. One day while his father was away, Ephraim Zalman borrowed some money from the woman to whom he was engaged, and he left Hrubeshov. After secretly staying with his sister in a nearby town, Ephraim Zalman managed to obtain a false passport and, with the little money he had borrowed, joined other Polish Jews who were headed for Galveston. Sailing from Bremen September 3, he arrived in Galveston September 28 with ten dollars in his pocket and was greeted there by the representatives of the Jewish Immigrants' Information Bureau. The JIIB sent Hoffman on to Fort Worth, Texas, where he was immediately given a job at the stockyards. After two days at work, his false passport was discovered, and he was fired.

Quite depressed, speaking hardly a word of English, Hoffman walked the streets of Fort Worth, not knowing what to do next. A kindly Jew, of German origin, found him sitting on the sidewalk crying, and he offered the pitiful greenhorn a job at his restaurant, working as a waiter at the bar. His Hebrew name proved to be too difficult for the kitchen help, so they began to call him "Charlie," which he later formalized to Charles. After a while, Charles Hoffman had collected enough tips to buy a partnership in a business known as the Star New York Supply Company, specializing in "silks, dresses and imported novelties," shipped in from New York. Actually, the company's headquarters consisted of a horse-drawn buggy, from which Charlie and his partner peddled their wares throughout all sections of Fort Worth, including the red light district. Its sometimes questionable clientele may have led to the company's eventual demise. According to company records, Charlie's partner, who was in charge of accounts receivable, accepted unspecified "services" when the customer's credit failed. Charlie's partner might have been forgotten by the Hoffman family were it not for the fact that one Sunday in the early part of 1915, his partner's future wife introduced Charlie to a girl friend of hers, named Sarah Bernstein, a Russian Jewess who had arrived at Galveston twelve days after Hoffman himself. By this time, Charlie, formerly Ephraim Zalman, had long since abandoned his own fiancée in Hrubeshov, and he married Sarah Bernstein before the year was out.

Sarah Bernstein's great-grandfather, Yehuda Gorelik, formerly of Paritz (or Parichi) in White Russia, had been an overseer in the forests around the town of Rechitsa when his son, Israel, had died in 1877. Israel's widow, Dvorah, remarried and remained in Paritz, but she sent her three-year-old daughter, Rachel, to live with her former father-in-law in Rechitsa. Sometime after 1890, a grandson of Yehuda's named Chaim Bernstein came to Rechitsa to tutor girls in the basics of reading and writing, and he fell in love with his cousin, Rachel. Chaim and Rachel were married in 1893, and Sarah was born a year later, the first of five children. In 1896, the Bernsteins moved back to the town of Paritz, renewing their acquaintance with Rachel's mother, Dvorah, and with her half-brothers and half-sisters. Over the following ten years, Sarah's grandmother, and most of her maternal uncles and aunts, joined the mass wave of emigration to New York City.[52]

In 1908 one of Sarah's uncles sent her fifty dollars, or one hundred rubles, to join him in New York. Since unaccompanied young girls were often denied admission, Sarah's parents arranged for her to be included on the passport of a woman who was already traveling with four of her own children. Unfortunately, the examining doctors at the Latvian port of Riga rejected Sarah, suspecting trachoma, because of the lingering redness of an eye infection, and the woman with whom she was traveling went on board the ship without her. Although she was told she could wait for the departure of the next ship in a few weeks, when the redness in her eye would be sure to disappear, Sarah decided to return to Paritz. She took the train to the city of Bobruisk, and from there she rode on a passenger sled for the remainder of the journey. Many years later, she was to recall the experience of being covered with blankets and tucked in for the cold and dark ride home. It was very early in the morning when Sarah finally arrived, but her mother was already in the kitchen preparing tea. The fourteen-year-old girl stood in the doorway crying from disappointment and embarrassment when her mother turned to her to say, "Why are you crying? . . . You are home." Thus ended Sarah Bernstein's first attempt to emigrate to America. The one hundred rubles, earmarked for Sarah's emigration, were set aside by the Bernstein family to be used on another occasion.

In November 1911 Sarah's father decided that the time had come for him to follow the stream of emigration to New York City. For this purpose he used Sarah's one hundred rubles, promising to send for her, as well as for the rest of his family, as soon as he became settled. For the first eight months, he tried to scratch out a living in New York as a Hebrew teacher, without too much success. Then, he was invited to Texas by a nephew, W. H. Novit, who was the first of a large group of family and friends settling in Texas. Novit had developed a successful trade selling bananas in Gatesville, where he settled. While still unripe, the fruit would be unloaded from a ship at Galveston onto a train traveling north through central Texas. The train's first main stop was in Waco, where it unloaded a portion of the bananas. Its next stop was Gatesville, where Novit obtained his portion. After that, the train continued to Hamilton, Comanche, and Dublin. Novit encouraged members of family in Russia to immigrate through Galveston and join him in the business of banana distribution. In 1912, he wrote to his uncle Chaim in New York, urging him to come to Texas and join him in this successful enterprise. Thus, Chaim Bernstein became a supplier of bananas to the citizens of Comanche, Texas, and within a year he made enough money to send for his daughter. This time, instead of heading for New York, Sarah Bernstein set sail for Galveston. Her cousin, Sol Novit, who accompanied her on the journey from Paritz, came with her to Texas. They embarked on the S.S. *Chemnitz*, which left Bremen on September 18, 1913.

Many years later, as an old woman, Sarah would retain vivid memories of that trip. She recalled the crowded conditions on board ship, and remembered that her cousin, Sol Novit, was sick during most of the journey and hardly ate a thing. Sol obliged Sarah, however, by standing in the food line with her, so that she could get double portions. Sarah ate so much on the trip that she was obliged to wear a girdle for the first time in her life. During the voyage, another Russian-Jewish immigrant fell in love with her, and by the time the trip was over he had unsuccessfully asked for her hand in marriage. Since Sarah spoke German, she was able to make friends with some of the members of the crew as well, and they invited her to accompany them ashore during the intermediate stop in Philadelphia. Giving little thought to the fact that her entry into the United States was illegal, Sarah joined the sailors, but she began to realize, after walking with them for several blocks, that she really had no business being there, legally or otherwise. She hurried back, and was, fortunately, readmitted to the ship without too many questions asked. She continued her passage without further incident.

Sarah Bernstein arrived in Galveston, together with about 250 other Jews from Eastern Europe, at 5:30 in the afternoon of Friday, October 10, 1913. This was the evening of Yom Kippur, which fell that year on a Sabbath. The next day's *Galveston Tribune* reported that the U.S. immigration officials thoughtfully made provisions for the Jewish immigrants to observe their holiest day of the year in solemn assembly. A room in the station was set aside during the day for use as a synagogue, and services were conducted by "one of the local rabbis." At the end of Yom Kippur, and during the following day, most of the Jewish immigrants were sent off to various destinations by the representatives of the Jewish Immigrants' Information Bureau.[53] Unlike most of the immigrants, Sarah Bernstein knew her destination in advance: she was going to Comanche to meet her father. While the JIIB did not have to help Sarah in getting settled, it did prove to be of service by forwarding her an envelope from her father with the ten dollars she needed to secure her admission to the United States.

After a day or two in Galveston, Sarah and her cousin Sol Novit took the train to Gatesville, Texas, where Sol joined his family. Sarah saw her father in Comanche, then returned to Gatesville, where she lived with the Novits for nine months, attending public school there and excelling in her studies. By July 1914, Sarah had moved to Fort Worth, where she was occupied at hemming dresses in the alterations department of a fine lady's shop. At the same time, Sarah continued her studies at a college for women, where she surpassed many of the "local" students with her capacity for learning. During the following year, as previously mentioned, Sarah Bernstein kept company with Charles Hoffman, and the couple was married on Wednesday, November 24, 1915, in the study of Rabbi Fox of Fort Worth. The Hoffmans raised their family in Texas.[54]

CHAPTER 9

1914: The End of a Movement

Ever since the beginning of 1913, Henry Berman, manager of the Jewish Immigrants' Information Bureau, had expressed the desire to leave Galveston.[1] He had agreed to remain, however, until a suitable replacement could be found. It was only toward the end of the year that his successor, Maurice Epstein, was sent to Galveston. Berman remained until the year's end to help acquaint Epstein with his tasks. The new manager was undertaking his duties at a difficult time, for the Galveston Movement was about to have its final confrontation with the United States immigration authorities.

During this period of transition, Berman took Epstein to see Dr. Bahrenburg, the United States marine surgeon for the Port of Galveston. Berman's main purpose in arranging the interview was not to introduce the new manager to the marine surgeon, but to confront Bahrenburg with a report implying that his medical examinations were unfair. The North German-Lloyd Steamship Company had asked three medical doctors at Bremen to reexamine fourteen Jewish immigrants who had arrived there after having been deported from Galveston. These physicians issued reports which flatly contradicted those of Dr. Bahrenburg and denied any grounds for deportation. With Epstein present, Berman now brought these reports to Bahrenburg's attention.

Dr. Bahrenburg vehemently denied the implication that he unjustly excluded immigrants who deserved to be admitted. He reminded Berman that during several examinations of these very same immigrants he, Berman, had been present and, despite his layman's limitations, had corroborated the fairness of Dr. Bahrenburg's findings. To emphasize his point, Dr. Bahrenburg read to Berman and Epstein from a copy of a letter which he had recently sent to his superiors in Washington concerning the subject of deportations. Dr. Bahrenburg's letter seemed to have been written in a humanitarian spirit, making no special mention of Jews nor, for that matter, of any ethnic group, and declaring that his main intent was to safeguard the interests of the unfit immigrant.

"I must confess," Berman wrote, "that I cannot, despite any searching of my memory over a considerable past, charge the Doctor with any prejudice. He is all thoughtfulness and patience in the handling of the immigrants, and he is most favorably interested in our work." Apparently, Berman concluded, Dr. Bahrenburg's only fault was that he took his job too seriously, not allowing any cases to slip through without a thorough examination.[2] Deportation of the ostensibly carefully selected Jewish immigrants who arrived in Galveston was proportionately seven times higher than that at Boston, six times that at Philadelphia, and four times that at New York. From these figures, Bressler agreed "that greater rigor is being exercised at Galveston than at any other port. That this rigor, however, is unfair, it would be an exceedingly difficult thing to establish. The record of the marine surgeon, Dr. Bahrenburg, is absolutely against it."[3] In fact, while general deportation from Galveston was forty-three per thousand, deportation of Jews was only forty per thousand, thus precluding any possible charges of discrimination.[4]

These statistics were quoted in early November 1913. Over the next four months, however, more and more Jewish immigrants were deported from Galveston. By the end of February 1914, it could be pointed out that deportation of Jewish immigrants for medical reasons significantly exceeded that of non-Jewish immigrants. During a period in which 311 medical certificates of rejection had been issued against immigrants arriving in Galveston, it was noted that although Jews constituted only 41 percent of all the arrivals, they made up over 60 percent of the medical rejects. Ominously, these alarming statistics were compiled by the United States Immigration Bureau and were included in a letter to Simon Wolf by Acting Commissioner General of Immigration F. H. Larned, a man who had, in the past, indicated intense hostility to the Galveston Movement.[5] In quoting these statistics, Larned meant to point out that, far from selecting medically sound specimens, the Galveston Movement was recruiting immigrants of doubtful physical fitness. Wolf confidentially forwarded Larned's letter to Schiff, who brought it to the attention of the Galveston Committee in New York.

The Galveston Committee understood the letter of the acting commissioner general of Immigration as a vindication of the harsh policy of exclusions being carried out in Galveston. In his letter, Larned indicated that he accepted the immigration inspectors' classification of a slight hernia and that of a relatively poor physique as falling into the category of "grave defects," which was sufficient grounds for deportation. The members of the Galveston Committee viewed Larned's letter as a notice that they could expect no relief from Washington for the severe restrictions being carried out in Galveston.[6]

Only a short time before, Larned had sent an earlier letter to Wolf, contrasting the cases of Jewish and non-Jewish immigrants who, sometime after admittance, were then deported after having had their cases reviewed. In that letter, Larned had made the point that it was not true that the Jews look after all their own unfortunates, since many of those Jewish immigrants were deported for having become public charges. Whatever the justification for this charge—and there was sufficient doubt as to its accuracy—the members of the Galveston Committee questioned the motives of the officials in Washington who were drawing up these reports contrasting the cases of Jewish and non-Jewish immigrants.[7]

In order to encourage the immigration authorities in Galveston to admit borderline cases, the JIIB often guaranteed Jewish immigrants against the possibility of deportation. If it was discovered later that these immigrants were being supported at the expense of the public, then they would be deported at the expense of the Jewish Immigrants' Information Bureau. During the Wilson Administration, more and more of these unfortunate immigrants were ferreted out and deported at the expense of the JIIB. During the month of February 1914, three warrants for deportation were issued at an expense to the JIIB of $100, and another case was pending where an expense bill of about $80 had already been rendered. Legally, it was irrelevant whether the "cause" of an alien becoming a public charge existed prior to landing or whether it developed after landing. Even in the latter case, the JIIB was still responsible for bearing the cost of deportation. The government had general methods for being informed of the names of all aliens who were found in hospitals, mental institutions, and almshouses, as public charges. Nevertheless, Bressler was convinced that the government made a special effort to track down cases which were guaranteed by the JIIB.[8]

Epstein, the new manager, became agitated at the prospect of sending back deported aliens. When one former beneficiary of the JIIB was arrested and in the process of being deported, Epstein defended the alien so vociferously that he was charged with misconduct. The U.S. Bureau of Immigration used this incident as a pretext to drop a hint that in the future it would no longer regard the JIIB's guarantees against immigrants becoming public charges with the same degree of confidence as before.[9]

The Galveston deportees soon developed a stratagem for regaining admittance to the United States. Often, upon return to Bremen, a deported immigrant would simply take the next boat to Philadelphia, sometimes altering his name to avoid detection. It was apparent that the immigration inspectors at Galveston were much harsher than those at northeastern ports, for many of these two-time immigrants easily gained admittance the second time around. Schiff made this charge in an address which he delivered to an audience which included Secretary of Labor Wilson. Anticipating that Schiff might be called upon to substantiate this charge, Bressler asked Jochelmann and Zangwill to send him the names and arrival dates of immigrants who, to their knowledge, were first rejected at Galveston and then admitted at Philadelphia. Zangwill supplied Bressler with the facts of several such cases.[10] As it developed, however, the Jewish Immigrants' Information Bureau was engaged in a losing battle with the United States government.

In October 1913, a delegation from the U.S. Immigration Bureau had visited Europe to prepare a report for the federal government. Dr. Jochelmann was among those who had greeted them and had tried to imbue them with a sympathetic attitude toward immigration.[11] The official report, issued five months later, had a profound effect on matters of immigration.

The report of the commissioner general of Immigration for 1913 served formal notice that a stricter interpretation of the laws would be applied during 1914. One paragraph, for example, stated as follows:

> Attention has been directed in previous reports to a misapprehension regarding one provision of the law that relates to physically defective aliens. There seems to be a somewhat common impression that an alien suffering from a physical defect can not be excluded from the country unless there is evidence indicating that he is likely to become a public charge. Those who hold this view overlook the fact that the

act of 1907 contained a new excluded class, described therein as persons who are found to be, and are certified by the examining surgeon as being, mentally or physically defective to an extent that interferes with their earning a livelihood.

As the JIIB's expert on immigration law, Max J. Kohler was called upon to analyze the commissioner general's report. He concluded that the department was "now committed to the view that such persons are excludable, though not likely to become public charges." In fact, Kohler wrote, "the Commissioner General's report phrases the departmental construction in more limited manner than his rulings in particular cases require. We have been afraid of this particular phraseology . . . We cannot help having such exclusions take place, and the ITO ought to be promptly advised thereof."[12] Like Kohler, Bressler too realized that "there is nothing that we can do at this time to influence a more favorable attitude on the part of the authorities."[13] In general, the other members of the Galveston Committee shared the same pessimistic outlook.

Aside from the hernia problem, which provided the principal grounds for deportation, the immigrant parties of 1914 had their share of tragic and otherwise unfortunate cases. The January ship carried a woman who was to have met her husband in Galveston. During the voyage, however, the woman became insane and was removed when the ship reached Philadelphia. She died in a hospital. The February party contained one man who was feeble-minded and two who were homosexuals. All three were deported.[14]

An additional three immigrants were excluded in March 1914, for reasons other than hernia. According to Epstein, "the general appearance of the [March] arrivals was very favorable and made a very good impression even on the Immigration authorities, bringing forth comment." Nevertheless, Epstein continued,

the number of those afflicted with hernia was far in excess of what we had been receiving in the past few months. In fact, Mr. Hampton dubbed this boat a "hernia boat". It is practically impossible, unless the attendant circumstances are exceptional, to get a hernia case by. I have great confidence in Dr. Bahrenburg. I do not think he is unduly severe, for he is a man who, aside from devotion to his duty, is moved by fine impulses. If the exclusions at this port are, in proportion, greater than what they are in other ports, I should say that this as a general proposition is due to the fact that because of the smaller immigration here examinations are more thorough, leaving out of account that in porportion to the size of immigration here, we may, perhaps, be receiving more afflicted cases than arrive elsewhere. The causes for which our people have been deported are not such as to raise any doubt as to the correctness of the diagnosis.[15]

In practical terms, it did not much matter whether or not the physicians were correct in their diagnoses. Whenever deportation judgments were appealed in Washington, the Department of Labor invariably denied the appeal. Even when a majority of the Board of Special Inquiry ruled that a Jewish immigrant be admitted to Galveston, as they did in April 1914, the department sustained the appeal of the dissenting member of the board and ordered the deportation of the immigrant.[16] It became apparent to the members of the Galveston Committee that they were fighting a losing battle, and they began to give serious thought to the possibility of ending the Galveston Movement.

The Galveston Movement was never meant to exist indefinitely. From its very inception, the Jewish Immigrants' Information Bureau was viewed as an organization with limited goals, which would one day outlive its usefulness. In October 1906, when Schiff first proposed to set aside $500,000 for the founding of the Galveston Movement, he wrote to Zangwill: "Half a million dollars should suffice to place from twenty thousand to twenty-five thousand people in the American 'Hinterland', and, I believe, with the successful settlement of such a number, others would readily follow of their own accord."[17] This was a goal which Zangwill re-endorsed in 1908.[18] In another letter to Zangwill written in August 1909, Schiff reaffirmed this numerical goal:

I impressed upon the [Galveston] Committee and upon Dr. [Henry] Cohen, that unless we could properly distribute and place at least an average of two hundred a month or two thousand-five hundred a year, so that within a decade we shall have, through the placement of twenty-five thousand, laid the seed for the natural inflow of a much larger Russian-Jewish population west of the Mississippi, I should not consider the movement a success.[19]

Three years later, in December 1912, Schiff sent Zangwill yet another letter in which he reasserted once again the temporary nature of the Galveston Movement:

We here are all convinced, and this is now confirmed by Dr. Jochelmann and Mr. Bressler, that the Galveston Movement has already made its impress, and had its effect in many directions, and if it can be continued in an increased volume for the next two or three years, the Galveston route will be firmly established and take care of itself, without the aid and stimulation which you and we are now giving it.[20]

In 1913, about three thousand Jewish immigrants arrived in Galveston, thus more than fulfilling Schiff's numerical criterion for success (a yearly minimum of two thousand-five hundred). During the first three months of 1914, however, the average number of arrivals dropped to 162 per month (compared to an average of 217 for the corresponding months of the preceding year). As the rate of Jewish immigration to Galveston decreased, moreover, the rate of deportations increased. During the fiscal year ending June 30, 1913, when the rate of exclusions and deportations of Jewish immigrants from all ports was 1.21 percent, from Galveston it was 2.75 percent. For the calendar year 1913, the rate of Jewish exclusion from Galveston was as high as 4.99 percent, and during the first quarter of 1914 it rose to 5.87 percent.[21]

In November 1913, the ITO was prepared to continue sponsoring the European end of the Galveston Movement for at least another year, perhaps longer.[22] At the same time, however, Dr. Jochelmann warned:

> If the conditions in Galveston remain as they are now, i.e., if the deportation of *the selected* emigrants from Galveston continues, . . . the efforts to deviate the stream of emigration towards Galveston will, during the few years which are left for our work, be of little avail.[23]

Four months later, Jochelmann was even more pessimistic, writing, on March 16, 1914:

> Unless the amazing and wholly unjustified conduct of the Immigration officials at Galveston gives place to a fairer and more tolerant enforcement of the law, the "movement" must fail of its purpose . . . Among the emigrant population itself, the harsh treatment at Galveston has become a by-word, so that now, in describing a particularly inquisitorial proceeding, one often hears, "they examine just like at Galveston."[24]

On Thursday, April 9, 1914, at 5:15 P.M., having been advised that "a matter of much importance" was to be presented, the members of the Galveston Committee assembled at 965 Fifth Avenue, home of the chairman, Jacob H. Schiff.[25] In his opening statement, Schiff stated the purpose of the meeting: to discuss the advisability of bringing the Galveston Movement to an end. In the ensuing discussion, the committee members recognized that their original goal in establishing the Galveston Movement, "the deflection of the stream of Jewish immigration from the northern seaports to the territory west of the Mississippi," had not been realized, nor did they expect it to be realized during the foreseeable future.[26]

The committee reviewed the disappointing results of its efforts. Since its inception, the Galveston Movement had handled and distributed between eight thousand and nine thousand men, women, and children during a period when over 564,000 Jewish immigrants had arrived in the United States. After an existence of seven years and an expense of $235,000 on the part of the JIIB, the volume of Jewish immigration to Galveston had not increased appreciably over the period before its formation. At no time had the yearly number of Galveston immigrants reached four per cent of total Jewish immigration to the United States.[27]

Schiff pointed out that there had been two great obstacles to the success of the Movement: the lengthy, tortuous voyage and the harsh restrictionist policy being implemented by United States immigration officials at Galveston. In spite of all attempts to persuade the North German-Lloyd Company or other shipping lines to establish reasonably comfortable service to Galveston, and despite all efforts to induce the United States government to change its harsh policy at that port, these two problems remained and showed no signs of being solved. Because of these two handicaps, Schiff said, the Galveston Movement had failed to deflect Jewish immigration in any appreciable volume.[28]

Despite the limited success of the JIIB, Schiff did not at all regret his efforts on its behalf. He felt that his money had been well spent in support of those immigrants who came and who, in turn, would set an encouraging example for others to follow in their footsteps. The popular "image" of Galveston, however, remained a problem of which Schiff was, perhaps, unaware. The JIIB had long insisted upon a select group of immigrants—young, skilled, able-bodied men who were willing to work at anything, and even on the Sabbath. Advertisement along these lines had served to foster the popular impression that the "Galveston Territory" was a spiritual wasteland which promised little but a hard life. Whatever the reasons, it had become clear by now that the masses would always be attracted to New York and other well-established centers of Jewish life in the United States.

In view of the above, Schiff recommended that the Jewish Immigrants' Information Bureau discontinue its activities after the month of September 1914. Until the end of the year, however, the JIIB would continue to provide one-half the railroad fare for the wives and children of removals who had arrived previous to the month of June. Since Schiff was the founder and sole financial backer of the JIIB, his opinions obviously carried great weight in the deliberations of its executive committee. As usual, the minutes of this meeting of April 9, 1914, show no record of dissension, and the motion was carried unanimously.[29] In a letter to Rabbi Cohen, informing him of the decision, Bressler wrote:

> Personally, I had hoped that we could hold out a little longer, but I was influenced in this largely by sentiment pure and simple, not because I dissented in any way from the judgment and opinion of the other members of the Committee.[30]

In separate letters, Schiff and Bressler informed Zangwill of the Galveston Committee's decision to close the Jewish Immigrants' Information Bureau.[31] To Schiff's surprise, Zangwill did "not take the Galveston liquidation proposition at all tragically."[32] Perhaps Zangwill even felt a bit relieved that the Galveston Movement was being abandoned at a time when the ITO was running out of funds to finance its European organization. In a letter to Bressler, however, Zangwill gave the following reason for his good cheer:

> As I have written to Mr. Schiff, I do not consider it at all a failure to have opened up a new port for Jewish immigration. The Reverend Henry Cohen has just written to me that of 7,419 arrivals at Galveston in 1913, no less than 3,003 were Jewish. I imagine this compared favorably with the Jewish immigration into Boston. I am of opinion, therefore, that for the public, announcement should be made that after the dispatch of the hundredth Party, we consider the stream of emigration can find its way via Galveston without further guidance.[33]

Bressler welcomed Zangwill's suggestion. The hundredth immigrant party, which would bring the number of arrivals up to about ten thousand, was expected anyway, around September 1914. By announcing that its goal would be reached with the arrival of the hundredth party, the JIIB would be able to close its doors with a feeling of satisfaction, rather than one of frustration. Bresler recommended to Schiff that he adopt Zangwill's suggestion and that no mention be made in the press release of the United States government's negative attitude.[34] While Schiff was happy to emphasize the positive accomplishments of his pet project, however, he did not wish to exonerate those who, he felt, were primarily responsible for its demise. Schiff insisted that any statement to be issued must strongly criticize the part that the government had played in bringing about the end of the Galveston Movement.[35]

Together with Galveston Committee members Cyrus L. Sulzberger and Reuben Arkush, Bressler was responsible for preparing the press release. Bressler promised Zangwill that he would send him a draft notice of the statement before releasing it to the press.[36] Sulzberger, however, who was chairman of the three-man subcommittee, prepared a statement of his own and, after showing it to Schiff, had it published in the May 29 issue of the *American Hebrew*.[37] Zangwill was characteristically insulted that he had not been consulted, but he accepted Bressler's explanation of the incident. Nevertheless, he wrote, "what is done cannot be undone. I see that our Zionist friend, Dr. Katznelsohn [*sic*], has already raised the cry of failure."[38] (This was a reference to Nissan Katzenelsohn, a leading Russian Zionist who was, at the time chairman of the committee for Jewish emigration in Lebau.)

Bressler replied:

> I do not particularly care what cry Dr. Katzenelsohn or anyone else raises about the Galveston movement. The word failure is as much associated with Galveston as common sense with a mad-house . . . I, for one, feel that we have virtually carried out what we started out to do—despite tremendous odds and obstacles. Others to the contrary notwithstanding, I deem the Galveston results the largest single contribution in the history of pioneer and constructive human endeavor. I say it fearlessly because I feel it and believe it. My only regret is that it should even appear necessary to take the defensive. But the day of "knockers" inspired by one motive or another, is, unfortunately, not gone.[39]

Zangwill was so impressed with Bressler's reply that he had it translated into German, in order that it be read at an international conference on Jewish emigration, sponsored by the Jewish Territorial Organization, which was to take place in Zurich during the first week of September.[40] Bressler felt that the proposed conference was unnecessary and might even be accompanied by some danger for European immigration into the United States (an opinion with which, incidentally, the Jewish Colonization Association agreed).[41] Nevertheless, he sent Zangwill a copy of his article entitled "The Results and Significance of the Galveston Movement," which appeared in *The Jewish Comment* on July 31, 1914, with permission that it be read at the conference.[42] Schiff, too, sent Zangwill an article on the Galveston Movement, which he had written for the

June 1914 edition of *Jewish Charities*, with the intention that it also be included among the "obituary notices" to be read at the conference.[43] A resumé by Henry Berman, which appeared in the *American Hebrew* on June 19 was also placed on the agenda of the conference.[44] Dr. Jochelmann planned to address the conference in person, and for that purpose prepared a special report summing up the work of the Galveston Movement. The conference was scheduled to end with a Saturday night banquet "in honor of Dr. Jochelmann and the Jewish Emigration Society of Kiev to celebrate the dispatch of the hundredth party of emigrants to Galveston and the successful winding-up of the work."[45] With the outbreak of World War I, however, neither the conference nor the banquet ever took place.[46]

The main reason that the Galveston Committee meeting on April 9, 1914, had decided to cease operations was that it had not been able to prevent the increased deportation of its immigrants. Ironically, once the decision was made to end the Galveston Movement, the efforts of the JIIB to prevent deportations began to show successful results. Of the fifty-two immigrants who arrived on April 29,[47] seven were excluded by the United States immigration authorities. Of these, two were admitted after detention.[48] Another two, who were excluded by the Board of Special Inquiry, were admitted by the Labor Department in Washington on an appeal made by Maurice Epstein.[49] Thus, only three immigrants were actually deported.[50] In May, another fifty-three immigrants arrived. This time, Bressler wrote to Schiff, "It gives me pleasure to advise you that there were no deportations from this boat."[51]

On June 6, 211 Jewish immigrants arrived in Galveston, of whom eighteen were held for further inspection by the Board of Special Inquiry. One of those who was not passed by the Board, due to the detection of a double inguinal hernia, was a 21-year-old carpenter who was accompanied by his wife. Epstein managed to have the young couple admitted under bond, on appeal to Washington. Another detainee, a 50-year-old tailor who arrived with a wife and two children, was certified for senility, a diagnosis which Epstein found to be completely untrue, causing him to appeal the case. In his appeal of this case, Epstein was helped by the fact that Inspector in Charge Alfred Hampton had been transferred from Galveston to New Orleans. Hampton's replacement as Acting Inspector in Charge, a Mr. Barkman, was a sympathetic man and personally recommended that the family of four be admitted, which they were. Eleven other immigrants were also admitted upon appeal of their cases. In the end, out of the 211 immigrants who had arrived, only one was actually deported.[52]

In his report on the June arrivals, Epstein wrote:

The news of the intended dissolution of the Bureau came as a surprise to the Galveston community. There is everywhere a sincere feeling of regret, while in some influential quarters the opinion has been expressed that our action was hasty, and that our differences with the Immigration authorities might have been adjusted.[53]

In making this statement, of course, Epstein had the benefit of hindsight. It is also possible that the Immigration authorities decided to be lenient with the last few immigrant parties, once they knew that no new batches would be coming after September.

The JIIB had announced that until the end of 1914 it would continue to provide one-half the railroad fare, from Galveston to the ultimate points of destination, for the wives and children of ITO immigrants who had arrived before June. Predictably, ships scheduled to arrive in June and the months following contained higher proportions of reunion cases than had previous ships. These families, of course, wished to take advantage of the JIIB's commitment before it would expire. Of the 211 Jewish immigrants who arrived in Galveston on June 6, fifty were joining the rest of their families. On July 6, 183 immigrants arrived, of which seventy were cases of family reunion.[54] On July 23, fifty-six Jewish immigrants arrived in Galveston, nineteen of whom were reuniting with previous ITO immigrants. The remaining thirty-seven were not sent by the ITO; they were people who had decided, on their own, to come to Galveston.[55] These were the last Jewish immigrants to arrive directly at Galveston on board a vessel of the North German-Lloyd Shipping Company.

On August 5, 1914, the North German-Lloyd's S.S. *Brandenburg* arrived in Philadelphia, with Galveston as its ultimate destination. Since, by this time, war had broken out in Europe, the ship deposited all of its passengers at Philadelphia, including 179 Jewish immigrants, and then headed back to Germany.[56] Most of these immigrants were sent to New York, where they boarded an American ship bound for Galveston. The fifty-nine cases of family reunion on board, however, included some who were destined for states far removed from Texas. These were sent by railroad directly from Philadelphia to their points of ultimate destination.[57] Three families who were threatened with deportation were admitted on bond, due to the war, and were shipped to Galveston at the end of August.[58] These were the last to be distributed by the Jewish Immigrants' Information Bureau.[59]

No sooner had the end of the Galveston Movement been announced than talk of its revival was begun. Dr. Paul Nathan of the *Hilfsverein der deutschen Juden* suggested that the ICA might be able to take over the recruitment process previously handled by the ITO. Dr. Nathan wrote that the *Hilfsverein* and the ICA worked far more discreetly than did the ITO, which had been anxious to capitalize on the publicity of its only successful venture. Perhaps a quieter approach would not antagonize the United States government, and thus accomplish more to further the aims of the Movement.[60] Bressler agreed with Nathan's proposal that the ICA be asked to take over the European recruitment campaign. He proposed, furthermore, that the Industrial Removal Office (which was sponsored by the ICA) quietly take over from the JIIB the problem of placement, by sending a permanent representative to Galveston who might have more success in reaching an understanding with the immigration officials.[61] Schiff made it clear, however, that he did not wish to be associated with the ideas put forward by Nathan and Bressler. Schiff wrote:

> If I did address the ICA, suggesting that its allowance to the Removal Office be increased to enable the latter to take care of any immigrants that might hereafter come into Galveston, the ICA Trustees would naturally come under the impression that the discontinuance of our Galveston work here was brought about largely for the purpose of shoving it upon the ICA.[62]

Nathan, Bressler, and Zangwill felt that the distribution work should continue in one form or another, particularly at a time when war might create an unprecedented number of refugees.[63] It was at this time, too, that the Panama Canal was opened, which promised to bring fresh economic opportunities to the Pacific states. They speculated that bureaus similar to the JIIB could be established in various port cities of the West Coast.[64]

Schiff, too, hoped that the opening of the Panama Canal would bring more Jewish immigrants to the West.[65] He did not preclude the possibility that some day, after the conclusion of the war, a project similar to the Galveston Movement might be resumed under a somewhat different, perhaps more ambitious arrangement.[66] In 1915, Schiff asked Cyrus L. Sulzberger to head up a committee which would plan such a project.[67] The World War, however, lasted

longer than anyone expected. Afterward, the idea of a second
Galveston Movement seems to have lost its appeal. Schiff's death
in October 1920 was mourned by Jews throughout the world, who
recalled the many acts of generosity that he had performed during
his lifetime. This prompted Zangwill to write:

> It is characteristic that the only constructive idea my dear friend Schiff
> ever had—Galveston—is the only one generally ignored . . . I fear
> the death of Mr. Schiff will not make the resumption of the Galveston
> work any easier.[68]

Indeed, the Galveston Movement was never resumed.

Bereft of a practical reason for its existence, the Jewish Territorial
Organization fell into disuse. After 1917, when the British government issued the Balfour Declaration, favoring the establishment
of a Jewish homeland in Palestine, the ITO lost even its theoretical
reason for existence. It was finally disbanded in 1925, followed by
Zangwill's death less than a year later.

In 1913, Dr. David S. Jochelmann had suffered a heart attack
during a visit to England, and he had been prevailed upon, by
Zangwill, to remain in that country. During the First World War
and its aftermath, Jochelman—he now spelled his name with one
"n"—threw himself selflessly into the effort to relieve the suffering
of Jews in Eastern Europe, founding several organizations for that
purpose. Despite his serious heart condition, he lived an active,
full life, serving as chairman of the Federation of Jewish Relief
Organizations up until the time of his death in 1941, at age seventy-
one.[69]

As a result of the drastic reduction in immigration, due to the
War, David M. Bressler resigned as manager of the Industrial
Removal Office in 1916. He continued to work wholeheartedly for
the relief of European Jewry, joining the newly-founded American
Jewish Joint Distribution Committee during World War I and
playing an important role in that organization. In 1917–1918, the
successful campaign of the "Joint" to raise an unprecedented $25
million for Jewish war sufferers was directed by Jacob Billikopf of
Kansas City. In 1919, Billikopf moved to Philadelphia to become
executive director of that city's Federation of Jewish Charities.
Morris D. Waldman, who had left Galveston in 1908 to become
managing director of the United Hebrew Charities in New York,
served in that position until 1917. Subsequently, he, too, took an
active part in the "Joint", organizing relief in the war-torn Jewish

communities of Europe in 1921 and 1922. Returning to America, Waldman traveled widely, throughout the country, setting up federations of Jewish Charity all over the United States. Eventually, he became executive secretary of the American Jewish Committee.[70]

Jochelman in England, and Bressler, Billikopf, and Waldman in the United States, were among the leading Jewish social workers of the time. The valuable experience they gained in working with the Galveston immigrants was eventually seen as an asset to their later careers.

Among all the participants in the project, one man remained inseparably identified with Galveston—Henry Cohen. Long after Galveston lost much of its importance as a port and as a city, Rabbi Cohen continued to serve faithfully as spiritual leader of Congregation B'nai Israel. When he died in 1952, he had occupied the same pulpit for sixty-four years, probably longer than any other rabbi in the United States. During his many years of service, Dr. Cohen played a distinctly prominent part in a large variety of public activities and worthwhile causes. With a special element of satisfaction, he often fondly recalled his participation in the project which brought ten thousand Jews to the port of Galveston during the years 1907–1914.[71]

As for the immigrants themselves, spread out as they were throughout the United States, they soon became indistinguishable from those who had arrived through other ports. Thus, with the passing of time, the Galveston Movement receded into the margins of history.

Retrospective

In establishing the Galveston Movement, Jacob H. Schiff had expressed the hope that he might outflank the maneuvers of those advocating legislation to restrict immigration. If Congress saw that immigrants were settling in sparsely populated parts of the country where they were most needed, Schiff reasoned, it would continue to maintain the traditionally liberal American immigration policy. Taken by itself, however, the Galveston Movement seems to have been a negligible factor in the fight against the restrictionists. Even if the Galveston Movement had actually succeeded in deflecting a significant number of Jewish immigrants from the Northeast, it is still highly doubtful that this would have prevented the almost inevitable enactment of restrictionist legislation. Furthermore, by its actions in deporting Jewish immigrants from Galveston, the government showed that it was not entirely in sympathy with the Movement. Ironically, if the project had actually succeeded in bringing more Jews to the West, it might even have served to promote restrictionist sentiment in that area of the country. Realistically, though, it could have made little difference either way, for the Galveston Movement was actually too small to have had a major impact on American public opinion.

In spite of this, the Galveston Movement did make an important, if indirect, contribution to the fight against immigration restriction, and to other Jewish causes, as well, by evoking a new, militant political approach on the part of the American Jewish leadership. During the deportation crisis of 1910, Schiff carefully escalated his attacks on the Taft Administration, culminating in a stormy confrontation with Secretary of Commerce and Labor Charles Nagel at a meeting in December of that year (as mentioned in chapter 5). Schiff's behavior at that meeting may have shocked his colleagues at the time, but they soon recognized the favorable results which it produced. Immediately afterward, the leaders of American Jewry adopted Schiff's sophisticated approach to political pressure. In this sense, the Galveston Movement has been seen as a "prelude" to the American Jewish Committee's successful crusade for abrogation of the American commercial treaty with Russia. With Schiff setting the pace, the committee began its aggressive campaign in January 1911, appealing to congressmen and other politicians, as well as directly to President Taft himself.[1] When Taft refused to support abrogation, Schiff further shocked his colleagues by personally expressing his anger to the president, in no uncertain terms.[2] The aggressive campaign for abrogation was eventually rewarded with success, thus encouraging the leaders of American Jewry to employ similar techniques in their pursuit of a liberal immigration policy.

Through their general lobbying efforts, Schiff and his colleagues in the American Jewish Committee helped to delay restrictionist legislation for several years. In 1917, over the veto of President Wilson, Congress finally passed a literacy test requirement for immigrants, although its effect on Jews was minimized by its specification of Hebrew and Yiddish as recognized languages and by its exemption of immigrants avoiding religious persecution. In 1921, a year after Schiff's death, the Johnson Bill was passed, severely restricting the number of admissible aliens on the basis of a temporary quota. Three years later, the quota system was made permanent—and much stricter—by the passage of the Johnson-Reed Bill. The 1924 measure limited immigration to no more than 2 percent of national groups who had been living in the United States in 1890, nationality to be determined by place of birth. This effectively brought to an end the era of mass Eastern and Southern European immigration to America.

The scheme to direct significant numbers of Jewish immigrants to the Western states through the port of Galveston ultimately failed. The length of the voyage and the poor travel conditions on the competition-free Bremen-to-Galveston route discouraged potential candidates. Also, the hostility of the Russian government toward the Jewish Territorial Organization hindered recruitment campaigns. Furthermore, periodic slumps in the economies of various Western states, beginning with the nationwide depression of 1907–1909, made placement of the immigrants a tricky business.

The Jewish Immigrants' Information Bureau would sometimes call for a certain number of immigrants from Russia only to discover, upon receiving these immigrants, that it had difficulty providing them with suitable jobs, due to a worsening of industrial conditions. For its part, the ITO often found it difficult to supply precisely the types and number of immigrants called for from time to time. Mutual recriminations between the ITO and the JIIB missed the point that in those unstable conditions complete coordination between supplier and receiver of immigrants was quite impossible. Finally, the deportation actions taken by the United States government against the protégés of the Galveston Movement cast a dark shadow upon the entire project.

Each of the problems mentioned above contributed toward the failure of the Galveston Movement in its attempt to settle large numbers of Jewish immigrants throughout the American West. Some of these obstacles might have been surmounted had the Galveston Movement succeeded, somehow, in capturing the imagination of the Jewish people as a fundamental solution to their problems. While Zangwill and Schiff scoffed at Zionism as being completely impracticable, at least the Land of Israel, unlike Galveston, satisfied a religious and national yearning for fulfillment among the Jewish people. Even the ideal of Zion, however, was not enough to attract the great masses of displaced Jews. The breathtaking image of the Statue of Liberty, lighting the way to America's most exciting metropolis, remained the main symbol of attraction for hundreds of thousands of Jewish immigrants.

The incentive of the Galveston alternative was that it offered a reasonably promising financial future to immigrants who were willing and able to work hard. The route to Ellis Island, however, seemed to offer about the same possibility. In addition, apart from its general attraction, New York offered Jews from Eastern Europe a full spectrum of religious and cultural life—Jewish educational centers and institutions, kosher food, Yiddish newspapers and theaters, and a wide choice of synagogues and benevolent societies (landsmanschaften) composed of members originating in the same cities and towns from which the immigrants came. The streets of the ghettos of New York and several other large cities in the East veritably pulsated with Jewish life. Out West, only Chicago, purposely excluded from the Galveston Movement, offered a ghetto environment on a comparable scale. It is no wonder that many disillusioned Galveston immigrants ended up in Chicago.

Certain other Western cities offered some of the above mani-
festations of ghetto life, though, of course, on a much smaller
scale. However, the Galveston Movement had no capability of
competing with the great Eastern ghettos, nor did it desire to do
so. By discouraging the participation of Sabbath observers, religious
functionaries, and spiritual leaders in his immigration plan, Schiff
demonstrated that he did not primarily concern himself here with
the creation of healthy, viable Jewish communities. Rather, the
immigrants were expected, somehow, to adjust themselves to the
possibility of their being forced to lead an unfamiliar style of life.
Most Jewish immigrants saw no reason to make this adjustment,
when it was more natural to become caught up in the mainstream
of immigration, which led to Ellis Island.

Thus, New York remained the "real America" for the great
masses of Jewish immigrants. In a way, America without New York
seemed to be like Zionism without Zion—a movement robbed of
its main center of attraction. Besides all this, the prospective Jewish
immigrant most likely had relatives or acquaintances living in the
Eastern cities—especially in New York, which was, already then,
the city with the world's largest Jewish population. His preference
for the East, therefore, was a natural one, and it rendered him
quite impervious to the propaganda of the Galveston Movement.

Of those Jewish immigrants who did join the Galveston Movement, many, like Leib Haft and Nathan Kaluzny, eventually drifted
eastward, almost instinctively. While Haft (mentioned in chapter
7) had generally neglected Jewish ritual observances during his
years in the West, he assumed religious as well as familial responsibilities after finally settling down in Wilkes-Barre, Pennsylvania.
Haft served on his synagogue's board of trustees and board of
education and hardly missed a Sabbath at services. He and his wife
succeeded in passing on a strong feeling of Jewish identity to their
children, both of whom, as adults, also became trustees of their
respective synagogues, actively involving themselves in Jewish affairs. They remained in the East.[3]

Nathan Kaluzny's decision to leave Galveston for New York (as
mentioned at the end of chapter 5) was unfortunate. For a while,
he worked as a night watchman, but he was unemployed more
often than not. Kaluzny spent many nights sleeping in Central Park,
covering his face with a newspaper. Sometimes, a policeman would
come by and tap his feet with a nightstick to wake him up. Kaluzny
would then shuffle off to another bench and go back to sleep.
After about two years of this life, Kaluzny received a letter from

a cousin in Detroit, telling him of the growing opportunities available in that city. Arriving in Detroit, Kaluzny decided to try his hand at peddling from a horse-drawn wagon. (He preferred to think of himself as a "teamster".) After about half a year in Detroit, Kaluzny finally sent for his wife and three children, who, fortunately, managed to embark for New York just before the outbreak of the First World War. Kaluzny remained with his family in Detroit and led a successful life there, but he always retained fond memories of Galveston.

Kaluzny began peddling fruit, then junk, and eventually found his way into the scrap iron business. His activities often took him to the wealthier sections of town, where his honest business methods were appreciated by his mostly non-Jewish customers, who fondly called him "Nate." By the late nineteen-twenties, the Kaluznys owned a four-family house in the suburbs and had ten thousand dollars in the bank. Then came the Great Depression and Kaluzny lost everything he owned. He and his family left the suburbs and moved back to the city. His wife, Dobruschka, an excellent cook, went to work preparing food for catered weddings. She died in 1965. "Nate" worked full-time until he was seventy-five years old. He never regained his wealth, but his good health remained with him. He died in 1971 at the age of ninety.

The Kaluznys spoke Yiddish. "Nate" was proud of the fact that, despite the hard times through which he passed, he never worked on the Sabbath and always remained faithful to Orthodox Jewish practices. Yet, as with other first-generation American Jews, he found it hard to pass on his values intact to the second generation. Of his eight children and fifteen grandchildren, some wandered far from the path of strict Jewish observance. When one of his daughters was widowed at a young age and left alone with an infant son, Kaluzny and his wife took in their daughter's baby and raised him to manhood, instilling in him a special reverence for the immigrant generation. The grandson, Robert Rockaway, went on to write a doctoral dissertation on the history of the Jews of Detroit, later published as a book. Rockaway eventually moved to Israel, where he secured a position at Tel Aviv University as a professor specializing in American Jewish history. By his own account, Rockaway's strong identity with the Jewish people was definitely instilled in him by his grandparents. Thus it transpired that a man who emigrated from Russia to America as part of a movement which had abandoned Zionist aspirations as hopeless, eventually inspired his grandson to lecture on Jewish history in the modern State of Israel.[4]

While many gravitated eastward, most of the Galveston immigrants remained west of the Mississippi, though not necessarily in the cities and towns to which they were originally sent. Sarah and Charles Hoffman and the three sons who were born to them remained in Central Texas (as mentioned at the end of chapter 8). Charles Hoffman bought a partnership in a Fort Worth food store, which stocked a wide variety of fruits, vegetables, and groceries. Unfortunately, despite its initial success, the business failed in 1922. Balancing their disappointment in business, however, was a joyful, long-awaited reunion which took place during that same year. As a result of the First World War, the Bolshevik Revolution, and the subsequent civil unrest in Russia, Sarah and her father had lost contact with their family there. It was not until 1921 that contact was reestablished through a small notice in a New York Yiddish newspaper which was placed by Sarah's mother and seen by a family member living in New York. Finally, in September 1922, Sarah's mother arrived in New York with her two surviving children, two others having died in Russia. After meeting with relatives in New York, they boarded a train bound for Texas, to be reunited as a family after eleven years.

In 1924 the Hoffmans moved to Comanche, where they opened a dry goods store. The Novits and other relatives and friends settled in various towns of central Texas such as Gatesville, Hamilton, Brownwood, Stephensville, and Dublin, where they remained as small Jewish minorities among the general population. To counter any feelings of isolation that they may have had, they developed the custom of celebrating the Jewish holidays together, taking turns playing host. This custom continued throughout the nineteen-twenties and thirties. Eventually, due to ill health, Charles Hoffman closed down the business. He and his wife moved to Austin where all three of their boys attended law school at the University of Texas.

Charles Hoffman died in 1945, but Sarah lived on to a ripe old age. In celebration of her eighty-fifth birthday in 1979, Sarah's grandson David, living in Austin, wrote a fascinating account of the family, based mainly on conversations he had with his grandmother. David's brother, and his grandfather's namesake, Charles Hoffman, moved to Israel and became a reporter for the *Jerusalem Post*.[5]

It would, perhaps, be intriguing to discover if the immigrants who participated in the Galveston Movement—and who remained in the West—were especially conscious of their Jewish heritage or whether, to the contrary, they had pronounced tendencies toward assimilation into American society as a whole. There is no evidence, however, to indicate that either was the case. Their Jewish or assimilationist tendencies, like their religious or secularist preferences, depended upon their individual personalities and backgrounds, upon sociological trends, and upon the particular communities in which they found themselves, rather than upon the curious fact that they had entered the United States through the port of Galveston, Texas. After they adjusted to life in these Western communities, the fact of their initial arrival in Galveston did not distinguish them in any way from other Jews from Eastern Europe, who had arrived and had, perhaps, tarried, in the Eastern port cities of America, before going West.

It would be wrong to assume automatically that the American West was a breeding ground for assimilation. Often, the opposite was true. Some of the Western cities developed remarkably active Jewish communities. Perhaps because of their very isolation, these first-generation Westerners from Eastern Europe often banded together more tightly, hungrily biting at every morsel of Jewish culture which came their way. If the "indigenous" had helped the indigent by welcoming their Yiddish-speaking coreligionists and finding them places of employment, the latter more than returned the favor by breathing new life into American Judaism.

During the third quarter of the twentieth century, many Jewish communities throughout the West marked a hundred years since the founding of these communities, usually by Jews from Germany and Central Europe. The Jews of Sioux City, Iowa, celebrated their centennial in 1969 by issuing a book telling the history of their community.[6] Significantly, although Sioux City received Jews from Galveston, on and off, between 1907 and 1914, not a word is mentioned of that fact in this otherwise informative book. Although the Galveston Movement must have aroused some interest there during the years in which it operated, this interest has long since passed into oblivion. A retrospective look, however, will point up an important development. By directing Jews from Eastern Europe to Sioux City, the Galveston Movement inadvertently participated in the building of a new type of Jewish community, which replaced the old one. This development had hardly been foreseen by the established Jews of the city.

Joseph Rauch, a Reform rabbi who served the community from 1905 to 1912, supervised the greeting of Galveston immigrants in Sioux City.[7] Rabbi Rauch was a moderate, having abolished some of the more radical reforms which had characterized his temple, such as the lack of a Torah scroll and the holding of weekly Sabbath services on Sundays. Rabbi Rauch's mild measures of counter-reformation, however, were insufficient to attract the growing numbers of Eastern European Jews, if that was at all his intention. By 1909, there were four Orthodox synagogues, including one which followed the Chassidic ritual.[8]

Sixty years later, an immigrant who arrived in 1910 was to recall:

> Jewish life among the immigrants was entirely different from today. They were far more religious and more observant of the laws of Kashruth. There was as many as four Jewish butcher shops in Sioux City, three of them located on West Seventh Street and one located on Court Street. Every block had several grocery stores, and there was a Jewish newspaper in every home.*
>
> The business section of West Seventh Street comprised such Jewish tradesmen as mechanics, electricians, plumbers, painters, carpenters, blacksmiths, tailors, harness-makers, bakers and builders.
>
> I can remember as many as a hundred Jewish merchants peddling their wares on the West Side, using horse and wagon, selling fruits and vegetables, fish, delivering milk from door to door and delivering bread.
>
> Yiddish stage shows and concerts came to Sioux City to be enjoyed by young and old.[9]

As in the ghettos of the East, the new arrivals established their own fraternal and benevolent associations in Sioux City, including a local branch of the Jewish Workmen's Circle (*Yiddisher Arbeiter Ring*), an organization which was frowned upon by the Jewish Establishment. Rauch's successor as spiritual leader of the Reform temple, Rabbi Emanuel Sternheim, dubbed the Workmen's Circle "an insurance organization of radical tendency." Its local secretary, in 1915, was Abraham Koval, who had arrived five years earlier as an immigrant at the port of Galveston.[10]

According to a study by Oscar Littlefield which comprises a chapter of the centennial history,[11] the first Jewish settlers of Sioux City had mixed freely with the Unitarians, and had practically merged with them before the coming of the Eastern European Jews in the late nineteenth century. Littlefield speculates that the Sioux City Jewish community would probably have faded into

* Two Yiddish newspapers catering to the Midwest were published in Chicago— *The Jewish Daily Courier* and the Chicago edition of the *Jewish Daily Forward.*

extinction, as did many small Jewish communities in the West and South, had it not been for the influx of Jews from Eastern Europe. Speculations aside, Littlefield offers the following impressions of Jewish life in Sioux City at the turn of the century:

The Eastern European migration swelled the Jewish community from a few hundred souls in 1890 to nearly 2,500 during World War I. It was this migration that gave the community its substance, its distinctive character, that produced its leaders and built its Jewish institutions. The German-Jewish pioneers who came first contributed mightily to the prosperity and growth of the city, but it was the second migration of east Europeans who molded Sioux City Jewry into what it is today.

. . . The east Europeans with very few exceptions arrived dirt poor. They went to work as packing-house laborers, as cobblers, tailors, blacksmiths, farm workers. A large number, however, soon became fruit and vegetable hucksters and peddlers of merchandise, who in time became grocers and general-storekeepers. Many moved into the small towns and villages of Western Iowa, South Dakota and Nebraska, but they considered Sioux City their home, because it was there they went to buy merchandise and there they went for synagogue, Jewish food and communal life.

It is not easy for one who has not lived through it and witnessed it personally, to recreate the feel and the essence of a community and a historic period, out of a few news items, some old pictures and a few fragmentary records. It does appear, however, that the Jewish community built by these first-generation immigrants, in its range and variety, in its intense *Yiddishkeit*, compares favorably with the Jewish culture of large cities in that pre-war period. In historic retrospect, the numbers who read the Yiddish dailies, who bought and read books by Yiddish authors, who patronized the touring Yiddish theater, who went to *Shul* [synagogue] mornings and evenings, who attended Zionist and labor-socialist meetings, who formed Jewish literary clubs, who contributed to Yeshivahs [rabbinical academies], orphanages and homes for aged in Jerusalem, suggest an infinitely richer and more varied Jewish cultural life than anything witnessed today . . .

. . . It was by no means a homogeneous community. The Sioux City immigrant generation included Chassidim, Yeshiva-trained scholars, free thinkers, labor Zionists, Marxists, atheists, scoffers, some who embraced Reform. Sioux City had considerably more varieties and shades of opinion and ideology in 1919 than it has in 1969.[12]

Sioux City's Conservative congregation was established in 1925. Jacob Kuntz, one of its most devoted members, was a Galveston immigrant. Kuntz had originally settled in Omaha, Nebraska. After living there for a while, he heard about someone opening up a jewelry store in Sioux City and went there to join him. Kuntz remained in Sioux City, where he served on his synagogue's board of directors. His two sons, both of whom became physicians, eventually moved to Los Angeles.[13]

The Jews of Colorado, who celebrated their centennial in 1959, retained memories of the arrival of Jewish immigrants from Galveston, associating it with the work of the Industrial Removal Office, which sent Jews from New York. According to records kept in the Denver community, 176 Jewish immigrants arrived in the city during the second half of 1907, including sixty-eight men, forty-two women and sixty-six children. About an equal number arrived during the following year. In 1910, the arrival of ninety-four Jewish immigrants was recorded in Denver, with an additional 235 arriving during the next year. These figures apparently include various Jewish immigrants who were helped by a local committee established for that purpose, not necessarily immigrants who had arrived through Galveston. Besides helping the new arrivals find jobs, the Jewish community of Denver also organized a settlement house in the heart of the immigrant neighborhood. This community center was used by over a thousand people, and was open three nights a week.[14]

As in the big cities of the East Coast, the Jewish immigrants in Denver crowded into their own neighborhood in the West Colfax section of town. In the Denver "ghetto"—inevitably, the term was used—the immigrants established a variety of organizations, representing their various social and political inclinations, and a large number of Orthodox synagogues, some of which were designed to attract people who stemmed from one locality or another in the Old Country. Even Yeshivas, or Hebrew Day Schools, were established, which were considered to be among the best in the West.[15]

The Jewish immigrants in Denver maintained a high level of religious, social, and cultural activity. In addition, Denver's dry and healthful climate—and the Jewish hospitals established there—made the "mile high city" a haven for tubercular-ridden refugees from the more congested ghettos of the East. Removed though they were from the main centers of Jewish population, Denver's Jews succeeded in building an enviable community.

Jewish immigrants from Galveston arrived in the smaller cities of Colorado as well, such as Pueblo and Colorado Springs, where they participated actively in Jewish life. Colorado Springs' first permanent synagogue was built in 1909 by Orthodox Jews, most of them immigrants from Russia, some of whom, it was noted, had arrived through Galveston. A *Mikveh*, or ritual bath, was built into the synagogue's basement, and kosher meat was no problem, since one of the members of the synagogue was a *schochet*, or ritual slaughterer.[16]

Another Colorado town which received Jewish immigrants from Galveston was Cripple Creek, which had been the scene of a gold strike during the last decade of the nineteenth century. By 1907, however, the Cripple Creek district was experiencing a decrease in population, due to a decline in production at the gold mines. After taking stock of the situation, most of the arriving Jewish immigrants joined the general exodus from the area.[17]

The experience at Cripple Creek was not the only example of Jewish immigrants being sent from Galveston to places of declining opportunity. In most such cases, it was not long before the immigrants realized that they must seek greener pastures. If they did not move to the East Coast, or to Chicago, they usually gravitated to larger neighboring cities offering more employment opportunities as well as more sizable Jewish communities. Thus, by the natural order of events, the arrivals from Galveston joined the removals from New York, and contributed their share to the growth of various Jewish centers throughout the West.

Of all the Jewish communities which cooperated with the Jewish Immigrants' Information Bureau by welcoming Jewish immigrants from Galveston on a regular basis, the most celebrated was that of Kansas City, Missouri, which received the most such immigrants, in addition to thousands who arrived there through other routes. The Reform Jews of Kansas City, who marked their temple's centennial in 1970, recalled with pride the part played by their predecessors in welcoming the immigrants to what they liked to refer to as "the most intensely American city in our country." Their active participation in the running of the Jewish Educational Institute, which was set up in the heart of the immigrant neighborhood, was greatly responsible for its reputation as one of the most successful settlement houses in the United States.[18]

Jacob Billikopf, superintendent of the United Jewish Charities, which sponsored the Jewish Educational Institute, apparently considered the running of the institute to be one of his most important tasks. His active cooperation with the Galveston Movement, which was noted with approval by the mayor of Kansas City, expressed a desire to bring more of his fellow Russian Jews to that city and to help them adjust to American life. The institute placed special emphasis on the evening classes, which were well attended, even after a hard day's work, by the struggling immigrants.[19]

191

In 1914–1915, one of the most enthusiastic teachers at the Jewish Educational Institute was twenty-two-year-old Isaac Don Levine, later to become well known as a writer and journalist. Levine had arrived as an immigrant barely three years before, through the Port of Boston. After applying himself assiduously to his studies in a Kansas City high school, he received his diploma and found, to his amazement, that he was now teaching English and other subjects to new immigrants, most of whom had arrived through Galveston. Thrilled at his recent mastery of the English language, Levine committed some of his experiences to writing, including the following anecdote:

> It was a short time ago that we had our first lesson in geography. The map of the world looked fascinating to most of the pupils. Here they come up to it and find Kansas City in one place, Vilna or Warsaw in another place, and right there is Bremen, the port from which they left Europe, while pretty close to Kansas City is Galveston, the place where they first landed in this country. But Mr. Ziablikofsky is not like the rest. He does not believe in the roundness of the world. You can see in his eyes a defiant statement. "No, you don't fool me!" is what it amounts to.
> At first I did my best to convince him that the world is round. I invited him to see me before class and after class, and made use of my eloquence in all the languages of the world, including that of gesticulation, all with the purpose of convincing Mr. Ziablikofsky that the world is round. But it was all useless. He was not moved from his original argument. "If the world is round," he says, "it must be round, but why is it flat? Noo, why is it flat?" he closes emphatically. Now go and talk to him![20]

While teaching English to immigrants, Levine also taught Hebrew to American-born youngsters at the Reform temple. Fifty-five years later, the contrast between the two remained vivid in his memory:

> A definite influence in my Americanization . . . was the class I taught at Sunday School, easy-going teen-agers with whom I got along famously . . . To me they were as American as apple pie which I loved, and as different from the 'green' immigrants . . . as Kansas City was from the New York ghetto.[21]

While the main purpose of the Jewish Educational Institute was to "Americanize" the Jewish immigrants, it should not be thought of as a vehicle for assimilation. Courses and lectures were offered on various topics of Jewish interest. Trained educators introduced the most advanced method of Hebrew instruction (*Ivrit b'Ivrit*: the use of Hebrew in the classroom as a means of teacher-pupil communication).[22] The immigrants regarded the institute not as a symbol of alien culture within their midst, but as an integral part of their community life, along with the many Orthodox synagogues which they established in Kansas City[23] and the various fraternal and political organization to which they belonged there. The religious, who attended the synagogues, the secularists, who joined the Yiddish labor movement[24] or other ideological groups, all freely gave concrete expression to their strongest inclinations within the mechanism of the Jewish immigrant community. Thus, the newcomers from Eastern Europe formed their own neighborhoods—little ghettos, if you will—even in the heartland of the country, feeling at the same time, that this was their way of participating in American life.

On April 12, 1915, nearly a year after the end of the Galveston Movement, Schiff visited Kansas City to see for himself how his former protégés were faring. Billikopf guided the stately philanthropist to the poorer sections of town, where they spent the day visiting the immigrants in their homes. As Billikopf later recalled, Schiff was visibly moved by "the sight of these men and women winning out in the struggle to adjust themselves spiritually and economically to their new environment." The most touching moments, however, came at the end of the day:

> [Schiff's] greatest joy came when . . . he visited a night school where a large group of immigrants had gathered, after a hard day's work, to grapple with the intricacies of the English language, its accent and construction. Th subject this class of immigrants was discussing that evening was "Abraham Lincoln." It had been planned that Mr. Schiff should deliver an address at a meeting of the Missouri Bankers Association, which had been moved forward a day from its scheduled date in order to take advantage of his presence in Kansas City. The expectation was, of course, that this famous banker, talking at a meeting of bankers, would dwell on some important phase of the subject of banking, or speak on some economic or financial subject. Now those who knew Mr. Schiff have a very vivid recollection of his punctuality. But at this meeting of the assembled bankers of the state of Missouri, of his western colleagues, he was late. He was late because he had been unable to tear himself away from that classroom full of immigrants. He made that explanation of his tardiness, when finally, after nearly an hour's delay, he arrived at the bankers' meeting. And then, touching only casually on the subject he was expected to discuss, he told, in detail, the wonderful story of the Galveston movement. It was plain that he had been stirred. So, too, was his audience. For he took as the text a composition written by an immigrant who had been in

this country only six months. The subject of the essay was "Abraham Lincoln," and from it Schiff read, and proceeded to develop his own conception of Americanization. To him, Americanization was a matter of soul, not of outer conformity—of clothing, of speech, of manners. Love for America, for its institutions, for its ideals—that was Americanization.[25]

If narrowly defined, in terms of Schiff's grand design to drastically diffuse the Jewish immigrant population, the Galveston Movement must be deemed a failure. In 1900, 57 percent of America's Jews lived in the Northeast. By 1930, the figure had risen significantly to 68 percent. This was during a time when the total proportion of Americans living in that region remained at a stable 28 percent.[26]

Thus, even when including the relatively greater results of the Industrial Removal Office, it must be acknowledged that the attempt to artificially direct the course of American Jewish demography was a hollow one. The *Forward* had known this all along, as it had editorialized in 1907 that "with tricks one can never go against the stream that pulls people to a different place where they can expect to live a life that they think will be better."[27]

Jews help form the character of the areas in which they settle, and they remain there as long as these areas continue to provide them with opportunities for success. The strong position maintained by Jews in American society, and their disproportionately large contribution to American culture, has often been attributed to their concentration in key areas of geographic as well as professional influence. Thus, the initial desirability of the goal of dispersal, with its consequences of dissipation, is open to serious question.

The first significant lessening of the concentration of American Jews in the Northeast began to occur in the 1960s and '70s, paralleling a similar move among the general population. This trend has been partially seen as a response to the spreading of high-level professional opportunities to other areas of the country. In addition, third- and fourth-generation American Jews may be less concerned with the necessity of living in areas of high Jewish density and with the importance of immediate family proximity in the age of jet travel. Thus, if dispersal continues, as many predict, it will demonstrate a normal socio-demographic pattern, rather than an artificially divergent one.[28]

From its inception, Schiff's goal of large-scale artificial dispersal probably stood little chance of realization at that time. Perhaps Schiff's grand design was necessary, however, in order to attract even the small following which it did. In its own small way, the

Galveston Movement contributed toward a continuing presence of Jewish communities in various cities of the American West. This, by itself, was an important factor in defining the place of Jewry in American society. The acceptance of Judaism as one of America's three great religious groups is due as much to the existence of viable Jewish communities throughout the country as it is due to the concentration of most of the Jewish population in the national centers of influence and communication.

The Galveston Movement should, perhaps, be ultimately measured on a human scale. Through it, ten thousand refugees from a brutal, oppressive regime found their way to a land of freedom and opportunity, where they were assisted in the formidable task of rebuilding their lives. For most of these people and their descendants, the Galveston Movement, with all its shortcomings, was ultimately a success.

Notes

1. Origins

1. Max L. Margolis and Alexander Marx, *A History of the Jewish People* (Philadelphia: Jewish Publication Society of America, 1956), p. 694.

2. Actually, Eastern European Jews had been coming to America since early Colonial times, but they had had little effect on the demography and character of American Jewry. See Henry L. Feingold, *Zion in America* (New York: Hippocrene Books, 1974), p. 113.

3. Elias Tcherikower, ed., *The Early Jewish Labor Movement in the United States*, translated and revised by Aaron Antonovsky (New York: YIVO Institute for Jewish Research, 1961), p. 106.

4. This thesis is developed by Esther L. Panitz in "The Polarity of American Jewish Attitudes toward Immigration (1870–1891)," *American Jewish Historical Quarterly* 53. 2 (December 1963): 99–130; reprinted in Abraham J. Karp, ed., *The Jewish Experience in America* (New York: Ktav Publishing House, 1969), vol. 4, pp. 31–62. The restrictionist attitude of the American Jewish leadership was abandoned, however, after 1891. See Esther L. Panitz, "In Defense of the Jewish Immigrant (1891–1924)," *American Jewish Historical Quarterly* 55. 1 (September 1965): 57–97; reprinted in Abraham J. Karp, ed., *The Jewish Experience in America* (New York: Ktav Publishing House, 1969), vol. 5, pp. 23–63.

5. In 1922, its name was changed to the Jewish Agricultural Society. Other immigrant groups, such as the Italians, organized similar agricultural colonies for the purpose of encouraging their people to leave the slums of the large cities. Most of these ventures, however, came to nothing. See Humbert S. Nelli, *The Italians in Chicago, 1880–1930: A Study in Ethnic Mobility* (New York: Oxford University Press, 1970), pp. 15–19.

6. Samuel Joseph, *History of the Baron de Hirsch Fund* (Philadelphia: Jewish Publication Society of America, 1935), p. 204.

7. Edmund J. James, et al., *The Immigrant Jew in America* (New York: B. F. Buck and Co., 1907), pp. 369–370.

8. Joseph, *History of the Baron de Hirsch Fund*, p. 41.

9. Jacob H. Schiff to Paul Nathan, December 28, 1904, Schiff Papers, Box No. 20.

10. Morris D. Waldman to David M. Bressler, July 24, 1905; Bressler to Industrial Removal Office, July 27, 1905, JIIB Papers.

11. Yehuda Slutsky, "Dr. Max Mandelstamm," *He-Avar* (a Hebrew periodical on the history of Jews and Judaism in Russia, published in Tel Aviv), Issue no. 4 (1956), pp. 56–76; Issue no. 5 (1957), pp. 44–68.

12. *The Letters and Papers of Chaim Weizmann*, Series A (Letters), Meyer W. Weisgal, general editor (London: Oxford University Press, 1971; 1972), volume II, biographical index, s.v. Jochelman, David S.; volume III, letter no. 124 (Weizmann to Ben-Zion Mossinson, November 27, 1903). Jochelmann's obituary appears in *The Jewish Chronicle*, July 18, 1941, p. 17. A reference to Jochelmann's initial organization of the ITO is found in Joseph Leftwich, *Israel Zangwill* (London: James Clarke & Co., Ltd., 1957), p. 219. Further information was obtained from Dr. Jochelmann's two surviving daughters, Mrs. Fanny Cockerell of London and Mrs. Sonia Benari of Ramat Gan, Israel, and from the latter's husband, Dr. Yehuda Benari.

13. In a sense, this prediction was partially fulfilled during the early years of World War I, when the Jewish population of Palestine was reduced by about one third, as a result of hardship, emigration, and expulsion by the Turks. The Turkish government launched a fierce attack upon the entire Zionist effort in Palestine and might have expelled the bulk of the Jewish population, but for various political considerations. See Howard M. Sachar, *The Emergence of the Middle East: 1914–1924* (New York: Alfred A. Knopf, 1969), pp. 193–194. See also Israel Cohen, *The Turkish Persecution of the Jews* (London: Alabaster, Passmore and Sons, 1918).

14. From a speech delivered at Derby Hall, Manchester, April 1905, found in Israel Zangwill, *Speeches, Articles and Letters*, selected and edited by Maurice Simon (London: The Soncino Press, 1937), p. 212. Apparently, Zangwill had uttered these phrases before, for they are also found in *The Maccabean* (December 1904), p. 280, as quoted by Marnin Feinstein, *American Zionism 1884–1904* (New York: Herzl Press, 1965), p. 274.

15. After the Balfour Declaration of 1917, when the idea of Palestine as a Jewish homeland gained international recognition, the ITO became anachronistic, and it was formally disbanded in 1925. See the *Encyclopaedia Judaica*, s.v. "Territorialism."

16. Cyrus Adler, *Jacob H. Schiff: His Life and Letters* (New York: Doubleday, 1928), vol. 2, p. 96.

17. Schiff to Leven, July 16, 1907, Schiff Papers, Box No. 4.

18. Schiff to Israel Zangwill, August 24, 1906; Schiff to Zangwill, November 8, 1906, Schiff Papers, Box No. 4.

19. Schiff to Nathan, August 27, 1906, Schiff Papers, Box No. 20.

20. Schiff to Cyrus L. Sulzberger, July 15, 1907, Schiff Papers, Box No. 20.

21. Schiff to Zangwill, October 25, 1906, Schiff Papers, Box No. 4.

22. Zangwill to Schiff, October 26, 1906; Schiff to Zangwill, November 8, 1906, ITO Papers, A36/41.

23. Waldman to Bressler, November 5, 1906, JIIB Papers. Also, Waldman's five-page report to the Industrial Removal Office, ITO Papers, A36/95.

24. Schiff hoped to enlist the support of Albert Ballin, head of the Hamburg-American passenger line, but Ballin refused to become involved. See Schiff to Nathan, January 3, 1907, Schiff Papers, Box No. 20.

25. Sulzberger to Henry Cohen, January 8, 1907; Schiff to Cohen, January 8, 1907 (letters of introduction regarding Morris D. Waldman), Henry Cohen Collection, Box No. 2536.

26. Schiff to Nathan, December 5, 1906; Schiff to Zangwill, February 14, 1907; Schiff to Oscar S. Straus, February 15, 1907, Schiff Papers, Box No. 20.

27. *Who's Who in American Jewry*, Vol. 3 (1938–1939), New York: National News Association, Inc., 1938, s.v. "Bressler, David Maurice;" "Waldman, Morris David." Also, see Encyclopaedia Judaica, s.v. "Bressler, David Maurice"; "Waldman, Morris David."

28. Schiff to Straus, February 15, 1907, Schiff Papers, Box No. 20.

29. "Plan for the Diversion of Immigrants by way of Galveston," ITO Papers, A36/45.

30. Maurice Wohlgelernter, *Israel Zangwill: A Study* (New York and London, Columbia University Press, 1964), p. 25.

31. According to a well-circulated, though apocryphal story, Schiff once refused to handle a crucial multimillion-dollar transaction because it was Saturday. See Stephen Birmingham, *"Our Crowd": The Great Jewish Families of New York* (New York: Harper and Row, 1967), pp. 206–207.

32. Schiff to Sulzberger, December 18, 1906; Schiff to Nathan, December 20, 1906; Schiff Papers, Box No. 20.

33. "Plan for the Diversion of Immigrants by Way of Galveston." ITO Papers, A36/45. The original wording was crossed out, and this became the official version.

34. Morris D. Waldman, "The Galveston Movement: Another Chapter from the Book Which May Never Be Written," *Jewish Social Service Quarterly* 41. 3 (March 1928): 197–205.

35. Ibid.

36. "Sailing of the First Party of Emigrants from Bremen to Galveston," in Yiddish and in English translation. ITO Papers, A36/95.

37. Ibid. In that Yiddish document, it is stated that eighty-six Jewish emigrants sailed from Bremen. There is, however, another document, in Russian, which states that eighty-seven Jewish immigrants arrived in Galveston. It is captioned "Celebration Welcoming Galveston Pioneers, Special Telegram from American T.B. [Telegraph Bureau], Galveston, Texas, July 2nd [1907]," and is found in the Central Archives for the History of the Jewish People, Inv./1589(3). This printed copy of the telegram was apparently used to stimulate interest among Russian Jews.

38. "Immigration Law," *Galveston Daily News*, July 1, 1907, p. 2; "Delay was Costly," *Galveston Daily News*, July 2, 1907, p. 10.

39. "Letter from Galveston," dated July 1, 1907, signed by members of the first immigrant party before they departed for various locations, *Yevreyski Golos*, no. 29, July 21, 1907 (Old Style; the New Style equivalent

is August 3, 1907), pp. 13–14. An English translation of this letter is found in the ITO Papers, A36/95.

40. "Jewish Immigrants," *Galveston Daily News*, July 2, 1907, p. 9.

41. The names of these three immigrants appear on the passenger manifest of the North German-Lloyd Co. ship which preceded the S.S. *Cassel* to Galveston in June 1907.

42. During the first nine months alone, Kansas City took in a hundred male immigrants from Galveston, or three times as many as any other city. See the *American Hebrew*, March 27, 1908, p. 542, and the *Novaya Eudaia* no. 1 (April 1908): 53–54.

43. "Names and Addresses of Immigrants Arriving on S.S. *Cassel* July 1st [1907] and Where Sent," ITO Papers, A36/95.

44. The names of some of the members of the second immigrant party appear crossed out on the passenger manifest of the S.S. *Cassel*, which carried the first party to Galveston.

45. "Names and Addresses of Immigrants [on] S.S. *Frankfurt* [arriving] July 14, 1907; also, where sent," ITO Papers, A36/95.

46. Waldman's report of July 26, 1907, quoted in Sulzberger to Zangwill, August 1, 1907, ITO Papers, A36/95.

47. Waldman's report of July 27, 1907, quoted in Sulzberger to Zangwill, August 1, 1907, ITO Papers, A36/95.

48. Waldman's report of July 27, 1907, quoted in Sulzberger to Zangwill, August 1, 1907, ITO Papers, A36/95.

2. 1907: Activity and Controversy

1. "Statistics of Jewish Immigrants Who Arrived at the Port of Galveston, Texas, During the Years 1907–1913 inclusive, handled by the JIIB of Galveston, Texas," Henry Cohen Collection, Box No. 2538.

2. "Names and Addresses of Immigrants Arriving on S.S. *Hanover*, August 6, 1907, and Where Sent," ITO Papers, A36/95.

3. Bressler to Zangwill, October 7, 1907, ITO Papers, A36/96b.

4. Bressler to Clement I. Salaman, November 20, 1907, ITO Papers, A36/95.

5. Report from W. Willner of Houston, Texas, to the Jewish Immigrants' Information Bureau, ITO Papers, A36/95.

6. Reports from Jacob Billikopf of Kansas City, Missouri, to the Jewish Immigrants' Information Bureau, ITO Papers, A36/95.

7. Bressler to Salaman, November 11, 1907, ITO Papers, A36/96b.

8. "Name[s] and Addresses of Immigrants Arriving on the S.S. *Chemnitz*, August 24th, 1907, Together With Trades Registered," ITO Papers, A36/95.

9. This complaint was relayed, together with other complaints, to the Jewish Emigration Society in Kiev, by one I.J. Plostchansky, in a letter from Zhivotov (Kiev province) dated September 4, 1907 (presumably Old Style; that is, according to the New Style calendar it would be September 17, 1907), ITO Papers, A36/95.

10. Report by Clement I. Salaman to the Jewish Territorial Organization Emigration Regulation Department dated September 10, 1907. In another,

almost identical version, the report is dated September 22, 1907 and left unsigned. ITO Papers, A36/95.

11. Ibid. Also see S. Wininger, *Grose Judische National-Biographie*, s.v. "Klatzkin, Jakob" (Czernowitz: "Arta," 1928), vol. 3, p. 456. In 1908, Klatzkin visited the United States, where he studied immigration matters on behalf of the *Hilfsverein*. See the *American Hebrew*, March 13, 1908, p. 495. (His name is misspelled there as "Kliatzkin.") For a sampling of Klatzkin's controversial views on Zionism, see Arthur Hertzberg, *The Zionist Idea* (New York: Atheneum, 1973, reprinted by arrangement with the Jewish Publication Society of America), pp. 314–327. Klatzkin's early Territorialist connection, found in the report by Clement I. Salaman, sheds light on his unique approach to Zionism. This connection has gone unnoticed by Klatzkin's biographers.

12. Continuation of abovementioned report by Clement I. Salaman, ITO Papers, A36/95 (see above, note 10). In the report, Rosenak's name is erroneously given as "Dr. Rosenbach." Reference to his activities is found in the *Univeral Jewish Encyclopedia*, s.v. "Rosenak, Leopold."

13. Continuation of abovementioned report by Clement I. Salaman, ITO Papers, A36/95 (see above, note 10).

14. Ibid.

15. "Names and Addresses of Immigrants Arriving September 14, 1907, S.S. *Frankfurt*, Together With Trades Registered," ITO Papers, A36/95.

16. "United States via Galveston," ITO Papers, A36/95.

17. Israel Zangwill, "Preface to the Emigration Pamphlet," ITO Papers, A36/95.

18. This complaint was relayed, together with other complaints, to the Jewish Emigration Society in Kiev (see above, note 9), ITO Papers, A36/95.

19. "Immigrants Who Arrived on S.S. *Frankfurt*, November 18, 1907," ITO Papers, A36/95.

20. "List of Immigrants Who Arrived at Galveston on S.S. *Koeln*, October 5th, 1907," ITO Papers, A36/95.

21. Henry Cohen, *The Galveston Immigration Movement*, p. 6. (This is an undated pamphlet which appeared during the years of the Galveston Movement.)

22. Salaman to the ITO Emigration Regulation Department, October 21, 1907 (marked "Strictly Confidential"), ITO Papers, A36/95.

23. Ibid. Also, the ITO Papers A36/95 contain several versions of agreements between the *Hilfsverein* and the North German-Lloyd Shipping Company. None of these documents, however, is signed, thus leaving in doubt which was the final version.

24. "Dr. Oscar Nacht's Report on the Voyage of the Eighth Group from Bremen to Galveston, Oct. 24-Nov. 18, 1907," dated Galveston, Nov. 20, [1907], with notes added in Bremen, December 17, 1907, ITO Papers, A36/95.

25. Ibid.

26. Ibid.

27. Ibid.

28. Ibid.

29. Ibid.

30. Ibid.

31. Ibid.

32. "Immigrants who Arrived on S.S. *Frankfurt*, November 18, 1907," ITO Papers, A36/95.

33. The JIIB's controversial guidelines banning "*schochtim, melamdim* and Jews who do not work on the Sabbath" was reworded more diplomatically due to pressure from the ITO. See above, chapter 1, note 33.

34. Billikopf to Schiff, October 14, 1907, ITO Papers, A36/95.

35. Report to Jewish Immigrants' Information Bureau by J. Billikopf of Kansas City, Missouri, ITO Papers, A36/95.

36. *Jewish Daily News* (*Yiddishes Taggeblatt*), November 27, 1907, p. 4. The names as they appear in the newspaper are at variance with the way they appear in the JIIB's list of immigrants. The latter version has been placed in brackets.

37. Zosa Szajkowski, "Paul Nathan, Lucien Wolf, Jacob H. Schiff and the Jewish Revolutionary Movements in Eastern Europe (1903–1917)," *Jewish Social Studies* 291. 1 and 2 (1967), p. 81, n. 152.

38. *Jewish Daily News* (*Yiddishes Taggeblatt*), November 29, 1907, p. 4.

39. Mary Church Terrel, "Peonage in the United States: The Convict Lease System and the Chain Gangs," *The Nineteenth Century and After* 57 (August 1907): 306–322.

40. *Jewish Daily Forward*, September 16, 1907, p. 4, partially reprinted in *Der Fraind*, no. 217 (October 7/20, 1907), p. 4 and in the *Folks Zeitung*, no. 21.

41. *Jewish Daily Forward*, November 23, 1907, p. 4.

42. Ibid.

43. *Jewish Daily Forward*, December 2, 1907, p. 1.

44. *Jewish Daily Forward*, December 6, 1907, p. 8. See also "Errors in the Press," *American Hebrew and Jewish Messenger*, vol. 82, no. 5, December 6, 1907, p. 111. The *American Hebrew* was published by Cyrus L. Sulzberger.

45. *Jewish Daily Forward*, December 6, 1907, p. 1.

46. *Jewish Daily Forward*, December 7, 1907, p. 4.

47. Zangwill to Sulzberger, November 20, 1907, JIIB Papers. Also, Schiff to Sulzberger, December 2, 1907, and Schiff to Sonnenfeld, December 18, 1907, Schiff Papers, Box No. 20.

48. William Charles Schluter, *The Pre-War Business Cycle 1907 to 1914*, Studies in History, Economics and Public Law, edited by the faculty of Political Science of Columbia University, vol. 108, no. 1 (whole no. 243) (New York: Columbia University Press, 1923), p. 14.

49. Report by Salaman to ITO Emigration Regulation Department, April 30, 1908, ITO Papers, A36/95.

50. Zangwill to Sulzberger, November 20, 1907, JIIB Papers.

51. Lists of "Immigrants Who Arrived on S.S. *Hanover*, December 7, 1907," "Distributed December 10, 1907," "Admitted But Not Yet Distributed," and "In Hospital under Observation," ITO Papers, A36/95.

52. JIIB Papers.

53. Ibid.

54. "Immigrants who arrived on S.S. *Chemnitz*, December 30, 1907," (This list was not completed until January 7, 1908, or over a week later), ITO Papers, A36/95.

55. "Immigrants who arrived on S.S. *Frankfurt,* January 21, 1908," ITO Papers, A36/95.

56. Report by Salaman to ITO Emigration Regulation Department, April 30, 1908, ITO Papers, A36/95.

57. Ibid.

58. Henry Cohen, *The Galveston Immigration Movement,* p. 7.

59. Report by Salaman to ITO Emigration Regulation Department, April 20, 1908, ITO Papers, A36/95.

60. Billikopf to Bressler, October 26, 1907, JIIB Papers.

3. 1908–1909: The Economic Depression

1. Henry P. Goldstein to Waldman, February 7, 1908, JIIB Papers.

2. L. K. Friedman (secretary of the Jewish Educational and Benevolent Society of Topeka, Kansas) to the Jewish Immigrants' Information Bureau, JIIB Papers.

3. Waldman to Bressler, February 19, 1908, JIIB Papers.

4. Telegram from Waldman to Bressler, February 19, 1908, JIIB Papers.

5. Bressler to Clement I. Salaman, March 5, 1908; Zangwill to Leopold de Rothschild, March 5, 1908, ITO Papers, A36/95.

6. See the *American Hebrew,* March 6, 1908, p. 460.

7. Henry Cohen, *The Galveston Immigration Movement,* p. 6.

8. Schiff to Bressler, June 15, 1908, Schiff Papers, Box No. 20. Also "Chronicle-Emigration and Colonization: Renewal of Emigration to Galveston," *Novaya Eudaia* 2 (May 1908): 44–45.

9. Schiff to Zangwill, April 4, 1908; Zangwill to Schiff, May 19, 1908, ITO Papers, A36/41.

10. Zangwill to Schiff, June 12, 1908, ITO Papers, A36/41.

11. Lists of Jewish immigrants arriving in Galveston during the year 1908, ITO Papers, A36/95.

12. Passenger manifests of inbound ship passengers at the port of Galveston, Texas, arriving during the year 1908.

13. *Commercial and Financial Chronicle,* vol. 89, July 10, 1909, p. 73.

14. Samuel Joseph, *Jewish Immigration to the United States from 1881 to 1910* (New York: Arno Press and the New York Times, 1969), pp. 134–135.

15. Goldstein to Bressler, October 2, 1908, ITO Papers, A36/95.

16. Ibid.

17. H. Riegelman to the Jewish Immigrants' Information Bureau, March 7, 1908, JIIB Papers.

18. Minutes of a meeting held at the residence of Jacob H. Schiff on October 20th [1908], ITO Papers, A36/95.

19. Ibid.

20. Schiff to Oscar S. Straus, December 8, 1908, Schiff Papers, Box No. 20.

21. Zangwill to Schiff, December 18, 1908, ITO Papers, A36/41.

22. Zangwill to Schiff, February 21, 1909, ITO Papers, A36/41.

23. Zangwill to Schiff, March 23, 1909, ITO Papers, A36/41.

24. Zangwill to Schiff, April 14, 1909, ITO Papers, A36/41.

25. Schiff to Bressler, July 6, 1909, Schiff Papers, Box No. 20.

26. Zangwill to Schiff, July 7, 1909; Zangwill to Schiff, July 23, 1909; Zangwill to Schiff, July 30, 1909, ITO Papers, A36/41.

27. Louis Greenberg to Bressler, February 19, 1909, JIIB Papers. Also, Greenberg to H. L. Sabsovich, March 12, 1909, Baron de Hirsch Fund Archives, "Immigration Statistics" File. Beginning with a report for January 1909, Greenberg sent monthly reports on the numbers of Galveston Jewish immigrants to Bressler and to H. L. Sabsovich, the general agent of the Baron de Hirsch Fund in New York.

28. "Jewish Immigration to Galveston, Texas, Feb. 1909," JIIB Papers and Baron de Hirsch Fund Archives, "Immigration Statistics" File. In Greenberg's monthly reports (see above, note 27), he included the totals of all Jewish immigrants arriving in Galveston, whether or not they had been sent by the ITO (with the help of the *Hilfsverein*).

29. "Immigrants Who Arrived on S.S. *Hanover* Feb. 13, 1909," ITO Papers, A36/95.

30. Greenberg to Bressler, March 15, 1909, JIIB Papers.

31. Bressler to Greenberg, March 18, 1909, JIIB Papers.

32. Greenberg to Bressler, April 12, 1909; Bressler to Greenberg, April 16, 1909, JIIB Papers.

33. Greenberg to Bressler, May 28, 1909, JIIB Papers.

34. Annual Report of the Industrial Removal Office, January 1, 1909 (for the year 1908), Industrial Removal Office Papers.

35. Bressler to Greenberg, June 9, 1909, JIIB Papers.

36. Ibid.

37. Greenberg to Bressler, June 13, 1909, JIIB Papers. Bressler defended Goldstein against Greenberg's charge by answering as follows: "It is rather late in the day to make criticism of Mr. Goldstein's methods of organization. We must assume that he did the best he could. I shall be more than glad to learn that you have been able to improve upon his work, and I say this in all good faith and with best wishes to you." Bressler to Greenberg, June 16, 1909, JIIB Papers.

38. Greenberg to Bressler, June 25, 1909, JIIB Papers.

39. Bressler to Jochelmann, June 28, 1909, JIIB Papers.

40. Bressler's letters to Waldman, Cohen, Arkush, and Loeb dated July 23, 1909, inviting them to become members of the Galveston Committee, JIIB Papers.

41. Sidney E. Goldstein to Bressler, January 20, 1909, JIIB Papers.

42. Schiff to Zangwill, August 8, 1909, Schiff Papers, Box No. 20.

43. Schiff to Bressler, July 6, 1909; Schiff to Zangwill, July 7, 1909, Schiff Papers, Box No. 20.

44. Zangwill to Schiff, July 23, 1909, ITO Papers, A36/41.

45. Schiff to Zangwill, August 9, 1909, Schiff Papers, Box No. 20.

46. Schiff to Bressler, October 21, 1909; Schiff to Zangwill, November 11, 1909; Schiff to Zangwill, December 2, 1909, Schiff Papers, Box No. 20.

47. Schiff to Zangwill, August 30, 1909, Schiff Papers, Box No. 20.

48. Zangwill to Schiff, December 16, 1909, ITO Papers, A36/41.

49. Minutes of the Galveston Committee meeting of December 20, 1909, JIIB Papers.

50. Ibid.

51. Schiff to Zangwill, January 7, 1910, Schiff Papers, Box No. 20.

52. Telegram from Schiff to Zangwill, December 15, 1909, ITO Papers, A36/41.

53. Ruth Phillips (ITO secretary) to Bressler, December 13, 1909, JIIB Papers.

54. Schiff to Bressler, January 13, 1910, Schiff Papers, Box No. 20.

55. Bressler to Schiff, December 13, 1909, Schiff Papers, Box No. 20.

56. Lists of "Immigrants Who Arrived on S.S. *Breslau*, Aug. 13, 1909;" ". . . on S.S. *Cassel*, Sept. 17, 1909;" ". . . on S.S. *Breslau*, Oct. 15, 1909;" and ". . . on S.S. *Cassel*, Nov. 20, 1909," ITO Papers, A36/95.

57. "Jewish Immigration to Galveston, Texas, August, 1909;" ". . . September, 1909;" ". . . October, 1909;" and ". . . November 1909," Baron de Hirsch Fund Archives, "Immigration Statistics" File. See above, notes 27 and 28.

58. Schiff to Bressler, January 13, 1910, Schiff Papers, Box No. 20.

59. "Jewish Immigration to Galveston, Texas" monthly reports, Baron de Hirsch Fund Archives, "Immigration Statistics" File.

60. Reports by the JIIB on arriving groups of ITO immigrants, ITO Papers, A36/95.

4. 1910: Deportations!

1. Oscar Handlin, *The Uprooted* (New York: Grosset and Dunlap, 1951), pp. 288–289.

2. Samuel Gompers, "Immigration—Up to Congress," *American Federationist* 18 (January 1911): 17–21, quoted in David Brody, ed., *Industrial America in the Twentieth Century* (New York: Thomas Y. Crowell Co., 1967), pp. 65–70.

3. U.S., Congress, Senate, *Reports of the Immigration Commission*, "Statements and Recommendations Submitted by Societies and Organizations Interested in the Subject of Immigration," Document No. 764, 61st Congress, 3rd Session (Washington, D.C.: Government Printing Office, 1911). (In the final printing of the Immigration Commission Reports, the "Statements and Recommendations" appear in Volume 41.) The reports issued in 1911, and encompassing forty-one volumes, constitute what is probably the most exhaustive survey of U.S. immigration ever made.

4. See Boris D. Bogen, *Jewish Philanthropy: An Exposition of Principles and Methods of Jewish Social Service in the United States* (New York: The Macmillan Co., 1917), pp. 107–111.

5. "Pittsburgh Manufacturers Answer Regarding Local Labor Conditions," *Iron Age*, March 24, 1910, pp. 670–671. George Walter, "Why Foreigners Are Needed in Steel Plants," *Iron Age*, August 1, 1923, pp. 331–332, quoted in David Brody, ed., above, note 2, pp. 70–78.

6. Esther L. Panitz, "In Defense of the Jewish Immigrant (1891–1924)," *American Jewish Historical Quarterly* 55. 1 (September 1965). Reprinted in Abraham J. Karp, ed., *The Jewish Experience in America*, 5 vols. (New York: Ktav Publishing House, 1969), vol. 5, pp. 23–63.

7. "In Defense of the Immigrant," Herbert Friedenwald, ed., *The American Jewish Year Book*, vol. 12 (1910–1911) (Philadelphia: The Jewish Publication Society of America, 1910), p. 19.

8. Simon Wolf, *The Presidents I Have Known From 1860 to 1918* (Washington, D.C.: Press of Byron S. Adams, 1918). See the chapter dealing with the presidency of William Howard Taft (pp. 292–402). For a contrast between Schiff's outspoken attitude and Wolf's soft-spoken one, see pp. 305–313.

9. Simon Wolf to Bressler, July 15, 1910; Bressler to Wolf, July 18, 1910; Morris Loeb to Bressler, December 8, 1910, JIIB Papers.

10. *Dictionary of American Biography*, 1933 ed., s.v. "Keefe, Daniel J."

11. Samuel Joseph, *History of the Baron de Hirsch Fund: The Americanization of the Jewish Immigrant* (Philadelphia: The Jewish Publication Society of America, 1935), pp. 239–240.

12. "Contractors Figuring on Immigration Station . . . Importance of Station Realized by the City," *Galveston Daily News*, Octoer 6, 1909, p. 10.

13. Louis Greenberg to Bressler (marked "confidential"), July 28, 1909, JIIB Papers.

14. Telegram from Henry Berman to Schiff, November 19, 1909, JIIB Papers.

15. "Immigration Statistics" File, Baron de Hirsch Fund Archives.

16. Bressler to Herbert Friedenwald, July 5, 1910, JIIB Papers.

17. Max J. Kohler to Bressler, March 28, 1910, American Jewish Historical Society.

18. Schiff to Bressler, March 22, 1910, Schiff Papers, Box No. 20. Also, Bressler to Nathan Bijur, March 23, 1910, JIIB Papers.

19. Kohler to Bressler, March 28, 1910. (Bressler accepted Kohler's advice. See Bressler to Kohler, March 31, 1910.) American Jewish Historical Society.

20. Schiff to Bressler, April 18, 1910, Schiff Papers Box No. 20. Also, Bressler to Friedenwald, July 5, 1910, JIIB Papers.

21. Examinations of Tobias Braitford (Tewja Breidberg); also reference to these examinations by Chairman of the Board of Special Inquiry M. Arthur Coykendall in letter to Inspector in Charge of U.S. Immigration Service at Galveston [Alfred Hampton], August 12, 1910. "Board of Special Inquiry Hearings Given Aliens Arriving Galveston, Texas, July 24, 1910, ex. S.S. *Frankfurt*," U.S. Immigration File No. 52779/29-C. See below, chapter 5, note 7.

22. Hampton to the Commissioner General of Immigration, May 6, 1910 (letter no. 22–10), U.S. Immigration File No. 52961/11.

23. Hampton to the Commissioner General of Immigration, August 22, 1910, U.S. Immigration File No. 52779/29-D.

24. Daniel J. Keefe to the Inspector in Charge of the Immigration Service at Galveston, Texas, June 13, 1910 (letter No. 52885/34), U.S. Immigration File No. 5296/11.

25. Bressler to Friedenwald, July 5, 1910, JIIB Papers.

26. Galveston Inspector in Charge Alfred Hampton to the Commissioner General of Immigration, July 3, 1910, U.S. Immigration File No. 52961/11.

27. Keefe to Commissioner of Immigration, and Inspectors in Charge at all Ports of Entry, June 21, 1910 (letter No. 52986/5). Keefe's letter appears among the "Papers on Rehearing in the Matter of the Appeals to the Secretary of Commerce and Labor of Galveston Immigrants, who arrived under the auspices of the Jewish Immigrants' Information Bureau," pp. 60–61. The letter is annexed to a memorandum by Max J. Kohler, who attacked it as being incorrect and illegal, since it misled government officers as to their duty (see below, chapter 5, note 44). These "Papers on Rehearing," which were printed as a pamphlet, can be found in U.S. Immigration File No. 52779/29 and also in the JIIB Papers. The pamphlet is also available at the Jewish National and University Library, Jerusalem, under call no. S/36B/1994.

28. Berman's telegram is quoted in Bressler's letter to William S. Bennet, July 7, 1910, JIIB Papers.

29. *Who Was Who in America, A Companion Volume to Who's Who in America*, vol. I, (1897–1942), 1943 edition, s.v. "Nagel, Charles."

30. Donald F. Anderson, *William Howard Taft: A Conservative's Conception of the Presidency* (Ithaca and London: Cornell University Press, 1973) pp. 196–197.

31. Charles D. Norton to Benjamin S. Cable, August 31, 1910, U.S. Immigration File No. 52779/29-E.

32. William Edward Hayes, *Iron Road to Empire: The History of One Hundred Years of the Progress and Achievements of the Rock Island Lines* (New York: Simmons-Boardman, 1953), pp. 102–105, 143–146, 152, 178–179. See also *Who Was Who in America, A Companion Volume to Who's Who in America*, vol. I (1897–1942), 1943 edition, s.v. "Cable, Benjamin Stickney" and "Cable, Ransom R."

33. Cyrus Adler, *Jacob H. Schiff: His Life and Letters* (New York: Doubleday, 1928), vol. I, pp. 131–140.

34. George Kennan, *E.H. Harriman, A Biography* (Boston and New York: Houghton Mifflin Company, 1922), vol. II, pp. 228–310, esp. pp. 229, 261, 298 and 306.

35. William Edward Hayes, above, note 32, pp. 165–179; Cyrus Adler, above, note 33, pp. 131–141.

36. *Biographical Directory of the American Congress 1774–1971*, s.v. "Bennet, William Stiles."

37. Cable's memorandum to the Commissioner General of Immigration, July 14, 1910, U.S. Immigration File No. 52779/29; Wolf to Bressler, July 15, 1910, JIIB Papers.

38. Cable to Bennet, July 14, 1910, American Jewish Committee Archives. This letter also appears among the "Papers on Rehearing", above, note 27, pp. 14–17, where it is annexed to the "Statement of Facts Submitted by David M. Bressler," which vigorously refuted the charges put forward here by Cable.

39. "Statement of Facts As Disclosed by an Examination of the Files of the Bureau of Immigration and Naturalization of the Department of Commerce and Labor Which Cover the Cases of Aliens Recently Applying for Admission at the Port of Galveston, Texas," U.S. Immigration File No. 52779/29-E.

40. The field reports of the various immigrant inspectors who participated in the investigation headed by Alfred Hampton are found in U.S. Immigration File No. 52961/11.
41. Immigrant Inspector M.F. Maguire to the Inspector in Charge of the Immigrant Service at Galveston, Texas, June 28, 1910, U.S. Immigration File No. 52961/11.
42. Immigrant Inspector O.J. Palmer to Alfred Hampton, Inspector in Charge of the U.S. Immigration Service at Galveston, Texas, June 29, 1910, U.S. Immigration File No. 52961/11.
43. Hunter M. Course to Commissioner of Immigration, New Orleans, Louisiana, June 25, 1910, U.S. Immigration File No. 52961/11.
44. Extracts from reports by Immigrant Inspector Samuel L. Whitfield, submitted on June 28 and June 29, 1910, to his superior, James R. Dunn, Inspector in charge of the U.S. Immigration Service at Saint Louis, Missouri. Dunn included these extracts and others in his letter to the Commissioner General of Immigration, July 9, 1910, U.S. Immigration File No. 52961/11. In these reports, as in the immigrant examinations, some of which are quoted in the following pages, the names of the individuals appear intact. In these documents, certain people are accused, rightly or wrongly, of treating the immigrants unfairly, but they are not confronted directly, and so are not given the opportunity here to defend themselves against these accusations. In order to protect the memory of those individuals, some of whose descendants may still live in these communities, their names appear here in abbreviated form.
45. Examination of Yudel Spivak, Des Moines, Iowa, June 30, 1910, U.S. Immigration File No. 52961/11.
46. Examination of Yudel Spivak, Des Moines, Iowa, June 30, 1910, U.S. Immigration File No. 52961/11.
47. Examination of Wolf Kaufman, Des Moines, Iowa, June 29, 1910, U.S. Immigration File No. 52961/11.
48. Examination of Jossel Chaim Lerman, Des Moines, Iowa, June 30, 1910, U.S. Immigration File No. 52961/11.
49. S. L. Whitfield to Saint Louis Inspector in Charge James R. Dunn, July 11, 1910, U.S. Immigration File No. 52961/11.
50. Extract from a report by Immigrant Inspector S. L. Whitfield; see above, note 44.
51. Examination of Abraham Werskow, Sioux City, Iowa, July 5, 1910, U.S. Immigration File No. 52961/11.
52. S. L. Whitfield to Saint Louis Inspector in Charge James R. Dunn, July 11, 1910, U.S. Immigration file No. 52961/11.
53. Examination of Wolf Burnstein (Velvel Burshtein), Council Bluffs, Iowa, July 8, 1910, U.S. Immigration File No. 52961/11.
54. S. L. Whitfield to Saint Louis Inspector in Charge James R. Dunn, July 11, 1910, U.S. Immigration File No. 52961/11.
55. Wishing to demonstrate that he had no problem communicating with his supervisor at work, a Jewish immigrant interviewed later by Whitfield and his new interpreter, told them, "I speak to the German foreman as well as I speak to this interpreter." Examination of Solomon Lewitan, Kansas City, Missouri, July 22, 1910, U.S. Immigration File No. 52961/11.

56. Examination of Salman Holodez (also known as Ben Golt), Omaha, Nebraska, July 11, 1910, U.S. Immigration File No. 52961/11.

57. Examination of Chaim Shapiro, Omaha, Nebraska, July 13, 1910, U.S. Immigration File No. 52961/11.

58. Ibid.

59. Examination of David Weiner, alias Itzchok Bassarabsky, Omaha, Nebraska, July 17, 1910, U.S. Immigration File No. 52961/11.

60. Ibid.

61. Examination of Isaac Furman, Omaha, Nebraska, July 15, 1910, U.S. Immigration File No. 52961/11.

62. Examination of Sam Chalek, Omaha, Nebraska, July 15, 1910, U.S. Immigration File No. 52961/11.

63. Whitfield to Dunn, July 18, 1910, U.S. Immigration File No. 52961/11.

64. Examination of Bessie Saglan, Omaha, Nebraska, July 14, 1910, U.S. Immigration File No. 52961/11.

65. Examination of Annie Weisman, Omaha, Nebraska, July 14, 1910, U.S. Immigration File No. 52961/11.

66. Examination of Meier Lawrinowich, Omaha, Nebraska, July 15, 1910, U.S. Immigration File No. 52961/11.

67. Ibid.

68. Whitfield to Dunn, July 18, 1910, U.S. Immigration File No. 52961/11.

69. Ibid.

70. Examination of Beier Koltan (also known as Boris Fabricant), Lincoln, Nebraska, July 18, 1910, U.S. Immigration File No. 52961/11.

71. Examination of Aaron Kuralopnick, Leavenworth, Kansas, July 20, 1910, U.S. Immigration File No. 52961/11.

72. Examination of Mendel Shrager, Kansas City, Missouri, July 22, 1910, U.S. Immigration File No. 52961/11.

73. Memoir by Jacob Billikopf found in the Schiff Papers, Box No. 4.

74. Whitfield to Dunn, July 27, 1910, U.S. Immigration File No. 52961/11.

75. Memoir by Jacob Billikopf found in the Schiff Papers, Box No. 4.

76. Whitfield to Dunn, July 25, 1910, U.S. Immigration File No. 52961/11.

77. Ibid.

78. Examination of Aron Usiel, Kansas City, Missouri, July 21, 1910, U.S. Immigration File No. 52961/11.

79. Examination of Chaikel Geifman, Kansas City, Missouri, July 21, 1910; Whitfield to Dunn, July 22, 1910, U.S. Immigration File No. 52961/11.

80. Examination of Berkin Fredkin, Kansas City, Missouri, July 22, 1910, U.S. Immigration File No. 52961/11.

81. Examination of Srul Bistrizky, Kansas City, Missouri, July 24, 1910, U.S. Immigration File No. 52961/11.

82. Whitfield to Dunn, July 25 and July 27, 1910, U.S. Immigration File No. 52961/11.

83. Testimony of Charles Juster, Minneapolis, Minnesota, June 25, 1910, U.S. Immigration File No. 52961/11.

84. Examination of Rochmiel Krakpolsky, Omaha, Nebraska, July 14, 1910, U.S. Immigration File No. 52961/11.

85. "Statement of Facts Submitted by David M. Bressler, Esq., Honorary Secretary, Jewish Immigrants' Information Bureau, July 21, 1910, on Rehearing of Galveston Appeals." This statement appears among the "Papers on Rehearing," above, note 27, pp. 1–13.

86. These sections of the Immigration Act of 1907 are quoted in the "Memorandum in Support of Appeals Submitted by Max J. Kohler, Esq., to the Department of Commerce and Labor (Rehearing of Galveston Appeals Cases)," July 23, 1910. This memorandum appears in the "Papers on Rehearing," above, note 27, pp. 30–42 (see, especially p. 31). A copy of Kohler's memorandum can also be found in the American Jewish Committee Archives.

87. Ibid., pp. 32–34.

88. See "Memorandum on Behalf of the Galveston Immigrants and of the Future Activity of the Jewish Immigrants' Information Bureau at that Port, by Hon. Nathan Bijur, Esq." This memorandum appears in the "Papers on Rehearing," above, note 27, pp. 17–29. A copy of Bijur's memorandum can also be found in the American Jewish Committee Archives.

89. This telegram as well as others that passed between Berman and Schiff, and between Hampton and the Bureau of Immigration and Naturalization on July 27, 1910, are quoted in Hampton's letter to the Commissioner General of Immigration, August 12, 1910, U.S. Immigration File No. 52779/29-D. At first, there may have been some confusion over the number of immigrants to be deported, due, perhaps, to a typographical error in a copy of one of the telegrams which passed between Berman and Schiff. The exact number of deported immigrants was twenty-nine.

90. Ibid.

91. Ibid.

92. Ibid.

93. Zangwill to Schiff, September 1, 1910, ITO Papers, A36/41.

5. The Battle of the Bureaus

1. Telegram from Hampton to Immigration Bureau, August 17, 1910, U.S. Immigration File No. 52779/29-D.

2. Examination of Nachman Kesselmann, "Board of Special Inquiry Hearings Given Aliens Arriving Galveston, Texas, July 24, 1910, ex. S.S. *Frankfurt*," U.S. Immigration File No. 52779/29-C.

3. Examination of Abraham Fridman, "Board of Special Inquiry Hearings Given Aliens Arriving Galveston, Texas, July 24, 1910, ex S.S. *Frankfurt*," U.S. Immigration File No. 52779/29-C.

4. Coykendall to Hampton, August 12, 1910, U.S. Immigration File No. 52779/29-C.

5. Examinations of Menasche Katz and Rubin Peckler, "Board of Special Inquiry Hearings Given Aliens Arriving Galveston, Texas, July 24, 1910, ex. S.S. *Frankfurt*," U.S. Immigration File No. 52779/29-C.

6. Telegram from Hampton to Immigration Bureau, August 17, 1910, U.S. Immigration File No. 52779/29-D.

7. Examinations of Tobias Braitford (alias Tewja Breidberg). See also reference to these examinations by Chairman of the Board of Special Inquiry M. Arthur Coykendall in a letter to Inspector in Charge of U.S. Immigration Service at Galveston [Alfred Hampton], August 12, 1910. "Board of Special Inquiry Hearings Given Aliens Arriving Galveston, Texas, July 24, 1910, ex. S.S. *Frankfurt,*" U.S. Immigration File No. 52779/29-C. See above, chapter 4, note 21.

8. Examination of Hirsch Zukerman, "Board of Special Inquiry Hearings Given Aliens Arriving Galveston, Texas, July 24, 1910, ex S.S. *Frankfurt,*" U.S. Immigration File No. 52779/29-C.

9. Examination of Rafael Giller, "Board of Special Inquiry Hearings Given Aliens Arriving Galveston, Texas, July 24, 1910, ex. S.S. *Frankfurt,*" U.S. Immigration File No. 52779/29-C.

10. "Memorandum to the Commissioner General of Immigration" from Benjamin S. Cable, August 18, 1910, U.S. Immigration File No. 52779/29-D.

11. F. H. Larned to Inspector in Charge, Immigration Service, Galveston, Texas, August 19, 1910, U.S. Immigration File No. 52779/29-D.

12. Hampton to the Commissioner General of Immigration, August 22, 1910, U.S. Immigration File No. 52779/29-D.

13. Larned to Inspector in Charge, Immigration Service, Galveston, Texas, August 27, 1910, U.S. Immigration File No. 52779–29D.

14. Hampton to the Commissioner General of Immigration, September 2, 1910, U.S. Immigration File No. 52779/29-E.

15. Hampton to Cable, August 23, 1910, U.S. Immigration File No. 52779/29-D.

16. Examination of Schevie and Rifke Lipkin, "Board of Special Inquiry Hearings Given Aliens Arriving Galveston, Texas, August 19, 1910, ex. S.S. *Hanover,*" U.S. Immigration File No. 52779/29-E.

17. Examination of Peisach Josmann, "Board of Special Inquiry Hearings Given Aliens Arriving Galveston, Texas, August 19, 1910, ex. S.S. *Hanover,*" U.S. Immigration File No. 52779/29-E.

18. Examination of Nissan Fradkin, "Board of Special Inquiry Hearings Given Aliens Arriving Galveston, Texas, August 19, 1910, ex. S.S. *Hanover,*" U.S. Immigration File No. 52779/29-E.

19. Hampton to the Commissioner General of Immigration, September 2, 1910, U.S. Immigration File No. 52779/29-E.

20. U.S. Immigration File No. 52779/29-E.

21. Examination of Aron Ullman, "Board of Special Inquiry Hearings Given Aliens Arriving Galveston, Texas, August 19, 1910, ex. S.S. *Hanover,*" U.S. Immigration File No. 52779/29-E.

22. Acting Secretary of Commerce and Labor to U.S. Senator Henry Cabot Lodge, September 17, 1910, U.S. Immigration File No. 52779/29-E.

23. Universal Jewish Encyclopedia, s.v. "Galveston."

24. Henry J. Dannenbaum to Schiff, December 18, 1911, Henry Cohen Collection, Box No. 2538. (The copy of this letter which appears in the Henry Cohen Collection is unsigned, but it bears the initials H.J.D. Also,

it refers to its author as having been a recent president of B'nai B'rith's District Seven, i.e., the southern district, which included Galveston. During part of 1910 and 1911, Henry J. Dannenbaum was president of this district. See the *Report of the Executive Committee of the Constitution Grand Lodge, Independent Order B'nai B'rith, for the Year 1910–1911*, pp. 36–37. This places Dannenbaum as the author of this letter.)

25. Berman to Bressler, September 9, 1910, JIIB Papers.

26. J. Lippman to Bressler, July 22, 1910, JIIB Papers. In quoting this passage, certain obvious errors in spelling, grammar and punctuation have been corrected by the present author.

27. Berman to Bressler, September 9, 1910, JIIB Papers.

28. The accused also wrote angry letters of denial to Bressler. See Max Schreiber to Bressler, September 13, 1910 and Bressler's answer to Schreiber, September 22, 1910, JIIB Papers.

29. Berman to Bressler, September 9, 1910, JIIB Papers.

30. See the *Jewish Daily News* (*Yiddishes Taggeblatt*), September 14, 1910, p. 4.

31. Minutes of the Galveston Committee meeting of September 19, 1910; Bressler to Schiff, September 20, 1910, JIIB Papers.

32. See *Hayehudi*, vol. 14, no. 26, July 28, 1910, p. 12.

33. "Bar Jews at Galveston," *New York Times*, August 21, 1910, p. 2.

34. Schiff to Cable, August 22, 1910, U.S. Immigration File No. 52779/ 29-D. A copy of this letter is found in the Schiff Papers, Box No. 4.

35. Cable to Schiff, August 24, 1910, U.S. Immigration File No. 52779/ 29-D.

36. Schiff to Charles D. Norton, August 29, 1910, Schiff Papers, Box No. 20.

37. "Taft Anxious About Political Outlook," *New York Times*, October 8, 1910, p. 3.

38. William Manners, *TR and Will: A Friendship That Split the Republican Party* (New York: Harcourt, Brace and World, 1969), p. 174.

39. Schiff to Zangwill, August 23, 1910, Schiff Papers, Box No. 20.

40. Zangwill to Schiff, September 1, 1910, ITO Papers, A36/41.

41. Schiff to Bressler, September 5, 1910, Schiff Papers, Box No. 20. A copy of this letter was sent to Zangwill.

42. Carl Stettauer to Zangwill, September 21, 1910, attached to the minutes of the Galveston Committee meeting of September 19, 1910, JIIB Papers. Stettauer, honorary secretary of the ITO's Emigration Regulation Committee (of London), was then in New York, where he attended a meeting of the Galveston Committee. In this letter to Zangwill, he reported the results of the committee's deliberations.

43. Schiff to Kohler, October 3, 1910, Schiff Papers, Box No. 20.

44. See Kohler to Cable, October 5, 1910. This letter appears in the "Papers on Rehearing," above, chapter 4, note 27, pp. 44–59.

45. See above, chapter 4, note 87.

46. See above, chapter 4, note 11.

47. Max J. Kohler to Mortimer L. Schiff, October 14, 1925, recalling the events of fifteen years before, Schiff Papers, Box No. 20.

48. Minutes of the Galveston Committee meeting of October 6, 1910, JIIB Papers.

49. "Taft Wants More Ports to Get Aliens," *New York Times*, October 19, 1910, p. 1.

50. "Think Taft Will Aid Immigration Plan," *New York Times*, October 22, 1910, p. 10.

51. Bennet to Bressler, October 29, 1910, thanking him for sending out a letter of endorsement, JIIB Papers.

52. Schiff to Zangwill, January 11, 1911, ITO Papers, A36/41. Also found in the Schiff Papers, Box No. 20.

53. Max J. Kohler to Mortimer L. Schiff, October 14, 1925, recalling the events of fifteen years before, Schiff Papers, Box No. 20.

54. Schiff to Zangwill, January 11, 1911, ITO Papers A36/41. Also found in the Schiff Papers, Box No. 20.

55. Schiff to Zangwill, January 11, 1911, ITO Papers, A36/41. Also found in the Schiff Papers, Box No. 20.

56. Schiff to Zangwill, January 23, 1911, Schiff Papers, Box No. 20.

57. Schiff to George W. Wickersham, February 8, 1911 (marked "personal"), Schiff Papers, Box No. 20.

58. Kohler to Bressler, March 4, 1911; Bressler to Kohler, March 9, 1911, JIIB Papers.

59. J. Lestschinsky, "Die Auswanderung der Juden nach Galveston," *Zeitschrift fur Demographie und Statistik der Juden* 6. 12 (December 1910): 183.

60. Lestschinsky, p. 184. The article mentions "Chodozkov," but this is probably a typographical error. See Jochelmann to Bressler, December 25/January 7, 1908/09, and the accompanying statement, in Yiddish, about immigrants from that town, JIIB Papers. A condensed English translation of this statement is found in the ITO Papers, A36/95.

61. Information about Nahum Shlomo (Nathan) Kaluzny was obtained through private interviews between the author and Kaluzny's grandson, Professor Robert Rockaway of Tel Aviv University. Further information about Kaluzny was obtained by the author from the passenger manifest of the S.S. *Frankfurt*, which left Bremen May 5, 1910, and arrived in Galveston May 30, 1910. His name appears on page 68 (list 7), line 7, as Nochim Schlema Kaljusny.

62. Examination of Chaim Shapira, Omaha, Nebraska, July 13, 1910, and Examination of Isaac Furman, Omaha, Nebraska, July 15, 1910, U.S. Immigration File No. 52961/11. Shapira referred to the druggist as Betzel Dutch, while Furman referred to him as Betzel Judowitz.

63. Examination of Chaim Shapira, above, note 62.

64. See below, "Retrospective."

65. See Lestschinsky, above, note 59, pp. 178–179.

66. Ibid., pp. 182–183.

67. David M. Bressler, "The Removal Work, Including Galveston," *Proceedings of the National Conference of Jewish Charities*, 1910, pp. 123–140. Bressler presented this report at the Sixth Biennial Meeting of the National Conference of Jewish Charities, Saint Louis, Missouri, May 17–19, 1910. See especially the table of Galveston statistics at the end of the report. This report also constituted the statement of the Jewish Immigrants' Information Bureau for the U.S. Immigration Commission. See U. S., Congress, Senate, *Reports of the Immigration Commission*, "Statements and

Recommendations Submitted by Societies and Organizations Interested in the Subject of Immigration," above, chapter 4, note 3. A condensed version of Bressler's report, without the table of statistics, appears in Robert Morris and Michael Freund, ed., *Trends and Issues in Jewish Social Welfare* (Philadelphia: The Jewish Publication Society of America, 1966), pp. 39–42.

6. *1911: A Weakened Movement Resumes Operations*

1. Schiff to Zangwill, January 23, 1911, Schiff Papers, Box No. 20.
2. Berman to Bressler, March 8, 1911; Berman to Bressler (marked "Confidential"), March 8, 1911; Berman to Bressler, March 10, 1911; Bressler to Zangwill, March 16, 1911; Zangwill to Bressler, March 29, 1911; Bressler to Zangwill, April 10, 1911, ITO Papers, A36/96b.
3. Bressler to Phillips, January 3, 1911, ITO Papers, A36/96b.
4. Phillips to Bressler, January 19, 1911; Bressler to Phillips, January 30, 1911; Bressler to Phillips, March 3, 1911, ITO Papers, A36/96b.
5. Bressler to Finkenstein, September 25, 1911, ITO Papers, A36/96b.
6. Ibid.
7. Berman to Bressler, December 17, 1912; Bressler to Berman, December 23, 1912; Bressler to Zangwill, December 23, 1912; ITO Secretary to Bressler, January 2, 1913, ITO Papers, A36/96b.
8. Max J. Kohler advised the JIIB that Bloch could "average" the cost of an emigrant's stay in Bremen only if an overcharged person was later recompensed and an undercharged person was later forced to make good the difference. Bloch to Bressler, May 27, 1912; Bressler to Zangwill, June 7, 1912, ITO Papers, A36/96b.
9. Berman to Bressler, January 23, 1911; Bressler to Zangwill, January 27, 1911; Zangwill to Bressler, February 7, 1911; Bressler to Stettauer, March 3, 1911, ITO Papers, A36/96b.
10. Zangwill to Bressler, June 27, 1911; Bressler to Zangwill, July 7, 1911; Zangwill to Bressler, July 18, 1911; Bressler to Zangwill, July 27, 1911, ITO Papers, A36/96b.
11. Seman to Stettauer, December 27, 1911; Stettauer to Seman, January 11, 1912; Bressler to Stettauer, January 23, 1912, ITO Papers, A36/96b.
12. Bressler to Zangwill, November 6, 1911 (quoting report from Berman), ITO Papers, A36/96b.
13. Schiff to Leven, July 16, 1907, Schiff Papers, Box No. 4. See above, chapter 1, note 17.
14. Zangwill to Bressler, February 1, 1912, ITO Papers A36/41; Zangwill to Bressler, August 7, 1912, ITO Papers, A36/96b.
15. Bressler to Stettauer, October 19, 1911 (quoting report from Berman), ITO Papers, A36/96b.
16. Bressler to Stettauer, October 19, 1911, ITO Papers, A36/96b.
17. Bressler to Zangwill, August 27, 1912 (quoting report from Berman) and Zangwill to Bressler, September 4, 1912, ITO Papers, A36/96b. See below, chapter 7, notes 34 and 35.
18. Bressler to Zangwill, November 6, 1911 (quoting report from Berman), ITO Papers, A36/96b.

19. Bressler to Stettauer, June 21, 1911; Bressler to Stettauer, August 7, 1911, ITO Papers, A36/96b.

20. Ellman to Bressler, May 29, 1911, ITO Papers, A36/96b.

21. Ellman to Bressler, May 29, 1911; Ellman to Berman, June 23, 1911; Berman to Bressler, July 18, 1911, ITO Papers, A36/96b.

22. Berman to Bressler, July 28, 1911, ITO Papers, A36/96b.

23. Bressler to Stettauer, July 28, 1911, ITO Papers, A36/96b.

24. Minutes of the Galveston Committee meeting of January 30, 1911, JIIB Papers.

25. Berman to Bressler, August 1, 1911, ITO Papers, A36/96b.

26. Zangwill to Bressler, July 16, 1912, ITO Papers, A36/96b.

27. Bressler to Berman, July 2, 1912, ITO Papers, A36/96b.

28. Berman to Bressler, February 9, 1911; Bressler to Zangwill, February 15, 1911; Berman to Bressler (letter forwarded to Stettauer), ITO Papers, A36/96b.

29. Zangwill to Schiff, October 4, 1911, ITO Papers, A36/96b.

30. Bressler to Zangwill, October 10, 1911, ITO Papers, A36/96b.

31. Passenger manifests of ships arriving at Galveston during January-August 1911. These figures essentially agree with those compiled by the National Jewish Immigration Council. See chart "Jewish Immigration in the United States During 1911," Baron de Hirsch Fund Archives, "Immigration Statistics" File. The figures are further supported by reports given on the embarkation or disembarkation of the Jewish immigrant parties to Galveston. These reports were included in correspondence passing between the Jewish Emigration Society in Kiev, the *Hilfsverein* in Bremen, the ITO in London, and the JIIB in Galveston and New York.

32. Technically, Bressler had called for 125 *per shipment*, but it was understood that shipments arrived about once a month. Thus, although there were actually nine shipments in January-August 1911, we may take the liberty of dividing the figure by eight.

33. Schiff to Zangwill, October 13, 1911, ITO Papers, A36/41.

34. Zangwill to Schiff, November 3, 1911, ITO Papers, A36/41.

35. Bressler to Schiff, November 16, 1911, ITO Papers, A36/41.

36. Zangwill to Schiff, December 20, 1911, ITO Papers, A36/41.

37. Zangwill to Schiff, December 20, 1911, ITO Papers, A36/41.

38. Schiff to Zangwill, January 2, 1912, ITO Papers, A36/41.

39. From figures compiled by the National Jewish Immigration Council. See chart "Jewish Immigration in the United States During 1911," Baron de Hirsch Fund Archives ("Immigration Statistics" File).

7. *1912: Difficulties in Recruitment*

1. Bressler to Cohen, October 27, 1911; Hampton to Commissioner-General of Immigration, November 7, 1911, Cohen Papers, Box No. 3M229.

2. Cohen to Bressler, November 15, 1911, Henry Cohen Collection, Box No. 2538.

3. Hampton to Bressler, November 17, 1911, Henry Cohen Collection, Box No. 2538.

4. Bressler to Cohen, November 20, 1911, Henry Cohen Collection, Box No. 2538.

5. Schiff to Cohen, November 22, 1911, Henry Cohen Collection, Box No. 2538.

6. Cohen to Schiff, November 28, 1911, Henry Cohen Collection, Box No. 2538.

7. Bressler to Cohen, January 18, 1912, Henry Cohen Collection, Box No. 2538.

8. Bressler to Sulzberger, February 27, 1912, JIIB Papers.

9. Schiff to Zangwill, January 19, 1912, Schiff Papers, Box No. 20.

10. Schiff to Zangwill, February 2, 1912, Schiff Papers, Box No. 20.

11. Bressler to Zangwill, October 10, 1911, ITO Papers, A36/96b; Bressler to Schiff, November 16, 1911, ITO Papers, A36/41; Bressler to Schiff, January 17, 1912, ITO Papers, A36/41.

12. Bressler to Schiff, November 16, 1911 (letter forwarded by Schiff to Zangwill), ITO Papers, A36/41.

13. Bressler to Zangwill, February 7, 1912, ITO Papers, A36/96b.

14. Zangwill to Bressler, January 26, 1912, ITO Papers, A36/96b.

15. Bressler to Zangwill, February 7, 1912, ITO Papers, A36/96b.

16. Zangwill to Bressler, January 26, 1912, ITO Papers, A36/96b.

17. Bressler to Zangwill, February 7, 1912, ITO Papers, A36/96b.

18. Zangwill to Bressler, January 26, 1912, ITO Papers, A36/96b.

19. Bressler to Zangwill, February 7, 1912, ITO Papers, A36/96b.

20. Zangwill to Bressler, January 26, 1912, ITO Papers, A36/96b.

21. Bressler to Zangwill, February 7, 1912, ITO Papers, A36/96b.

22. Schiff to Dr. Katzenelsohn, February 19, 1912, Schiff Papers, Box No. 20.

23. Samuel Joseph, *Jewish Immigration to the United States from 1881 to 1910* (New York: Columbia University Press, 1914), p. 138.

24. Bressler to Zangwill, March 20, 1912 (quoting report from Berman), ITO Papers, A36/96b.

25. Bressler to Zangwill, January 23, 1912 (quoting report from Berman), ITO Papers, A36/96b.

26. Bressler to Zangwill, May 14, 1912 (quoting report from Berman), ITO Papers, A36/96b.

27. Bressler to Zangwill, August 1, 1912; Bressler to Zangwill, August 22, 1912, ITO Papers, A36/96b.

28. Phillips to Bressler, January 8, 1912; Bressler to Phillips, January 22, 1912, ITO Papers, A36/96b.

29. Finkenstein to Bressler, August 21, 1912 (quoting report from Bloch), ITO Papers, A36/96b.

30. Berman to Bressler, September 14, 1912, ITO Papers, A36/96b.

31. Bressler to Zangwill, August 22, 1912, ITO Papers, A36/96b.

32. Berman to Bressler, August 18, 1912, ITO Papers, A36/96b.

33. Zangwill to Bressler, September 3, 1912, ITO Papers, A36/96b.

34. Bressler to Zangwill, August 27, 1912 (quoting report from Berman), ITO Papers, A36/96b.

35. Zangwill to Bressler, September 4, 1912, ITO Papers, A36/96b.

36. Bressler to Zangwill, September 17, 1912, ITO Papers, A36/96b. See also, Jochelmann's "Report on the Condition of the Emigration Movement via the port of Galveston," ITO Papers, A36/31.

37. Bressler to Phillips, December 26, 1912, ITO Papers, A36/96b.

38. Bressler to Seman, November 9, 1912, JIIB Papers.

39. Information about Leib Haft was obtained through private correspondence between the author and Haft's daughter, Mrs. Sylvia Firschein, of Wayne, New Jersey, who has corresponded with her father's sister in Russia. Further information about Haft was obtained by the author from the passenger manifest of the S.S. *Rhein*, which left Bremen Nov. 15, 1912, and arrived in Galveston Dec. 8, 1912. Haft is listed in the manifest on page 167 (list 15), line 6. For a follow-up on Haft's life, see below, Retrospective.

40. Schiff to Zangwill, July 22, 1912, Schiff Papers, Box No. 20.

41. Bressler's "Brief Statement with Regard to Trip," filed among the minutes of the Galveston Committee meeting of November 30, 1912, JIIB Papers. The immigrants' complaints which are summarized in the pages ahead are taken from this "Brief Statement."

42. Jochelmann's "Report on the Condition of the Emigration Movement via the Port of Galveston," ITO Papers, A36/31.

43. Jochelmann's "Report on the Condition of the Emigration Movement via the Port of Galveston," ITO Papers, A36/31. Also, see Handbill issued in 1908 by the North German-Lloyd Steamship Co. advertising its Galveston Line, JIIB Papers.

44. See above, chapter 1, note 38.

45. Bressler to Schiff, August 21, 1908, JIIB Papers.

46. Schiff to Zangwill, October 4, 1907, ITO Papers, A36/41.

47. Examination of Solomon Lewitan, Kansas City, Missouri, July 22, 1910, U.S. Immigration File No. 52961/11.

48. Examination of Srul Bistrizky, Kansas City, Missouri, July 24, 1910, U.S. Immigration File No. 52961/11.

49. Examination of Mendel Shrager, Kansas City, Missouri, July 22, 1910, U.S. Immigration File No. 52961/11.

50. Examination of David Schwesky, Kansas City, Missouri, July 24, 1910, U.S. Immigration File No. 52961/11.

51. Examination of Moische Kaufman, Kansas City, Missouri, July 23, 1910, U.S. Immigration File No. 52961/11.

52. Examination of Aaron Mirapolsky, Kansas City, Missouri, July 23, 1910, U.S. Immigration File No. 52961/11.

53. Examination of Berkin Fredkin, Kansas City, Missouri, July 22, 1910, U.S. Immigration File No. 52961/11.

54. Berman to Bressler, February 1, 1911; Bressler to Zangwill, February 10, 1911; Stettauer to Bressler, May 11, 1911; Bressler to Zangwill, July 27, 1911; Bressler to Stettauer, June 30, 1911; Bressler to Stettauer, July 28, 1911, ITO Papers, A36/96b.

55. Original Yiddish, and English translation of letter, with signatures, ITO Papers, A36/96b.

56. Bressler to Zangwill, August 3, 1911, ITO Papers, A36/96b.

57. Finkenstein to Bressler, August 18, 1911, ITO Papers, A36/96b.

58. Finkenstein to Bressler, August 24, 1911; Bressler to Finkenstein, September 5, 1911, ITO Papers, A36/96b.

59. Zangwill to Schiff, October 4, 1911, ITO Papers A36/41.

60. Schiff to Cohen, January 30, 1912, Henry Cohen Collection, Box No. 2538.

61. Zangwill to Bressler, September 3, 1912, ITO Papers.

62. Bressler's "Brief Statement with Regard to Trip," filed among the minutes of the Galveston Committee meeting of November 30, 1912, JIIB Papers.

63. Schiff to North German-Lloyd Steamship Co., January 28, 1913, ITO Papers, A36/96b.

64. Bressler to Sulzberger, January 3, 1913; Sulzberger to Bressler, January 22, 1913; Bressler to Sulzberger, January 23, 1913, JIIB Papers.

65. Warburg to North German-Lloyd Steamship Co., March 13, 1913, ITO Papers, A36/96b.

66. Schiff to Zangwill, September 4, 1913; Schiff to Nathan, October 7, 1913, Schiff Papers, Box No. 20. Also, Schiff to Cohen, October 27, 1913, Henry Cohen Collection, Box No. 2538.

67. Schiff to Bressler, July 24, 1908, Schiff Papers, Box No. 20.

68. Schiff to Sulzberger, November 24, 1908, Schiff Papers, Box No. 20.

69. Schiff to Zangwill, December 3, 1912, ITO Papers, A36/41.

70. Bressler to Jochelmann, March 29, 1913, Felix M. Warburg Papers, Box No. 165.

71. Bressler to Zangwill, July 29, 1913 (quoting report from Berman), ITO Papers, A36/96b.

72. See above, note 10, referring to Schiff's letter to Zangwill, February 2, 1912, stating, "There will be no difficulty to place from 125 to 200 proper immigrants a month."

73. Schiff to Zangwill, December 3, 1912, ITO Papers, A36/41.

74. Galveston Committee meeting minutes of November 30, 1912, JIIB Papers.

75. Schiff to Bressler, December 19, 1912, Schiff Papers, Box No. 20.

8. 1913: The Rothschilds Withdraw and a Hernia "Epidemic" Breaks Out

1. A. H. Archer to Zangwill, March 27, 1907, ITO Papers, A36/24.

2. Table of "Expenses of the Emigration Regulation Department," ITO Papers, A36/24.

3. See above, the end of chapter 6.

4. Leopold de Rothschild to Zangwill, December 20, 1911; Zangwill to Leopold de Rothschild, December 21, 1911, ITO Papers, A36/24.

5. Leopold de Rothschild to Zangwill, November 22, 1912, ITO Papers, A36/24.

6. Jochelmann to Zangwill, February 23, 1913, ITO Papers, A36/31. Although Jochelmann does not mention Levin by name, the latter fits Jochelmann's description of a leading Zionist who was Brodski's private secretary. Interestingly enough, Levin himself had once advocated settling

Russian Jews in the American West where, according to U.S. law, they could apply for statehood after reaching a population of 60,000. Levin, who had proposed this idea in 1881 as an alternative to settlement in the Land of Israel, abandoned it within a year and joined the ranks of the budding Zionist movement, where he remained, ever since. See Ya'acov Tsur, *"Dyokanah shel Ha-T'futsah"* [Anatomy of the Diaspora] with documents and sources compiled and edited by Israel Bartal (Jerusalem: Keter Publishing Co., 1975), Document No. 15, pp. 298–300, taken from *Ha-Maggid*, 25. 39 (Oct. 6. 1881): 321–322.

7. *Vestnik Yevreiskoi Emigratzii E Colonizatzii*, no. 12, p. 8 (Dr. Max Goldberg, editor). Quoted in Yehuda Slutsky, *"Ha-Itonut Ha-Yehudit-Russit Ba-Meah Ha-Esrim, 1900–1918"* [The Russian-Jewish press in the Twentieth Century, 1900–1918], (Tel Aviv: Tel Aviv University, 1978), p. 317, note 69.

8. Zangwill to Schiff, January 28, 1913, appended to the Galveston Committee minutes of the meeting held on February 12, 1913, JIIB Papers.

9. Schiff to Zangwill, February 13, 1913, appended to the Galveston Committee minutes of the meeting held on February 12, 1913, JIIB Papers. This letter is also found in the Schiff Papers, Box No. 20. Zangwill's reactions to Schiff's letter are expressed in his own letter to Jochelmann dated February 25, 1913, ITO Papers, A36/31.

10. Schiff to Philipson, February 13, 1913. Letter in original German appended to Galveston Committee minutes of the meeting held on February 12, 1913, JIIB Papers.

11. Bressler to Phillips, January 23, 1913, quoting Berman's report, ITO Papers, A36/96b. Berman reported to Bressler on the arrival of every immigrant group.

12. Bressler to Phillips, February 26, 1913, ITO Papers, A36/96b.

13. Bressler to Warburg, February 25, 1913, quoting Berman's report; Warburg to Bressler, February 26, 1913; Bressler to Warburg, February 28, 1913, JIIB Papers.

14. Bressler to Warburg, March 11, 1913, quoting Berman's report, JIIB Papers. Same Berman report also quoted in Bressler to Phillips, March 12, 1913, and Bressler to Phillips, March 17, 1913, ITO Papers, A36/96b.

15. Bressler to Warburg, April 15, 1913, quoting Berman's report, JIIB Papers. Same Berman report quoted in Bressler to Zangwill, April 15, 1913, ITO Papers, A36/96b.

16. Zangwill to Bressler, March 27, 1913, ITO Papers, A36/96b.

17. Bressler to Warburg, April 15, 1913, quoting Berman's report, JIIB Papers. Same Berman report quoted in Bressler to Zangwill, April 15, 1913, ITO Papers, A36/96b.

18. (a) Bressler to Warburg, May 13, 1913, JIIB Papers, and Bressler to Zangwill, May 13, 1913, ITO Papers, A36/96b. Both letters quote the same report from Berman. (b) Bressler to Warburg, May 28, 1913, JIIB Papers, and Bressler to Zangwill, May 28, 1913, ITO Papers, A36/96b. Both letters quote another report from Berman. (c) Bressler to Zangwill, September 2, 1913, quoting still another report from Berman, ITO Papers, A36/96b.

19. Bressler to Warburg, May 20, 1913, JIIB Papers.

20. Bressler to all members of the Galveston Committee, June 9, 1913, JIIB Papers.

21. M. Sarschawsky and D. Feinberg (Saint Petersburg) to Jewish Colonization Association (Paris), August 13, 1913, JIIB Papers. Also, Schiff to Zangwill, October 27, 1913, Schiff Papers, Box No. 20.

22. Table of general and Jewish immigration comparing January-October 1912 to January-October 1913, Baron de Hirsch Fund Archives, "Immigration Statistics" File.

23. Schiff to Feinberg, October 21, 1913, Schiff Papers, Box No. 20.

24. Bressler to Zangwill, July 29, 1913, quoting Berman's report, ITO Papers, A36/96b.

25. Bressler to Zangwill, September 3, 1913, quoting Berman's report, ITO Papers, A36/96b.

26. Among influential circles in the field of Jewish social work, the view was often expressed that men had an obligation to support their families rather than be dependent on charity, even if it meant working on the Sabbath. See B. A. Palitz, "Desecration of Sabbath or Desertion of Family," *Jewish Charities* 1.11 (June 1911).

27. Bressler to Zangwill, September 16, 1913, quoting Berman's report, ITO Papers, A36/96b.

28. Ibid.

29. Bressler to Zangwill, July 29, 1913, quoting Berman's report; Bressler to Zangwill, August 1, 1913, ITO Papers, A36/96b.

30. Bressler to Zangwill, September 3, 1913, quoting Berman's report, ITO Papers, A36/96b.

31. Bressler to Zangwill, September 16, 1913, quoting Berman's report, ITO Papers, A36/96b.

32. Bressler to Zangwill, September 30, 1913, quoting Berman's report, ITO Papers, A36/96b.

33. Bressler to Zangwill, October 9, 1913, ITO Papers, A36/96b.

34. Bressler to Zangwill, October 21, 1913, ITO Papers, A36/96b.

35. Bressler to Zangwill, October 28, 1913, quoting report from Galveston office, ITO Papers, A36/96b.

36. Bressler to Zangwill, December 9, 1913, ITO Papers, A36/96b.

37. Bressler to Zangwill, February 11, 1914, ITO Papers, A36/96b.

38. Bressler to Zangwill, January 2, 1914, ITO Papers, A36/96b.

39. Bressler to Kohler, October 9, 1913, JIIB Papers.

40. Bressler to Zangwill, September 16, 1913, quoting Berman's report, ITO Papers, A36/96b.

41. Zangwill to Bressler, September 24, 1913, ITO Papers, A36/96b.

42. Zangwill to Bressler, October 23, 1913, ITO Papers, A36/96b.

43. Zangwill to Bressler, September 24, 1913, ITO Papers, A36/96b.

44. Schiff to Zangwill, November 24, 1913, Schiff Papers, Box No. 20.

45. Bressler to Kohler, November 14, 1913, referring to the latter's letter of November 7 to Secretary of Labor William B. Wilson, JIIB Papers.

46. See *The Dictionary of American Biography*, Dumas Malone, ed., s.v. "Post, Louis Freeland" (New York: Charles Scribner's Sons, 1935).

47. Elkus to Schiff, November 11, 1913; Elkus to Bressler, November 11, 1913; Bressler to Elkus, November 12, 1913, JIIB Papers.

48. Anonymous letter to Zangwill, December 3, 1913, ITO Papers, A36/3.

49. Presumably, Schiff's support for Wilson was based on considerations other than the latter's position on immigration matters. Schiff supported Wilson once again in 1916, during the president's successful campaign for reelection. See *The Dictionary of American Biography*, Dumas Malone, ed., s.v. "Schiff, Jacob Henry" (New York: Charles Scribner's Sons, 1935).

50. *I.T.O.*, Officieel Organ van de Ito-Federatie in Nederland 4. 3 (Maart 1914): 2.

51. Information about Ephraim Zalman (Charles) Hoffman was obtained from *A Family Portrait, Part I: Russia, Emigration, Fort Worth*, researched and written by the subject's grandson, David Hoffman, of Austin, Texas, and privately published by him in 1979. Further information about Hoffman was obtained by the present author from the passenger manifest of the S.S. *Wittekind*, which left Bremen September 3, 1913, and arrived in Galveston September 28, 1913. He is listed on page 118 (list 7), line 26, as Schie Gofmann.

52. Information about Sarah Bernstein Hoffman was obtained from *A Family Portrait, Part I: Russia, Emigration, Fort Worth*, researched and written by the subject's grandson, David Hoffman, of Austin, Texas, and privately published by him in 1979, in honor of his grandmother's eighty-fifth birthday. (He gleaned most of the information from conversations with his grandmother.) Further information was obtained by the present author from the passenger manifest of the S.S. *Chemnitz*, which left Bremen September 18, 1913, and arrived in Galveston October 10, 1913. Sarah Bernstein appears on page 139 (list 5), line 27.

53. "Aliens Arrive; Are Cared For," *Galveston Tribune*, October 11, 1913, as quoted in *A Family Portrait*, above, notes 51 and 52.

54. See below, Retrospective.

9. 1914: The End of a Movement

1. Schiff to Bressler, January 9, 1913, Schiff Papers, Box No. 20.

2. Berman to Bressler, December 1, 1913, ITO Papers, A36/96b.

3. Bressler to Zangwill, December 18, 1913, ITO Papers, A36/96b.

4. Jochelmann to ITO Emigration Regulation Department in London, November 15, 1913, American Jewish Archives.

5. See above, chapter 5, note 11, referring to Larned's expressed disappointment in the low number of deportations in August, 1910.

6. Bressler to Kohler, February 26, 1914, JIIB Papers.

7. Kohler answered Larned's charge by pointing out "that more than half the cases involved insane persons where we have purposely and wisely refrained from establishing special Jewish institutions." Kohler to Bressler, February 27, 1914, JIIB Papers.

8. Bressler to Kohler, February 28, 1914; Kohler to Bressler, March 2, 1914, JIIB Papers.

9. Wolf to Schiff, April 4, 1914; Bressler to Schiff, May 12, 1914, JIIB Papers.

10. Zangwill to Bressler, January 13, 1914; Bressler to Zangwill, February 19, 1914 (marked "personal & confidential"); Zangwill to Bressler, March 4, 1914; Bressler to Zangwill, March 14, 1914; Bressler to Zangwill, March 24, 1914; Zangwill to Bressler, April 3, 1914; Phillips to Bressler, April 16, 1914; Zangwill to Bressler, April 27, 1914; Bressler to Zangwill, May 14, 1914, ITO Papers, A36/96b. Also, Bressler to Schiff, May 15, 1914, JIIB Papers.

11. Schiff to Zangwill, November 24, 1913, Schiff Papers, Box No. 20. Among those greeted by Jochelmann was Mr. Husband, chairman of the delegation.

12. Kohler to Bressler (quoting excerpts from report of Commissioner General of Immigration for 1913), March 16, 1914, JIIB Papers.

13. Bressler to Kohler, March 13, 1914, JIIB Papers.

14. Bressler to Zangwill, January 19, 1914; Epstein to Bressler, March 9, 1914, ITO Papers, A36/96b.

15. Bressler to Zangwill, April 2, 1914 (quoting from Epstein's report), ITO Papers, A36/96b.

16. Bressler to Zangwill, March 27, 1914, ITO Papers, A36/96b. Also, Bressler to Schiff, March 27, 1914, JIIB Papers. (In both letters, Bressler quotes the same report from Epstein.)

17. Schiff to Zangwill, October 25, 1906, ITO Papers, A36/41.

18. In an address to ITO members, Zangwill gave the goal as 20,000 to 30,000 immigrants, who would serve as magnets for others. See the *Novaya Eudaia* no. 4 (July 1908): 32–35.

19. Schiff to Zangwill, August 30, 1909, ITO Papers, A36/41.

20. Schiff to Zangwill, December 3, 1912, ITO Papers, A36/41.

21. Minutes of the JIIB Executive Committee meeting of April 9, 1914, Henry Cohen Collection, Box No. 2538.

22. Schiff to Feinberg, October 31, 1913, Schiff Papers, Box No. 20.

23. Jochelmann to the ITO Emigration Regulation Department in London, November 15, 1913, American Jewish Archives.

24. Letter quoted in minutes of JIIB Executive Committee meeting of April 9, 1914, Henry Cohen Collection, Box No. 2538.

25. Bressler to all members of the JIIB Executive Committee, April 6, 1914, JIIB Papers. Of all the members, only Felix M. Warburg failed to attend. See minutes of JIIB Executive Committee meeting of April 9, 1914, Henry Cohen Collection, Box No. 2538.

26. Minutes of JIIB Executive Committee meeting of April 9, 1914, Henry Cohen Collection, Box No. 2538. The proceedings of this meeting were also summarized by Bressler in his letter to Zangwill dated April 16, 1914. This letter is available in the Henry Cohen Collection, Box 2538, and also in the ITO Papers, A36/96b.

27. Ibid.

28. Ibid.

29. Ibid.

30. Bressler to Cohen, April 16, 1914, Henry Cohen Collection, Box No. 2538.

31. Schiff to Zangwill, April 14, 1914, Schiff Papers, Box No. 20. Also, Bressler to Zangwill, April 16, 1914, which is available in both the Henry Cohen Collection, Box No. 2538, and in the ITO Papers, A36/96b.

32. Schiff to Bressler, May 4, 1914, JIIB Papers.

33. Zangwill to Bressler, April 27, 1914, ITO Papers, A36/96b.

34. Bressler to Schiff, May 12, 1914, JIIB Papers.

35. Bressler to Sulzberger, May 14, 1914, JIIB Papers.

36. Bressler to Zangwill, May 14, 1914, ITO Papers, A36/96b.

37. Bressler to Zangwill, June 9, 1914, ITO Papers, A36/96b.

38. Zangwill to Bressler, June 17, 1914, ITO Papers, A36/96b.

39. Bressler to Zangwill, July 3, 1914 (original English, and German translation), ITO Papers, A36/3.

40. Zangwill to Bressler, July 13, 1914, ITO Papers, A36/96b.

41. Abraham Solomon to Bressler, July 27, 1914, JIIB Papers.

42. Bressler to Zangwill, July 29, 1914, ITO Papers, A36/96b. See *The Jewish Comment* 43. 18 (July 31, 1914): 205–207. The German translation of most of this article can be found in the ITO Papers, A36/3.

43. Schiff to Zangwill, June 9, 1914, Schiff Papers, Box No. 20. See *Jewish Charities*, 4. 11 (June 1914): 5–6. Schiff's first draft of his article can be found in the Schiff Papers, Box No. 4.

44. Zangwill to Berman, June 30, 1914. The German translation of this article can be found in the ITO Papers, A36/3.

45. The agenda for the planned Conference of the International Council of the ITO, 1914, *Neue Volkshaus*, Zurich, September 1, 2, 3, and 4, is available in both English and German in the ITO Papers, A36/3.

46. Phillips to Bressler, August 13, 1914, ITO Papers, A36/96b.

47. Bressler to Zangwill, May 19, 1915, ITO Papers, A36/96b. Also, Bressler to Schiff, May 19, 1914, JIIB Papers.

48. Bressler to Zangwill, May 22, 1914, ITO Papers, A36/96b.

49. Bressler to Zangwill, May 19, 1914, ITO Papers, A36/96b.

50. Bressler to Zangwill, May 26, 1914, ITO Papers, A36/96b.

51. Bressler to Schiff, May 26, 1914, JIIB Papers.

52. Bressler to Zangwill, June 23, 1914 (quoting part of Epstein's report); Bressler to Zangwill, June 30, 1914; Bressler to Zangwill, July 3, 1914, ITO Papers, A36/96b.

53. Bressler to Schiff, June 22, 1914 (quoting Epstein's full report), JIIB Papers. Bressler left out this part of Epstein's report when he quoted it to Zangwill in his letter to him dated June 23, 1914. (See above, note 52.)

54. Solomon to Zangwill, July 29, 1914 (quoting Epstein's report), ITO Papers, A36/96b. Also, Solomon to Schiff, July 29, 1914 (quoting the same report from Epstein), JIIB Papers.

55. Bressler to Zangwill, August 7, 1914 (quoting Epstein's report), ITO Papers, A36/96b. Also, Bressler to Schiff, August 7, 1914 (quoting the same report from Epstein), JIIB Papers.

56. Bressler to Schiff, July 28, 1914 (quoting Epstein's report), JIIB Papers.

57. Solomon to Bressler, August 17, 1914, JIIB Papers.

58. Bressler to Schiff, August 25, 1914, JIIB Papers.

59. Technically, the distinction of being the last Galveston Movement immigrant might belong to one M. Lange, although he probably arrived in New York, as evidenced by the following letter from Zangwill to Bressler, dated July 23, 1914: "Mr. M. Lange, the bearer of this letter, has been

doing some work in the Office, but on account of the war there is nothing further for him to do. He is now going to try his luck in America, and it would be a real kindness if you could stretch the Galveston operations so as to include him by sending him to some town where you think he would be able to earn his livelihood." ITO Papers, A36/96b.

60. The JIIB Papers contain an excerpt from a German letter which seems to have been written by Nathan to Schiff on July 7, 1914. Schiff's answer to Nathan, dated July 21, 1914, refers to such a letter, and the German excerpt would seem to fit the description. Schiff's reply, translated from German, can be found in the Schiff Papers, Box No. 20.

61. Bressler to Schiff, July 29, 1914, JIIB Papers.

62. Schiff to Bressler, July 30, 1914, JIIB Papers.

63. Bressler to Schiff, August 3, 1914, JIIB Papers.

64. See above, note 60. See also Zangwill to Bressler, July 4, 1912, and Bressler to Zangwill, July 17, 1912, ITO Papers, A36/96b.

65. Schiff to Ballin, January 13, 1914, Schiff Papers, Box No. 20.

66. Bressler to Schiff, February 1, 1915; Schiff to Bressler, February 2, 1915, JIIB Papers. Also, Schiff to Sulzberger, November 2, 1914, Schiff Papers, Boxes No. 4 and 20. Also, Schiff to Cohen, November 4, 1914, Henry Cohen Collection, Box No. 2538.

67. Schiff to Zangwill, April 9, 1915, Schiff Papers, Box No. 4.

68. Zangwill to Arthur Meyerowitz, Schiff Papers, Box No. 20.

69. *The Letters and Papers of Chaim Weizmann*, Series A, Volume II, Meyer W. Weisgal, general editor (London: Oxford University Press, 1971), biographical index, s.v. Jochelman, David S. Also, obituary in *The Jewish Chronicle*, July 18, 1941, p. 17. These sources give the year of Jochelman's birth as 1868, making him age seventy-three at his death in 1941. However, according to an article in *The Jewish Chronicle*, February 27, 1920, p. 23, Jochelman was celebrating his fiftieth birthday at about the time of the article's appearance. Thus, Jochelman was born in 1870 and died at the age of seventy-one. This has been confirmed by Jochelman's daughter, Mrs. Fanny Cockerell of London, who gives her father's birthdate as April 1, 1870.

70. *Who's Who in American Jewry*, Vol. 3 (1938–1939), (New York: National News Association, Inc., 1938), s.v. Billikopf, Jacob; Bressler, David Maurice; Waldman, Morris David. Also, see *Encyclopaedia Judaica*, s.v. Billikopf, Jacob; Bressler, David Maurice; Waldman, Morris David.

71. Henry Cohen's life has been recounted in Anne (Cohen) Nathan and Harry I. Cohen, *The Man Who Stayed in Texas* (New York and London: Whittlesey House, a division of McGraw-Hill, 1941), and in A. Stanley Dreyfus, *Henry Cohen, Messenger of the Lord* (New York: Bloch Publishing Co., 1963).

Retrospective

1. Judith Goldstein, *The Politics of Ethnic Pressure: The American Jewish Committee as Lobbyist, 1906–1917* Ph.D. dissertation, Columbia University, 1972, pp. 137–139, 154–155.

2. Simon Wolf, *The Presidents I have Known from 1860 to 1918* (Washington, D.C.: Press of Byron S. Adams, 1918), pp. 305–313.

3. Information about Leib Haft was obtained from Haft's daughter, Mrs. Sylvia Firschein, of Wayne, New Jersey. See above, chapter 7, note 39.

4. Information about Nathan Kaluzny was obtained from his grandson, Professor Robert Rockaway. See above, chapter 5, note 61. Prof. Rockaway's book on the Jews of Detroit, untitled at the time of this writing, will soon be published by Wayne University Press, Detroit, Michigan.

5. David Hoffman's *A Family Portrait, Part I*, above, chapter 8, notes 51 and 52, extends to 1924. At the time of the present writing, Part II has not yet appeared. Further information about the Hoffman family was obtained by the present author through an interview with Charles Hoffman, the reporter.

6. Bernard Shuman, *A History of the Sioux City Jewish Community, 1869 to 1969* (Sioux City, Iowa: Bolstein Creative Printers, Inc., for Jewish Federation, Sioux City, Iowa, 1969).

7. On passenger manifests as well as in the JIIB Papers, up to the year 1912, Rabbi Joseph Rauch is listed as the man in Sioux City to whom the Galveston Jewish immigrants were destined.

8. Bernard Shuman, above, note 6, pp. 13–17, 23.

9. Ibid., pp. 42–43, quoting the reminiscences of Morris Lazriowich.

10. Emanuel Sternheim, *History of the Jews in Sioux City*, c. 1916, as quoted in Shuman, above, note 6, p. 35. Abraham Koval's name appears as Abram Berko [?] Kowal on the passenger manifest of the S.S. *Hanover*, which left Bremen April 7, 1910, and arrived in Galveston April 28, 1910. He is listed on page 44 (list 10), line 21, as being destined for Rabbi Joseph Rauch in Sioux City.

11. Oscar Littlefield, "A Point of View," in Shuman, above, note 6, pp. 161–172 (chapter 16).

12. Ibid., pp. 162–163.

13. From a private interview between the author and Rabbi Hyman R. Rabinowitz of Jerusalem, who served as spiritual leader of Sioux City's Conservative synagogue, Shaare Zion, from 1925 to 1958.

14. Allen duPont Breck, *The Centennial History of the Jews of Colorado, 1859–1959*. The University of Denver, Department of History Series "The West in American History," No. 1 (Denver, Colorado: Hirschfeld Press, 1960), pp. 107–109.

15. Ibid., pp. 93, 110–119.

16. Ibid., p. 151.

17. Ibid., p. 155.

18. William Clendenin, "Kansas City, The Workshop of the West," addendum to Ethel R. Feineman, "A History of the Jews of Kansas City," *The Reform Advocate* (Chicago), March 28, 1908, pp. 9–56 (quote appearing on p. 56). Quoted in Frank J. Adler, *Roots in a Moving Stream: The Centennial History of Congregation B'nai Jehuda of Kansas City, 1870–1970* (Kansas City, Missouri: The Temple, Congregation B'nai Jehuda, printed by Spangler Printers, Kansas City, Mo., 1972), p. 130.

19. Frank J. Adler, *op. cit.*, pp. 112, 130–132.

20. "Isaac Don Levine: Letters of an Immigrant," (part of "The East European Immigrant Jew in America, 1881–1981"), *American Jewish Archives* 33. 1 (April, 1981): 53–83, reprinted, with some deletions, from various editions of the *Kansas City Star* which appeared between July 5, 1914, and January 31, 1915. The quoted excerpt is from p. 82, which was reprinted from the January 31, 1915 edition.

21. Frank J. Adler, *op. cit.*, p. 137, quoting a letter to Adler from Isaac Don Levine, written April 7, 1970.

22. Ibid., p. 245n.

23. Ibid., p. xiii, introduction by Jacob R. Marcus.

24. Ibid., p. 255.

25. Cyrus Adler, above, chapter 1, note 16, vol. 2, pp. 111–113, quoting a slightly condensed version of Billikopf's reminiscences about Schiff. The complete version is found in the Schiff Papers, Box No. 4.

26. Sidney Goldstein, "Jews in the United States: Perspectives from Demography," *American Jewish Year Book*, vol. 81 (1981), (New York and Philadelphia: The American Jewish Committee and the Jewish Publication Society of America, 1980), pp. 30–32, especially table 5 on p. 31.

27. *Jewish Daily Forward*, December 7, 1907, p. 4. See above, chapter 2, note 46.

28. Sidney Goldstein, above, note 26.

Bibliography

1. Archival Sources

For the varying significance of these archival sources, see the Preface. In the notes throughout this study, these archival sources are referred to in their shortened forms, as they appear here in italics.

American Jewish Committee Archives: New York, N.Y. The American Jewish Committee. Archives.

Baron de Hirsch Fund Archives: Waltham, Massachusetts. The American Jewish Historical Society. The Baron de Hirsch Fund Archives. "Immigration Statistics" File.

Central Archives for History of Jewish People: Jerusalem, Israel. The Central Archives for the History of the Jewish People. Inv./1589(3).

Cohen Papers: Austin, Texas. The General Libraries of the University of Texas at Austin. The Barker Texas History Center. The Henry Cohen Papers. Boxes No. 3M226–234 and 3M323.

Henry Cohen Collection: Cincinnati, Ohio. The American Jewish Archives. The Henry Cohen Collection. Box No. 2538.

Industrial Removal Office Papers: Waltham, Massachusetts. The American Jewish Archives. The Industrial Removal Office Papers.

ITO Papers: Jerusalem, Israel. The Central Zionist Archives. The Jewish Territorial Organization (ITO) Papers. Section A36.

JIIB Papers: Waltham, Massachusetts. The American Jewish Historical Society. "Galveston Immigration Plan." These are the papers of the Jewish Immigrants' Information Bureau, which were selected from among the Industrial Removal Office Papers.

Kohler Papers: Waltham, Massachusetts. The American Jewish Historical Society. The Max J. Kohler Papers.

Passenger Manifests: San Francisco, California. United States Department of Justice, Immigration and Naturalization Service. Records. Passenger manifests of inbound ship passengers at the Port of Galveston, Texas, dated prior to December 1, 1954, and arranged in chronological order,

226

micro-photographed by the Immigration and Naturalization Service. There are fifteen microfilm rolls, numbers 4 through 18, which cover the years 1907–1914.

Schiff Papers: Cincinnati, Ohio. The American Jewish Archives. The Jacob H. Schiff Papers, on microfilm. The two microfilm rolls which I used are Roll No. 4, which is a copy of the original Box No. 4 (marked "Galveston") of the Schiff Papers, and Roll No. 18, which is a copy of the original Box No. 20 (marked "Galveston Project"). Under the cataloguing system of the American Jewish Archives, these microfilm rolls are referred to as Nos. 678 and 692, respectively. (Rolls No. 700 and No. 714 are positive copies of Nos. 678 and 692.)

U.S. Immigration Files: Washington, D.C. National Archives and Records Service. Legislative, Judicial, and Fiscal Branch. Civil Archives Division. United States Department of Commerce and Labor, Bureau of Immigration and Naturalization. Record Group No. 85. Immigration Files. The immigration files I have used are No. 52,779/29 and No. 52,961/11.

Warburg Papers: Cincinnati, Ohio. The American Jewish Archives. The Felix M. Warburg Papers, Box No. 165.

2. Contemporary Newspapers and Periodicals

In the United States:

American Hebrew and Jewish Messenger
Commercial and Financial Chronicle
Galveston Daily News
Galveston Tribune
Jewish Charities
Jewish Comment
Jewish Daily Forward (Yiddish)
Jewish Daily News (Yiddishes Taggeblatt) (Yiddish)
New York Times

In Russia:

Der Fraind (Yiddish)
Folks Zeitung (Yiddish)
Novaya Eudaia (Russian)
Vestnik Yevreyskoi Emigratzii E Colonizatzii (Russian)
Yevreyski Golos (Russian)

In Germany:

Hilfsverein der Deutschen Juden Geschaftsbericht, Vols. 6–13 (1907–1914). (German)

BIBLIOGRAPHY

In the Netherlands:

  I.T.O. (Dutch)

In Austria:

  Die Wahrheit (German)
  Dr. Bloch's *Osterreichische Wochenschrift* (German)

In England:

  Hayehudi (Hebrew)
  Jewish Chronicle

3. Encyclopedias and Biographical Dictionaries

Biographical Directory of the American Congress, 1774-1971. S.v. "Bennet, William Stiles." Washington, D.C.: Government Printing Office, 1961.
Dictionary of American Biography. Dumas Malone, ed. S.v. "Keefe, Daniel J.," "Post, Louis Freeland," and "Schiff, Jacob H." New York: Charles Scribner's Sons.
Encyclopaedia Judaica. S.v. "Territorialism." Jerusalem: Keter Publishing House, Ltd., 1971.
S. Wininger's *Grose Judische National-Biographie.* S.V. "Klatzkin, Jakob," (vol. 3, p. 456). Czernowitz: Arta, 1928.
Universal Jewish Encyclopedia. S.v. "Galveston," and "Rosenak, Leopold." New York: Universal Jewish Encyclopedia Co., Inc., 1941.
Who Was Who in America, A Companion Volume to Who's Who in America. vol. I (1897–1942). S.v. "Cable, Benjamin Stickney," "Cable, Ransom R.," and "Nagle, Charles." Chicago: A.N. Marquis Co., 1942.
Who's Who in American Jewry. vol. 3 (1938–1939). S.v. "Billikopf, Jacob," "Bressler, David Maurice," "Waldman, Morris David," New York: National News Association, Inc., 1938.

4. Unpublished Dissertation

Goldstein, Judith. "The Politics of Ethnic Pressure: The American Jewish Committee as Lobbyist, 1906–1917". Ph.D. dissertation, Columbia University, 1972.

5. Published Works

Adler, Cyrus. *Jacob H. Schiff: His Life and Letters.* 2 vols. New York: Doubleday, 1928
Adler, Frank J. *Roots in a Moving Stream: The Centennial History of Congregation B'nai Jehuda of Kansas City, 1870–1970.* Kansas City, Missouri: The Temple, Congregation B'nai Jehuda, (Spangler Printers,) 1972.

Anderson, Donald F. *William Howard Taft: A Conservative's Conception of the Presidency*. Ithaca and London: Cornell University Press, 1973.

Best, Gary Dean. "Jacob H. Schiff's Galveston Movement: An Experiment in Immigration Deflection, 1907–1914." *American Jewish Archives*. 30.1 (April 1978): 43–79.

Birmingham, Stephen. *"Our Crowd": The Great Jewish Families of New York*. New York: Harper and Row, 1967.

Bogen, Boris D. *Jewish Philanthropy: An Exposition of Principles and Methods of Jewish Social Service in the United States*. New York: The Macmillan Co., 1917.

Breck, Allen du Pont. *The Centennial History of the Jews of Colorado, 1859–1959*. The University of Denver, Department of History Series "The West in American History," No. 1, Denver, Colorado: Hirschfeld Press, 1960.

Bressler, David M. "The Removal Work, Including Galveston." *Proceedings of the National Conference of Jewish Charities*, 1910.

Brody, David. *Industrial America in the Twentieth Century*. New York: Thomas Y. Crowell Co., 1967.

Cohen, Henry. *The Galveston Immigration Movement*. (An updated pamphlet which appeared during the years of the Galveston Movement.)

Cohen, Israel. *The Turkish Persecution of the Jews*. London: Alabaster, Passmore and Sons, 1918.

(Cohen) Nathan, Anne and Cohen, Harry I. *The Man Who Stayed in Texas*. New York and London: Whittlesey House (a division of McGraw-Hill), 1941.

Dreyfus, A. Stanley. *Henry Cohen, Messenger of the Lord*. New York: Bloch Publishing Co., 1963.

Feingold, Henry L. *Zion in America*. New York: Hippocrene Books, 1974.

Feinstein, Marnin. *American Zionism 1884–1904*. New York: Herzl Press, 1965.

Friedenwald, Herbert, ed. "In Defense of the Jewish Immigrant." *American Jewish Year Book*, vol. 12 (1910–11). Philadelphia: The Jewish Publication Society of America, 1910.

Goldstein, Sidney. "Jews in the United States: Perspectives from Demography." *American Jewish Year Book*, vol. 81 (1981). New York and Philadelphia: The American Jewish Committee and the Jewish Publication Society of America, 1980.

Handlin, Oscar. *The Uprooted*. New York: Grosset and Dunlap, 1951.

Hayes, William Edward. *Iron Road to Empire: The History of One Hundred Years of the Progress and Achievements of the Rock Island Lines*. New York: Simmons-Boardman, 1953.

[Hoffman, David] *A Family Portrait, Part I: Russia, Emigration, Fort Worth*. Austin, Texas: (privately published,) 1979.

James, Edmund J., et al. *The Immigrant Jew in America*. New York: B.F. Buck and Co., 1907.

Joseph, Samuel. *History of the Baron de Hirsch Fund*. Philadelphia: Jewish Publication Society of America, 1935.

Joseph, Samuel. *Jewish Immigration to the United States from 1881 to 1910*. New York: Columbia University, 1914, reprint ed., New York: Arno Press and the New York Times, 1969.

Kennan, George. *E. H. Harriman, A Biography.* Boston and New York: Houghton Mifflin Co., 1922.

Leftwich, Joseph. *Israel Zangwill.* London: James Clarke & Co., Ltd., 1957.

Lestschinsky, J. "Die Auswanderung der Juden nach Galveston." *Zeitschrift fur Demographie und Statistik der Juden* 6. 12 (December 1910).

Levine, Isaac Don. "Isaac Don Levine: Letters of an Immigrant" (part of "The East European Immigrant Jew in America, 1881–1981"). *American Jewish Archives* 33. 1 (April, 1981): 53–83. Reprinted, with some deletions, from various editions of the *Kansas City Star* which appeared between July 5, 1914, and January 31, 1915.

Manners, Ande. *Poor Cousins.* New York: Coward, McCann and Geoghegan, Inc., 1972.

Manners, William. *TR and Will: A Friendship that Split the Republican Party.* New York: Harcourt, Brace and World, Inc., 1969.

Margolis, Max L. and Marx, Alexander. *A History of the Jewish People.* Philadelphia: Jewish Publication Society of America, 1956.

Morris, Robert and Freund, Michael, ed. *Trends and Issues in Jewish Social Welfare.* Philadelphia: Jewish Publication Society of America, 1966.

Nelli, Humbert S. *Italians in Chicago, 1880–1930: A Study in Ethnic Mobility.* New York: Oxford University Press, 1970.

Panitz, Esther L. "In Defense of the Jewish Immigrant (1891–1924)." *American Jewish Historical Quarterly* 55. 1 (September 1965): 57–97. Reprinted in Abraham J. Karp, ed., *The Jewish Experience in America,* 5 vols. (New York: Ktav Publishing House, 1969), vol. 5, pp. 23–63.

Panitz, Esther L. "The Polarity of American Jewish Attitudes toward Immigration (1870–1891)." *American Jewish Historical Quarterly* 53. 2 (December 1963):99–130. Reprinted in Abraham J. Karp, ed., *The Jewish Experience in America,* 5 vols. (New York: Ktav Publishing House, 1969), vol. 4, pp. 31–62.

Papers on Rehearing in the Matter of the Appeals to the Secretary of Commerce and Labor of Galveston Immigrants, who arrived under the auspices of the Jewish Immigrants' Information Bureau. (These papers, which were printed as a pamphlet, can be found in U.S. Immigration File No. 52,779/29 and also in the JIIB Papers. The pamphlet is also available at the Jewish National and University Library, Jerusalem, under call no. S/36B/1994.)

Report of the Executive Committee of the Constitution Grand Lodge, Independent Order B'nai B'rith, for the Year 1910–1911.

Sachar, Howard M. *The Emergence of the Middle East: 1914–1924.* New York: Alfred A. Knopf, 1969.

Schluter, William Charles. *The Pre-War Business Cycle 1907 to 1914.* Studies in History, Economics, and Public Law edited by the Faculty of Political Science of Columbia University, vol. 108, no. 1 (whole no. 243). New York: Columbia University, 1923.

Shpall, Leo. "Spreading the Jewish Migrant in America (the Galveston Experiment)." *The Jewish Forum* 28. 6, 7, and 8 (June, July, and August 1945): 119–120, 139–140, 144, 156–158.

Shuman, Bernard. *A History of the Sioux City Jewish Community, 1869–1969.* Sioux City, Iowa: The Jewish Federation, (Bolstein Creative Printers,) 1969.

Slutsky, Yehuda. *"Ha-Itonut Ha-Yehudit-Russit Ba-Meah Ha-Esrim, 1900–1918"* (The Russian-Jewish Press in the Twentieth Century, 1900–1918). Tel Aviv: Tel Aviv University, 1978, (especially chapter 6, pp. 308–320, on "The Territorialist Press").

Szajkowski, Zosa. "Paul Nathan, Lucien Wolf, Jacob H. Schiff and the Jewish Revolutionary Movements in Eastern Europe (1903–1917)." *Jewish Social Studies* 29. 1 and 2 (1967): 3–26, 75–91.

Tcherikower, Elias, ed. *The Early Jewish Labor Movement in the United States.* Translated and revised by Aaron Antonovsky. New York: YIVO Institute for Jewish Research, 1961.

Terrel, Mary Church. "Peonage in the United States: The Convict Lease System and the Chain Gangs." *Nineteenth Century and After* 62 (August 1907): 306–322.

Tsur, Ya'acov (Jacob). *"D'yokanah shel Ha-Tefutsah"* (Anatomy of the Diaspora), with documents and sources compiled and edited by Israel Bartal. Jerusalem: Keter Publishing House, 1975. (From Keter Library "Am Yisrael V'Tarbuto," Part B: "Golah.")

U.S. Congress, Senate. *Reports of the Immigration Commission.* "Statements and Recommendations Submitted by Societies and Organizations Interested in the Subject of Immigration," Document No. 764, 61st Congress, 3rd Session. Washington, D.C.: Government Printing Office, 1911. (In the final printing of the Immigration Commission Reports, the "Statements and Recommendations" appear in vol. 41.)

Waldman, Morris D. "The Galveston Movement: Another Chapter from the Book Which May Never be Written." *The Jewish Social Service Quarterly* 4. 3 (March 1928): 197–205.

Waldman, Morris D. *Nor By Power.* New York: International Universities Press, Inc., 1953.

Wischnitzer, Mark. *To Dwell in Safety: The Story of Jewish Migration Since 1800.* Philadelphia: Jewish Publication Society of America, 1949.

Wohlgelernter, Maurice. *Israel Zangwill: A Study.* New York and London: Columbia University Press, 1964.

Wolf, Simon. *The Presidents I have Known from 1860 to 1918.* Washington, D.C.: Press of Byron S. Adams, 1918.

Zangwill, Israel. *Speeches, Articles and Letters.* Selected and edited by Maurice Simon. London: The Soncino Press, 1937.

Credits for Illustrations

1. Casualties of the Kishinev pogrom of 1903. From *Hilfsverein der Deutschen Juden Geschaftsbericht,* vol. 2 (1903), p. 17, Berlin, 1904.

2. Wounded casualties of the Kishinev pogrom of 1903. From *Hilfsverein der Deutschen Juden Geschaftsbericht,* vol. 2 (1903), p. 23, Berlin, 1904.

3. Wilkomir, in the province of Rovno, one of the cities in which many Jewish families were burned out of their homes, in 1904. From *Hilfsverein der Deutschen Juden Geschaftsbericht,* vol. 3 (1904), p. 27. Berlin, 1905.

4. Well before the inauguration of the Galveston Movement, Jacob H. Schiff was acknowledged as the financial leader of American Jewry, as is evidenced by this call, appearing in the *American Israelite,* Nov. 16, 1905.

5. Jacob Henry Schiff, founder and sponsor of the Galveston Movement. From Frontispiece of American Jewish Year Book 5682 (vol. 23), Philadelphia: Jewish Publication Society of America, 1921.

6. Dr. Paul Nathan, secretary of the Hilfsverein der Deutschen Juden. From Photograph collection, Central Zionist Archives, Jerusalem.

7. Israel Zangwill leaving the hall after his main speech to the Seventh Zionist Congress in Basle, July 30, 1905. From Photograph collection, Central Zionist Archives, Jerusalem.

8. A Jewish Territorial Organization membership card. From ITO Papers, A 36, Central Zionist Archives, Jerusalem.

9. Dr. Max Emmanuel Mandelstamm, president of the ITO's Jewish Emigration Society, in Kiev. From Photograph collection, Central Zionist Archives, Jerusalem.

10. David M. Bressler. From Joint Distribution Committee Archives, N.Y.

11. Morris David Waldman, first manager of the Jewish immigrants' Information Bureau at Galveston. From The Universal Jewish Encyclopedia. S. v. "Waldman, Morris David". New York: Universal Jewish Encyclopedia Co., Inc. 1941.

12. A letter of complaint by Galveston immigrant Moshe Opotowski, printed on the front page of the *Jewish Daily Forward,* December 2, 1907.

13. Dr. David S. Jochelmann, secretary and manager of the ITO's Jewish Emigration Society, based in Kiev. From *The Jewish Chronicle*, May 25, 1917, p. 14.

14. Rabbi Dr. Henry Cohen of Galveston. From Stanely A. Dreyfus. *Henry Cohen, Messenger of the Lord*. New York: Bloch Publishing Co., 1963.

15. Jacob Billikopf, superintendent of the United Jewish Charities in Kansas City, Missouri, who actively participated in the settling of immigrants from Galveston. From Frank J. Adler. *Roots in a Moving Stream: The Centennial History of Congregation B'nai Jehuda of Kansas City, 1870–1970, p. 114,* Kansas City, Missouri: The Temple, Congregation B'nai Jehuda, (Spangler Printers,) 1972.

16. Promotional literature prepared in 1907 by Jacob Billikopf of Kansas City. From ITO Papers, A 36, Central Zionist Archives, Jerusalem.

17. "Announcement, to be posted in synagogues, study houses, and elsewhere." From ITO Papers A 36/95 (278), Central Zionist Archives, Jerusalem.

18. ITO identification card carried by immigrants to Galveston. From ITO Papers A 36/95 (275), Central Zionist Archives, Jerusalem.

19. Cover page of an 11-page pamphlet printed in Zhitomir in 1907 by the "ITO Central Emigration Bureau for all of Russia, in Kiev", entitled *Important Information about Emigration to Galveston (State of Texas)*. From ITO Papers A 36/8, Central Zionist Archives, Jerusalem.

20. Last page of a pamphlet printed in Zhitomir in 1907 by the "ITO Central Emigration Bureau for all of Russia in Kiev", entitled *Important Information about Emigration to Galveston (State of Texas)*. Waldman added his comments at the bottom of the page.

21. Report sheet from Jacob Billikopf of Kansas City, Missouri, on progress of immigrants sent to him from Galveston. From ITO Papers A 36/95 (275), Central Zionist Archives, Jerusalem.

22. A conference of the Jewish Territorial Organization, with Israel Zangwill standing in the center. From *The Jewish People, Past and Present,* vol. 2, p. 321, N. Y.: Jewish Encyclopedic Handbooks, Inc., Central Yiddish Culture Organization (CYCO), 1948. In that book the white-bearded figure was mistakenly identified as Mandelstamm but is actually I. Jasinowski.

23. Israel Zangwill, founder and president of the Jewish Territorial Organization (ITO). From Frontispiece of *In Memory of Israel Zangwill,* New York: Zangwill Memorial Committee, 1926.

24. Galveston-bound emigrants in Bremen, with representatives of the Hilfsverein. From *Hilfsverein der Deutschen Juden Geschaftsbericht,* vol. 6 (1907), p. 106. Berlin, 1908.

25. Boarding ship in Bremen for the voyage to Galveston. From *Hilfsverein der Deutschen Juden Geschaftsbericht,* vol. 6 (1907), p. 102. Berlin, 1908.

26. Immigrants arriving at Galveston. From The Rosenberg Library, Galveston, Texas.

27. Ephraim Zalman (Charles) Hoffman, an immigrant who settled in Fort Worth after arriving at Galveston in 1913. From [David Hoffman.] *A Family Portrait, Part 1—Russia, Emigration, Fort Worth.* Austin, Texas, (privately published,) 1979.

28. W. H. Novit, a Jewish immigrant from Russia, selling bananas in Gatesville, Texas (c. 1912). From [David Hoffman] *A Family Portrait, Part 1—Russia, Emigration, Fort Worth.* Austin, Texas, (privately published,) 1979.

29. Sarah Bernstein and Ephraim Zalman (Charles) Hoffman, two immigrants who arrived separately in Galveston in 1913, met in Fort Worth, and got married in 1915. From [David Hoffman] *A Family Portrait, Part 1—Russia, Emigration, Fort Worth.* Austin, Texas, (privately published,) 1979.

30. Ephraim Zalman (Charles) Hoffman (left), an immigrant who arrived at Galveston in 1913, as half-owner of a fruit, vegetable, and grocery store in Fort Worth (c. 1913–20). From [David Hoffman] *A Family Portrait, Part 1—Russia, Emigration, Fort Worth,* Austin, Texas, (privately published,) 1979.

Index

Made in the USA
Columbia, SC
02 August 2018